Educating Economists

The Teagle Discussion on Re-evaluating the Undergraduate Economics Major

ALSO FROM EDWARD ELGAR

The Making of a European Economist
David Colander, *Christian A. Johnson Distinguished Professor of Economics, Middlebury College, USA*

'In this captivating volume, David Colander scrutinizes economics in Europe, which is currently undergoing a radical process of convergence, standardization and metrication. While he acknowledges that the USA is the world leader in terms of journal publications in economics, he also suggests that the scholarly breadth and practical orientation of much economics research in Europe is worth preserving and enhancing. No-one who wishes to make economics more relevant should ignore Colander's painstaking study.'
– Geoffrey M. Hodgson, University of Hertfordshire, UK

David Colander's highly original and thought provoking book considers ongoing changes in graduate European economics education. Following up on his earlier classic studies of US graduate economic education, he studies the 'economist production function' in which universities take student 'raw material' and transform it into economists. In doing so he provides insight into economists and economics.

He argues that until recently Europe had a different 'economist production function' than did the US; thus European economists were different from their US counterparts. However, this is now changing, and Colander suggests that the changes are not necessarily for the best. Specifically, he suggests that in their attempt to catch up with US programs, European economics is undermining some of their strengths—strengths that could allow them to leapfrog US economics in the future, and be the center of 21st century economics. Student views on the ongoing changes and ensuing difficulties are reported via surveys of, and interviews with, students in global European graduate programs. The conclusion draws broad policy implications from the study, and suggests a radically different market approach to funding economic research that Colander argues will help avoid the pitfalls into which European economics is now falling.

July 2009   200pp
Hardback 978 1 84844 639 7
Paperback 978 1 84844 641 0

Educating Economists

The Teagle Discussion on Re-evaluating the
Undergraduate Economics Major

Edited by

David Colander

*Christian A. Johnson Distinguished Professor of Economics,
Middlebury College, Vermont, USA*

KimMarie McGoldrick

Professor of Economics, University of Richmond, USA

Edward Elgar
Cheltenham, UK • Northampton, MA, USA

Published by
Edward Elgar Publishing Limited
The Lypiatts
15 Lansdown Road
Cheltenham
Glos GL50 2JA
UK

Edward Elgar Publishing, Inc.
William Pratt House
9 Dewey Court
Northampton
Massachusetts 01060
USA

A catalogue record for this book
is available from the British Library

Library of Congress Control Number: 2009933411

Mixed Sources
Product group from well-managed
forests and other controlled sources
www.fsc.org Cert no. SA-COC-1565
© 1996 Forest Stewardship Council

ISBN 978 1 84844 579 6 (cased)
ISBN 978 1 84844 580 2 (paperback)

Printed and bound by MPG Books Group, UK

Contents

PART 1   THE TEAGLE REPORT

PART 2   CHALLENGING THE CONTENT: WHAT DO WE TEACH?

PART 3   CHANGING THE WAY WE TEACH ECONOMICS

PART 4   STRUCTURAL PROBLEMS AND THE
INTERDISCIPLINARY NATURE OF ECONOMICS

PART 5   VIEWS FROM THE ADMINISTRATION

Figures

Contributors

Bradley W. Bateman is Provost and Executive Vice-President of Denison University, Ohio. He received his BA from Alma College, Michigan and his PhD in economics from the University of Kentucky. Previously, he was the Gertrude B. Austin Professor of Economics at Grinnell College, Iowa. His fields of specialty include the history of economic thought, monetary, and macroeconomics. He is the author of *Keynes's Uncertain Revolution* and the editor, with Roger Backhouse, of *The Cambridge Companion to Keynes*. His current research interests focus on the role of religion in the formation of economics.

David W. Breneman is a University Professor and Director of the Public Policy Program in the Batten School of Leadership and Public Policy at the University of Virginia. From 1995 to 2007 he served as Dean of the Curry School of Education at the University of Virginia. He received his PhD in economics from the University of California at Berkeley. He was a Visiting Professor at the Harvard Graduate School of Education from 1990 to 1995, where he taught graduate courses on the economics and financing of higher education, on liberal arts colleges, and on the college presidency. As a Visiting Fellow at The Brookings Institution he conducted research for a book, *Liberal Arts Colleges: Thriving, Surviving, or Endangered?* From 1983 to 1989, he served as President of Kalamazoo College, a liberal arts college in Michigan. Prior to that, he was a Senior Fellow at Brookings from 1975 to 1983, specializing in the economics of higher education and public policy toward education.

David Colander is the Christian A. Johnson Distinguished Professor of Economics at Middlebury College, Middlebury, Vermont. He has authored, co-authored, or edited over 40 books (including a principles and intermediate macro text) and 100 articles on a wide range of topics. His books have been, or are being, translated into a number of different languages, including Chinese, Bulgarian, Polish, Italian, and Spanish. He has also been a consultant to Time-Life Films, a consultant to Congress, a Brookings Policy Fellow, and a Visiting Scholar at Nuffield College, Oxford. In 2001–02 he was the Kelly Professor of Distinguished Teaching at Princeton University. He is a former President of both the Eastern

ix

Economic Association and History of Economic Thought Society, has been on numerous editorial boards, and is currently Associate Editor for Content for the *Journal of Economic Education*.

Mahesh Dahal is a student at Middlebury College, Middlebury, Vermont who worked as a Christian A. Johnson Fellow after his sophomore year. He is from Nepal. He is majoring in economics and mathematics, and is planning to go to graduate school to study international and development economics.

George Daly serves as Professor and Dean of the McDonough School of Business at Georgetown University, Washington, DC. Previously, he was the Albert Fingerhut Professor of Business at the Stern School of Business of New York University. He also served as Dean of the Stern School from 1993 through 2002. In addition to his academic roles, he has served in the federal government and as a consultant to the National Football League. He serves on a number of corporate and non-profit boards. He received his BA from Miami University in Ohio and received his PhD from Northwestern University.

Benjamin M. Friedman is the William Joseph Maier Professor of Political Economy and formerly the Chairman of the Department of Economics at Harvard University. He received both his BA and PhD from Harvard University. His latest book is *The Moral Consequences of Economic Growth*, and his best-known previous book is *Day of Reckoning: The Consequences of American Economic Policy Under Reagan and After*, which received the George S. Eccles Prize from Columbia University for excellence in writing about economics. His current professional activities include serving as a director and member of the editorial board of the *Encyclopaedia Britannica*, a director of the Council for Economic Education, and an adviser to the Federal Reserve Bank of New York. He was the 2005–06 recipient of the John R. Commons Award, presented every two years in recognition of achievements in economics and service to the economics profession, and in 2008 he received the Medal of the Italian Senate.

Richie Fuld graduated from Middlebury College, Middlebury, Vermont in 2008 with a degree in economics, where, among other things he played on the hockey team. He is currently working for an investment bank in New York.

Robert F. Garnett is Associate Professor of Economics at Texas Christian University. His writings on the philosophy, history, and teaching of economics have appeared in *Rethinking Marxism*, the *Journal of Economic*

Issues, the *Review of Political Economy*, the *Review of Austrian Economics*, the *Review of Social Economy*, the *Eastern Economic Journal*, the *Journal of Markets and Morality*, *Studies in Philosophy and Education*, the *Atlantic Economic Journal*, and the *Post-Autistic Economics Review*. His current projects examine the goals and methods of liberal learning in undergraduate economics education, the value and requirements of pluralism in economic inquiry, and the relationship between commercial and philanthropic forms of economic cooperation.

Arthur H. Goldsmith is the Jackson T. Stephens Professor of Economics at Washington and Lee University. He received his PhD in economics from the University of Illinois in 1979 and his primary area of specialization is labor economics. He teaches a wide range of interdisciplinary courses including, The Economics of Race and Ethnicity, The Economics of Social Problems, and Economic Themes in Literature and Film, as well as traditional or mainstream economics courses such as the Principles of Economics and Intermediate Macroeconomics. His research combines insights from economics, psychology, sociology, anthropology, and history to explore questions regarding wages, employment, unemployment, psychological well-being, access to health care, and educational accumulation. He is currently Vice-President of the Southern Economics Association and serves on the Editorial Board of both the *Journal of Economic Psychology* and the *Journal of Socio-Economics*.

Paul W. Grimes is a Professor of Economics and Associate Dean in the College of Business at Mississippi State University. He also serves as the Director for the MSU Center for Economic Education and Financial Literacy. A native of Missouri, Paul earned his BS and MS degrees in economics from Pittsburg State University in Pittsburg, Kansas. In 1984 he received his PhD in economics from Oklahoma State University. In recent years, he has been heavily involved in the field of economic education – in terms of both research and program delivery. He is the author of more than 70 scholarly research articles, notes, and book reviews, and he works closely with the Mississippi Council on Economic Education to train public school teachers across the state. In 2005 he was recognized for his economic education research with the Henry H. Villard Award presented by the National Council on Economic Education. In 2009 he served as president of the National Association of Economic Educators and is currently an Associate Editor of the *Journal of Economic Education*.

W. Lee Hansen is Professor Emeritus of Economics at the University of Wisconsin at Madison. He received his BA and MA from UW-Madison and his PhD in political economy from the Johns Hopkins University. He has been a Senior Staff Economist for the President's Council of Economic Advisers, Research Fellow at the Brookings Institution, a Post-doctoral Fellow in Political Economy at the University of Chicago, a Guggenheim Fellow, and a Fulbright Scholar at the University of Sydney. He is the author, co-author, or editor of ten books and has written extensively on the economics of higher education. He is the recipient of a UW-Madison Distinguished Teaching Award, the Hilldale Award for Distinguished Professional Achievement, and elected membership in the Teaching Academy. He has also been recognized widely for his teaching and research in economic education, including the Marvin Bower Award from the National Council on Economic Education, the Leavey Award for Excellence in Private Enterprise Education, and the Henry H. Villard Research Award. He is currently working on a book about his "expected proficiencies" approach to the economics major.

Catharine Hill is President and a Professor of Economics at Vassar College. She graduated summa cum laude from Williams College, Massachusetts, and also earned BA and MA degrees at Brasenose College, Oxford University. She received her PhD in economics from Yale University. She is a noted economist whose work focuses on higher education affordability and access, as well as on economic development and reform in Africa. Her publications include the study co-authored with Gordon C. Winston "Access to the Most Selective Private Colleges by High-ability, Low-income Students: Are They Out There?" and "Affordability: Family Incomes and Net Prices at Highly Selective Private Colleges and Universities," co-authored with Gordon C. Winston and Stephanie Boyd. She has been selected for a number of scholarly awards, grants, and fellowships from organizations including the American Council of Learned Societies, Brookings Institution, National Science Foundation, and Social Science Research Council.

Eric Hoest graduated from Middlebury College, Middlebury, Vermont in 2008 with a degree in economics. In addition to conducting research on the undergraduate economics major, he also assisted in researching political control of the economy. Eric currently works in New York City at a leading investment bank, and is co-founder of Betasab, a non-profit organization devoted to providing a stable home and education to orphaned children in Ethiopia.

Jessica Holmes is Associate Professor of Economics at Middlebury College, Vermont. She received her BA from Colgate University, New York and received her PhD from Yale University. She teaches courses in microeconomics, statistics, public finance, health economics, and the economics of social issues. Prior to joining the Middlebury faculty, she taught at Colgate University and worked as a litigation consultant for National Economic Research Associates, conducting economic analyses for companies facing lawsuits involving securities fraud, product liability, and intellectual property. Her research fields include health economics and economic development, and her research has been published in journals such as *Population Research and Policy Review, Economics of Education Review, Clinical Pediatrics*, and *Southern Economic Journal.*

Steven Jones is a student at Middlebury College, Middlebury, Vermont, Class of 2009. He is an economics major and a Chinese minor, and his studies have included a year abroad in Hangzhou, China at the C.V. Starr-Middlebury School. He was also a Christian A. Johnson Fellow at Middlebury College. He is currently researching economic disparities between ethnic groups in Xinjiang, China.

David Kennett is Elizabeth Stillman Williams Professor of Economics at Vassar College, where he served as the Director of the Program in International Studies until June 2007. He received his BA from the University of Sussex, UK and his PhD from Columbia University, New York. He has taught at University College London, the Economic University of Varna, Bulgaria, Sciences Po, Paris, and Ochanomizu University in Tokyo, and is senior specialist for the Fulbright Program. His current research focuses on comparative economics, the changes in economic systems provoked by the recent crisis and the potential for liberal arts education in a non-US context. His recent publications include *A New View of Comparative Economic Systems* and "William S. Vickrey's Legacy: Innovative Policies for Social Concerns." He is now working on "New Challenges to the Global Economy: Are There State-level Solutions?"

Mark Maier teaches economics at Glendale Community College (California). He has been co-principal investigator for three National Science Foundation projects: establishing an economics pedagogy portal at the Science Education Resource Center; adapting successful pedagogies from the natural sciences in economic education; and developing just-in-time teaching methods in economics. Between 2001 and 2004 he was a scholar and lead scholar in the CASTL program at the Carnegie Foundation for the Advancement of Teaching. He has published several articles on cooperative learning and is the author of three books: *Introducing Economics: A Critical Guide for Teaching* (with Julie Nelson),

The Data Game: Controversies in Social Science Statistics; and *City Unions: Managing Discontent in New York City*.

Stephen A. Marglin holds the Walter S. Barker Chair in the Department of Economics at Harvard University. He became a tenured professor at Harvard in 1968, one of the youngest in the history of that institution. His published papers and books have ranged from the foundations of cost–benefit analysis, the workings of the labor-surplus economy, and the organization of production to the relationship between the growth of income and its distribution and the process of macroeconomic adjustment. His work has been translated into many languages, including Spanish, French, German, and Japanese. His recent work, reflected in his latest book, *The Dismal Science: How Thinking Like an Economist Undermines Community* (Harvard University Press, 2008), has focused on the foundational assumptions of economics and how these assumptions make community invisible to economists. In addition to teaching and research, Marglin has been adviser to governments and international agencies, for-profit concerns, and non-profit organizations in many different countries.

KimMarie McGoldrick is Professor of Economics at the University of Richmond. She currently serves on the American Economic Association's Committee on Economic Education and on the Board of Editors of the *Journal of Economic Education*. Her research spans a wide range of education topics including service-learning, undergraduate research, cooperative learning, and liberal education skills as applied in economics. Her research regularly appears in leading education journals including the *Journal of Economic Education*. In 2008, she received the highest award for faculty achievement in the state of Virginia, the State Council of Higher Education of Virginia Outstanding Faculty Award. McGoldrick is Co-PI (along with Scott Simkins, Mark Maier and Cathy Manduca) on a National Science Foundation (DUE 0817382) project, Starting Point: Teaching and Learning Economics. Starting Point will make it easier for economists to find out about teaching innovations both within and beyond their discipline and provide them with the tools to begin integrating and assessing these innovations in their own classrooms. In addition, the portal will increase economists' knowledge of fundamental research findings from the learning sciences and illustrate how those findings can inform classroom teaching to improve student learning. McGoldrick has (co-)organized 11 economics education workshops since 1996. Her most recent efforts contribute to the Teaching Innovations Program (TIP), a National Science Foundation (NSF)-funded project designed to improve undergraduate education in economics by offering instructors an opportunity to expand their teaching skills and participate in the scholarship of teaching and learning.

Brendan O'Flaherty is Professor of Economics at Columbia University. His primary research interests are in the areas of urban economics and race. His published works include *City Economics*, an urban economics textbook, and *Making Room: The Economics of Homelessness*. He is a member of the Columbia Center on Homelessness Prevention Studies and the research advisory board of the New York City Department of Homeless Services. He has also been Chief Financial Officer for the City of Newark, New Jersey. At Columbia he has been Director of the MPA program, and Director of Graduate Studies for the economics department.

Ann L. Owen is Professor of Economics at Hamilton College, New York. She has published widely on long-run growth, income distribution, human capital accumulation, and the impact of culture on economic behavior in journals such as *American Economic Review, Economic Journal, Journal of Monetary Economics, Journal of Environmental Economics and Management, Journal of Economic Growth*, and *European Economic Review*. The recipient of a college-wide teaching award, Owen also has established expertise as an educator, having published several articles on pedagogy in the economics classroom, presented in many venues on economics education, and written textbook supplements that facilitate innovative teaching methods. She has also co-authored several refereed publications with Hamilton undergraduates. Owen teaches courses in monetary policy, economic growth, macroeconomic theory, and economic statistics. Prior to joining Hamilton College in 1997, Owen was an economist at the Federal Reserve Board in Washington, DC. She earned her PhD in economics from Brown University in 1995, an MBA from Babson College in 1989, and a BA in economics from Boston University in 1985. In addition to her work at the Federal Reserve, Owen's experience outside of academe includes product management at a regional Boston-based commercial bank.

Joseph Persky is a Professor of Economics at the University of Illinois at Chicago. He received his PhD from Harvard University. He has written extensively on the distributional implications of urban and regional economic growth. He is currently a member of the Illinois Governor's Council of Economic Advisers. His recent publications include *Does "Trickle Down" Work? Economic Development Strategies and Job Chains* *in Local Labor Markets*. He also has a long-standing interest in the history of economic thought and acts as the informal editor of the Retrospectives feature of the *Journal of Economic Perspectives*.

Michael K. Salemi is Bowman and Gordon Gray Professor of Economics at the University of North Carolina at Chapel Hill. He received his PhD from the University of Minnesota, Minneapolis. Salemi is the author of more than 50 published articles in macroeconomics, domestic and international monetary theory, and economic education. His recent projects deal with optimal monetary policy, generalized method of moment estimation, strategies for reforming the college-level principles of economics courses, and using discussion of classic and current articles to teach undergraduate economics. In 2005, Edward Elgar published his *Discussing Economics: A Classroom Guide to Writing Discussion Questions and Leading Discussions* co-authored with W. Lee Hansen. Michael Salemi has been involved with teacher education since 1974. In recent years, he was Chair of the Committee on Economic Education of the American Economic Association. He is currently Co-PI for an AEA-NSF project to promote interactive teaching strategies in college-level economics courses. He was awarded the Bowman and Gordon Gray Professorship for Excellence in Undergraduate Instruction by the University of North Carolina in 1987 and again in 2004, the Bower Medal by the National Council on Economic Education in 1998, and the Villard Research Award by the Association of Economic Educators in 2001.

John J. Siegfried is a Professor of Economics at Vanderbilt University. He earned a BS from Rensselaer Polytechnic Institute, New York and a PhD in economics from the University of Wisconsin at Madison. His professional roles have included President of the Southern Economic Association and the Midwest Economics Association and Senior Staff Economist on President Ford's Council of Economic Advisers. He has been Secretary-Treasurer of the American Economic Association since 2000. His more recent publications have appeared in the *Journal of Economic Education*, the *American Economic Review*, and the *Economics of Education Review*. His edited book *Better Living Through Economics*, appeared in 2009. His current research interests include graduate education in economics and trends in undergraduate economics degrees.

Scott Simkins is the director of the Academy for Teaching and Learning and Associate Professor of Economics at North Carolina A&T State University in Greensboro, NC. He earned his PhD in economics from the University of Iowa in 1988. Over the past decade he and Mark Maier

(Glendale Community College, California) have led two NSF-funded projects exploring the adaptability of STEM (science, technology, engineering, and math) discipline teaching innovations in economics (NSF DUE #0088303 – Developing and Implementing Just-in-Time-Teaching [JiTT] Techniques in the Principles of Economics Course and DUE #0411037 – Implications of STEM Discipline Research for Instructional Innovation and Assessment in Economic Education). In August 2008 Simkins, Maier, KimMarie McGoldrick and Cathy Manduca (Carleton College, Minnesota) were awarded a large NSF grant to develop a national economics pedagogic portal highlighting innovative pedagogical practices developed both inside and outside of economics for use in undergraduate economics courses (NSF DUE #081738 – Developing an Economics Pedagogic Portal). Scott is a frequent presenter on scholarship of teaching and learning (SoTL) topics at workshops and conferences regionally, nationally, and internationally. His work focuses on pedagogical innovations in economics as well as cross-disciplinary sharing of educational research and pedagogical practices. His economic education research has appeared in the *Journal of Economic Education* as well as other journals and focuses on the adaptation and implementation of pedagogical innovations in economics and their effect on student learning.

Neil T. Skaggs is a Professor of Economics at Illinois State University. He received his PhD from Duke University, NC. He teaches Economic Development and Growth, History of Economic Thought, Macroeconomics, and large sections of Principles of Economics. Neil's research specialty is the history of monetary economics and his work has appeared in the *Canadian Journal of Economics, History of Political Economy, Southern Economic Journal*, and *Public Choice*. He has published numerous articles on the development of British monetary theory and policy in the nineteenth century and is currently working on a monograph that traces the influence of the ideas of Henry Thornton.

Michael Watts is a Professor of Economics and the Director of the Center for Economic Education at Purdue University, Indiana. He has served as President of the National Association of Economic Educators and the Society of Economics Educators, as Vice-President of the Midwest Economic Association, and as a member and Chair of the American Economic Association's Committee on Economic Education. His main teaching interests include microeconomics, labor economics, managerial economics, public policy analysis, and history of economic thought. His major publications include *The Literary Book of Economics*, "Chalk and Talk: A National Survey on Teaching Undergraduate Economics" (with W. Becker), "What Students Remember and Say about College Economics Years Later" (with S. Allgood, W. Bosshardt, and H.W. van der Klaauw), "Is Sexy Economics and Economics Teaching Necessary or Sufficient?," "Student Gender and School District Differences Affecting the Stock and Flow of Economic Knowledge," and "How Instructors Make a Difference: Panel Data Estimates from Principles of Economics Courses" (with W. Bosshardt). He has served as a consultant for such organizations as the National Council on Economic Education, Agency for Instructional Technology, The College Board, the IMF, the US Information Agency, and Microsoft.

James Wible is Professor of Economics at the Whittemore School of Business and Economics at the University of New Hampshire. He received his BA from Wheaton College, Illinois and his PhD from The Pennsylvania State University. Previously he served as Interim Dean and Associate Dean of the Whittemore School, as Chair of the Economics Department, and as the Graduate Teaching Supervisor in the Cognate in College Teaching. He specializes in macroeconomics and monetary theory, economics of science and philosophy of science, and law and economics. His recently published research includes "The Economic Mind of Charles Sanders Peirce," "Macroeconomics, Pragmatism, and Cognitive Scarcity: Keynes Should Have Read C.S. Peirce on Probability and Evolutionary Complexity," "Toward a Process Conception of Rationality in Economics and Science," and *The Economics of Science: Methodology and Epistemology as if Economics Really Mattered*.

Jonathan B. Wight is Professor of Economics at the Robins School of Business at the University of Richmond. Jonathan received his BA from Duke University and his PhD from Vanderbilt University, Tennessee. Jonathan's recent work focuses on the moral foundations of capitalism and the ethical basis for economic analysis. Books include *Saving Adam Smith: A Tale of Wealth, Transformation, and Virtue* (Prentice-Hall, 2002), an academic novel that develops Smith's theory of how social and moral capital are created through social interaction – and how these concepts relate to business and economics. Along with John Morton, Jonathan also published *Teaching the Ethical Foundations of Economics* (National Council on Economic Education), which contains a set of ten lessons on ethics for economics teachers. He received the University of Richmond's Distinguished Educator Award in 2002 and the John Templeton Foundation's In Character prize in 2006.

Preface

Michael Watts

In fall 2006 the Teagle Foundation awarded $75 000 grants to investigate the role of majors from each of six different academic disciplines in promoting undergraduate liberal education. One of the grants was made to the American Economic Association's Committee on Economic Education (AEA CEE); the other five grants went to the American Academy of Religion, the American Society for Biochemistry and Molecular Biology, the Center for Hellenic Studies, the Modern Language Association, and the National History Center. A summary of the six projects, with links to white papers prepared for each of the disciplines, is available at http://www.teaglefoundation.org/grantmaking/grantees/disciplines.aspx (accessed 17 April 2009).

Teagle's request for proposals for this initiative arrived shortly after I began my first term as Chair of the AEA CEE. I knew enough history of the Committee and the AEA to understand how some key institutional features would affect any participation by the AEA CEE in the project. Most important, an explicit objective of the AEA has been, since its founding in the late 1800s and its incorporation in 1923, "The encouragement of perfect freedom of economic discussion. The Association as such will take no partisan attitude, nor will it commit its members to any position on practical economic questions" (http://www.vanderbilt.edu/AEA/gen_info.htm, accessed 17 April 2009).

Given that long-standing and, for the most part, scrupulously observed policy, there was never a question of producing an "official" AEA or AEA CEE document on what economics departments should do to provide the best possible liberal education for economics majors, and for students in other majors who take economics courses – which is a far larger number of students. What might have been done instead, and has been done in the past, was to establish an independent committee to prepare such a report. For example, in 1961 a document titled *Economic Education in the Schools* was published by a National Task Force on Economic Education, with members appointed by the AEA and funding provided by the Committee on Economic Development. The report was influential, with over a quarter of a million copies of the booklet distributed to US schools. But within the economics profession the report and its national distribution led to a heated debate, featuring such prominent economists as Paul Samuelson, George Stigler, and Lee Bach, on the questions of whether or not it makes sense to teach economics at all at the secondary level, and if so whether the recommendations of the National Task Force – or for that matter any "official" recommendations – were the best way to go about doing that. That episode may demonstrate the wisdom of the AEA policy promoting freedom of discussion while keeping the association itself out of the business of directly adopting statements on practical questions, including even questions about how and when to teach economics. It may also offer some support for George Bernard Shaw's quip about economists laid end to end not reaching a conclusion.

For the Teagle project in 2006, after consulting with John Siegfried at the AEA and several others, I opted not to set up a large independent committee, not from any fear of the controversy such a report might engender, but rather just the opposite. In my experience, today academic committee reports all too often turn out to be so bland and general that they are neither useful nor memorable. Instead they are more likely to become long and bulky documents by trying to provide balanced discussions of all reasonable points of view. If specific recommendations are offered – frequently that is left as something to be done by "the next" committee, which may never be appointed – they are often presented as such broad statements (or even platitudes) on desirable goals that almost everyone accepts them, and already did before the committee was appointed.

To try to ensure that this project, if funded, would attract attention and promote active discussion and debate among economists who are seriously concerned about undergraduate liberal education – which is perhaps not the representative or majority group of US academic economists, but is certainly a large and important group – it seemed more promising to choose two co-authors to write the white paper. The authors should be working at schools with good liberal education programs, and known both for holding strong views on these topics and for regularly engaging in free and open discussions about the goals and practice of teaching undergraduate economics. Dave Colander and KimMarie McGoldrick came quickly to mind. They generously agreed to serve, first by writing the proposal. As this volume makes clear, they embraced the goal of promoting a discussion of ideas on a wide range of topics and specific recommendations, including several that were always expected to be controversial. They never envisioned the report as trying to set out a settled body of conclusions on best practices for all schools or even all liberal education programs. And they understood that neither their white paper, nor the responses to the white paper that they hoped to elicit and publish, would be viewed as official documents or position statements of the American Economic Association or of the AEA CEE. The discussion and proposals would have to stand or fall on their own merits, and on the authors' powers of persuasion. As was true in the 1960s, these are still not areas in which economists are noted for agreeing to make changes. That is particularly true in times when, as now, undergraduate enrollments in economics majors and courses are high and rising. Why tamper with a major that is already passing the test of the marketplace? The answer, of course, is that even in good times there may be some serious problems with the economics major and how we teach undergraduate economics, and some of those problems may be getting worse rather than better.

But we all knew specific claims about problems with the way undergraduate economics is taught, and specific recommendations on how to make things better, were almost certain to generate disagreements, counterarguments, and counterproposals. In fact, that was an integral part of the intended outcome from this discussion. To make sure it happened and was at least partly documented, the white paper was presented and revised over a period of more than a year, at two small conferences specifically on the white paper, at several paper sessions in national and regional professional meetings, and in other venues. That helped shape the recommendations and arguments in the final draft of the white paper, and brought the discussion to a larger audience. But the intent was not to have all of the objections and disagreements reflected in the white paper. Instead, the goal was to sharpen the arguments and recommendations in the white paper, and to provide ways for those who disagreed – or more often who partly agreed and partly disagreed – to speak for themselves. And so this book also emerged from the project, and will now be distributed to chairs of US economics departments.

I attended the conferences at Middlebury and Richmond that were organized for the project, and some of the other sessions in which various drafts of the report were presented and discussed. As other participants in those meetings can testify, I can be included among those who disagree with several of the major arguments and proposals in the white paper. But in this Preface I have a different role to play, reflecting on what I heard at the earlier discussions and, now, in reading these chapters. So having set the stage with a bit of background on the report and how it came about, I will now risk suggesting some "points of emphasis" readers may want to take special note of as they read the following pages.

First, in Chapter 1, Colander and McGoldrick note that in framing their recommendations their focus was on "the economics discipline within research liberal arts colleges" (p. 21). They hope some of their ideas will also be useful at other types of schools and in other disciplines, but do not claim that they will be. I have not heard or seen responses from people in other disciplines, but as other economists responded to the white paper there were, not surprisingly, clear examples of a different focus in many of the responses from those who work at research universities or other schools in which liberal undergraduate education is not the key focus of the school or the economics department. What is perhaps more surprising is how much disagreement there is in the responses from other economists who are also employed at schools where liberal education is the key focus of the faculty. Clearly economists' individual "perspectives" – a term that appears in many of the responses – shape their ideas and many of their reactions to specific points in the white paper. Those perspectives are certainly influenced by the kinds of schools at which the authors are working or have worked in the past, but just as clearly, that occupational influence is not so strong or so uniform in its effect as to establish a standard set of positions on questions about how the economics major contributes to or limits a liberal education, or whether the sources of those positive and/or negative effects are rooted in the discipline itself or in how economists are trained (or not trained) to research and teach, or in the incentives they face from departments and central administrations at their schools.

More generally, there seems to be considerably more disagreement than consensus among the authors on many of the specific arguments and recommendations in the white paper, including:

- whether the discipline of economics represents – and prepares faculty and students to understand and discuss – "big think" or "little think" ideas;
- whether economics, as it is practiced today, has become narrow and perhaps imperialistic, or is instead more likely than ever to draw ideas from other disciplines and therefore fit naturally with interdisciplinary initiatives, including public policy programs;
- whether individual economics courses and/or the economics major promote too much depth and too little breadth (or vice versa, some argue), both in absolute terms and compared with undergraduate coursework and majors in other disciplines – particularly other social sciences and the natural sciences;
- whether breadth or depth is a more effective way to teach undergraduate economics content to economics majors or to non-majors taking only two or three economics courses, and a more effective way to promote a lifelong passion for learning;
- whether particular breadth courses (such as economic history and the history of economic thought, according to Colander and McGoldrick) should be required courses for undergraduate students,

and for graduate students in economics who want to teach in liberal education and interdisciplinary programs;

● whether special credentialing programs for faculty who take jobs at schools that stress undergraduate liberal education would be well received by individual faculty members, economics departments, and schools, and whether the best way to provide those credentials would be in new or existing doctoral programs (in economics or, perhaps, from economics programs in public policy schools), or as post-doctorate programs;

● whether teaching and research are, in theory and/or practice, substitutes or complements, or perhaps operate in different combinations for economists at different kinds of schools; and

● whether bottom-up or top-down reforms at colleges and universities have the best chance of being adopted and succeeding – unless top-down programs must have enough support from faculty and departments, and bottom-up programs must have enough support from central administrators that the differences are not really as important as they sound.

There is no list of arguments and recommendations from the white paper with which all of the respondents explicitly agreed, but there is a short list of ideas that at least some respondents supported and with which I do not remember hearing or reading any substantive disagreements from other respondents. Even that limited consensus may reflect only a considerable degree of selection bias in those who were invited to the conferences and who chose to attend. And it is also possible that there were some respondents who did not agree with these points but did not say that because they cared more about expressing their thoughts on other points they considered more important. But with those caveats, it seems to me the following few points of agreement are also worth noting:

● Economics instruction for liberal education, and for that matter all other kinds of education, could be improved by training economists to use more innovative, student-centered teaching methods, either as graduate students or as new faculty members.

● We can probably do more to tailor undergraduate courses (especially principles classes) for different groups of students – mostly for non-economics majors.

● Not surprisingly, almost all academic economists agree that incentives are important, and can be used to promote more attention to good teaching. But exactly how, where, and when to do that, and who should do it, is not so clear. For example, is it better to promote

Educating economists: the Teagle discussion

a culture that values teaching through existing school and department structures, or to set up special units or schools to provide general education or interdisciplinary programs, with promotion, tenure, and salary decisions residing at least partly in those units?

I had seen almost all of the papers printed here, or at least earlier versions of them, at the conferences or sessions in which they were first presented. Rereading them to prepare this Preface left me with two very general impressions. First, it was more fun to hear people making these points and arguing these points face-to-face, because what has been lost in the printed pages is a good deal of humor and general goodwill, even when the oral disagreements were sharp and sometimes more pointed. That suggests that there is still a role for those kinds of forums.

On the other hand, in reading the papers together without the generally pleasant distractions of individual personalities and group and subgroup dynamics, I was left with a stronger sense of how important the overall issue of an educational culture (to use a term from Brad Bateman's response) at any kind of school can be. Understandably, the culture at a school that prides itself first and foremost on the quality of its undergraduate liberal education will often be different from the culture at a school that ranks itself based on doctoral or master's programs. But it is also worth noting there are some large research universities that manage to put more emphasis on undergraduate education than others, and that's a culture issue, too.

Ultimately a school and department's culture sinks through and affects the behavior of individual faculty, even with those who are stellar researchers *and* stellar teachers of both undergraduate and graduate students. If you can keep that kind of faculty member in the undergraduate classroom, he or she will inspire students' passion for learning in ways that most non-researchers can't. And the faculty member will find the experience rewarding and worthwhile, and derive satisfaction from building up the size and reputation of the undergraduate economics major. At schools where the university and department cultures encompass excellence in undergraduate teaching, this can be a stable equilibrium. But if the culture of the department and school is focused on doctoral or master's programs (as in business schools that are ranked on MBA programs), and the undergraduate program comes to be valued primarily because that justifies faculty slots that can be used to bolster rankings for the graduate programs, the handwriting is on the wall. And so after reading these chapters again, I wondered how many of the problems raised in the white paper might be addressed if it were possible to change the culture in departments and schools, perhaps through our graduate programs or perhaps in post-doctoral programs, so that the value of good teaching in good undergraduate programs at any kind of school is regularly seen as a more important part of what it means to be a professor. It would be interesting to compare the characteristics and histories of the large research universities where that seems to happen to those where it does not.

I hope these brief summary impressions and the short lists of major questions addressed in this volume show that the discussion Dave and KimMarie have started takes in a large number of interesting and important questions. Some of the questions are what they call "big think" questions, with no simple answers, and some are "little think" questions, or recommendations that may or may not be worth pursuing, compared with alternative approaches. I am extremely grateful to Dave and KimMarie for agreeing to accept the risks of developing the proposal, and then doing all of the hard work that came along when the proposal was funded. They drew together a wonderfully diverse and engaging group of respondents, who served in many respects as collaborators in developing the project and this volume. And of course without the funding and initiative from the Teagle Foundation none of this would have happened, so sincere thanks are due there, too.

It was a privilege for the Committee for Economic Education of the American Economic Association to support and facilitate this project, even though I must repeat that the white paper and responses are not official statements of the AEA or the AEA CEE.

Michael Watts, Chair
American Economic Association Committee on Economic Education

Acknowledgments

We would like to take this opportunity to thank the many people and organizations that supported this project through its various stages. First and foremost, the Teagle Foundation provided financial support for both developing and distributing this volume. Many of the reflections included in this volume originated out of conferences held at Middlebury College, Vermont and the University of Richmond; both institutions provided financial and administrative support throughout the project. The generosity of the Christian A. Johnson Foundation, notably Julie Kidd, provided additional support for this endeavor.

A number of people played key roles in bringing this volume into existence. Members of the American Economic Association's Committee on Economic Education encouraged us not only to take on this project, but to be provocative to promote discussion. The Committee also provided opportunities to jump-start this discussion first by providing their own reflections on early drafts of the lead discussion paper and second by sponsoring a session at the 2009 Allied Social Science Associations (ASSA) meetings. Many others provided comments on the many drafts of this discussion paper, through conference presentations, listserv postings, and personal prodding. Special thanks to Tim Taylor of Macalester College, Minnesota, Dave Colander's history of economic thought class, and Janine Podraza. A special thanks to the people at Edward Elgar Publishing – Edward, Jo Betteridge and Suzanne Mursell. They warmly received our vision to turn the white paper into a unique volume, and did a great job with a fast production schedule. Finally, we have to say a special thank you to Carol Jones and Pat Colander for their support. Without it this project would have been a much more difficult task.

Introduction: a discussion, not a report

David Colander and KimMarie McGoldrick

When the AEA's Committee of Economic Education (CEE) was asked to develop a report on the economics major as part of a liberal education, there was a real question of whether the CEE wanted to undertake this endeavor.* While the Committee believed that the issue was both relevant and important, the question was whether a traditional, association-compiled report would make any difference. Decisions about the major are made at the department level, and unless there are incentives to change at that level, a report is unlikely to make any difference, regardless of what it contains. Economists, probably rightly, don't pay much attention to reports.

Every so often a report comes along that seems to be influential in creating change, but generally, its influence is derived from it being written at the right time and place. In other words, the situation on the ground was already ripe for change. There is a correlation, but no causation between reports and change. When the Committee asked itself whether the economics major was ripe for change, the consensus was no. The economics major is doing quite well, and while there are issues being debated, there is also a balance of views on those issues so that little overall change was expected. Thus, it was probable that a traditional report would only receive a cursory review before being moved to the back shelf.

Ultimately the Committee decided to do the report, not because it expected to bring about change in the major, but in order to encourage more discussion of the issues that the Committee felt were important. That's why this book is entitled a "Discussion" and not a "Report." But instead of trying to organize a blue-ribbon panel reflecting the various views on the major to generate a report that everyone would sign on to, the CEE asked two of its more provocative members to provide a thought-provoking piece on the economics major and its relation to a liberal education. The assignment was to write a report that would generate discussion and promote the continued debate of important issues.

We quickly decided that the goal of the report would not be to determine a set of best practices for the major – we believe that there are many best practices. We also weren't going to identify a set of lousy practices

– we believe that there are many lousy practices, but they are generally not practices borne out of ignorance, but conducted out of lack of caring, so a report ranting against them would have little effect. Instead, we decided to address some provocative questions that would encourage readers to look at the major in a slightly different light than is typically considered. What is the appropriate training for a person who will be teaching in a liberal arts school? Is it highly correlated with the PhD as currently constructed, or does it entail a quite different set of courses? What incentives would motivate the creation of institutional value through teaching and not simply research? What is the best way to teach introductory economics, and are we training anyone to do it? Is the disciplinary nature of undergraduate education squeezing out the big think questions, and replacing them with little think questions? That report is Chapter 1 of the book.

The initial draft report was distributed to numerous economists who were asked for comments. We organized two conferences designed to discuss the issues raised by the report – one at Middlebury College and one at the University of Richmond. Based on those comments and conferences we revised the report. The reflections of those who reviewed initial drafts of the report and attended the conferences were extremely insightful. Based on those comments, and comments from many others to whom we sent the report, including all the members of the Committee of Economic Education for the AEA, we revised and sharpened our arguments. We then sent the revised report to that same group of people, along with a few others to try to get a wide diversity of views, and invited them to submit revised versions of their comments, or new comments for the book. Those comments make up Parts 2, 3, and 4 of the book. One chapter in those comments, Chapter 12 is longer than the others. That is by design. As we were going through the comments, we found that W. Lee Hansen had developed his "proficiencies" approach to economics in more detail, and we thought it would be much more helpful to readers to see a fuller discussion of his ideas. So we asked him to allow us to publish his longer paper on the subject and he kindly agreed. Finally, the report was presented at the 2009 AEA meetings, at which we asked three economists who have also served as administrators, to comment. Their comments, along with comments from Bradley Bateman, who made the transition from professor to administration between when he first wrote his comments, and when he finished his comments, make up Part 5 of the book.

Writing about the major is usually only done by professors and administrators. But there is another important group – students – who have a large stake in the major and views about the major. Part 6 represents their views. It reports the results of two surveys – one at research liberal arts schools, and one a random survey of a variety of economics majors – that Dave Colander's Middlebury College students conducted.

A discussion has no conclusion, and we see this book as a discussion, not a report. The point of the discussion is to raise questions, not to provide answers or conclusions. However, we felt that some type of concluding chapter would be useful and Part 7 provides a short summary and overview of the discussion by John Siegfried. We believe that John is in a unique position of having headed the committee that compiled the last report describing the status and prospects of the economics major (Siegfried et al., 1991b).

NOTE

* This work was generously supported by a grant from the Teagle Foundation as part of their Fresh Thinking: Working Groups on the Disciplines and Undergraduate Education program, http://www.teaglefoundation.org/grantmaking/grantees/disciplines. aspx (accessed 17 April 2009).

PART 1

The Teagle report

1. The Teagle Foundation report: the economics major as part of a liberal education

David Colander and KimMarie McGoldrick

The goal of this report is to consider the relationship between the goals and objectives of the economics major and the goals and objectives of a liberal education. Is the economics major playing its part in meeting those objectives? Should it be changed? And if it should be changed, how should change be brought about?

The report is structured as follows. We first discuss the goals of a liberal education and the complaints that have developed about the major's role in general (and the economics major's role in specific) in meeting those broader goals. Second, we discuss the goals of the economics major – what it is meant to do, and what it isn't, and how those goals relate to a liberal education. Third, we discuss the reasons for differences in goals, and whether those differences should be of concern. Fourth, we discuss some structural changes that might lead to a better fit between the two. Finally, we discuss the role of pedagogy in a liberal education, and some changes that might better promote goals of the economics major within this broader context.

THE GOALS OF A LIBERAL EDUCATION

According to the Association of American Colleges & Universities (AAC&U), a liberal education should involve more breadth and less depth than it currently does. They see a liberal education as one that empowers students with broad knowledge and transferable skills.[1] They see it as an education that instills in students a strong sense of values, ethics, and civic engagement. Accordingly, they see a liberal education as a way of learning rather than as learning specific content. In their Liberal Education and America's Promise (LEAP) report, the National Leadership Council suggests "narrow preparation in a single area – whether that field is

3

chemistry or information technology or history – is exactly the opposite of what graduates need from college" (p. 17).[2] They argue that this is true both from a vocational standpoint and from a broader liberal education standpoint. We agree.

We do not intend for this report to address the question of what is meant by a liberal education, or whether the LEAP report's interpretation of a liberal education is the correct one. However, because the issue is so central, a few comments are necessary to frame the narrative in our report. Education is a never-ending process, and a student's learning in the major, or even in college, is only a small part of that education. Total classroom contact of students with faculty at college involves less than 1 percent of the students' first 21 years of life, with the major being only about one-third of that. This suggests to us that the success or failure of a liberal education, or of the major, depends far more on how the educational process influences a student's passion for learning than it does on the specifics of what they learn in their major. In our view, classroom education is best thought of as a catalyst for education as much as it is thought of as the education. The implication of this view is that colleges will succeed in providing a liberal education almost independently of what they teach if they instill a passion for learning in the students.

Conveying a passion for learning is best done by bright, passionate teachers who care about their subject, and care about teaching their subject, whatever that subject may be. The catalyst function of education can work almost regardless of content because the inquisitiveness and passion for learning that a successful liberal education creates in students carries over to other fields and areas. A successful liberal education creates a lifelong learner, who then picks up knowledge in other areas on his or her own. So, while the major is important to study as part of a liberal education, the catalyst role of the major, not the specific content of the major, should be seen as key.

THE ROLE OF THE MAJOR IN A LIBERAL EDUCATION

According to Derek Bok (2006), the major enters into the discussion of a liberal education because the student's major is an important part of their education, accounting for a third to a half of the total course load. Further, he finds that the major needs to be reconsidered in relationship to liberal education goals because majors "rarely attract serious scrutiny from the faculty as a whole" (p. 46). Bok quotes the AAC&U, arguing that:

the major in most colleges is little more than a gathering of courses taken in the department, lacking structure and depth, as is often the case in the humanities, or emphasizing content to the neglect of the essential style of inquiry on which the content is based, as is too frequently true in the natural and physical sciences. (p. 46)

He further writes that majors "often become so focused on covering their field of knowledge that they neglect or even undermine the teaching of good writing, critical thinking, and other important goals" (p. 47).

We agree with both Bok and with the National Leadership Council that looking specifically at the major is warranted.[3] However, we also believe that there is a more fundamental way in which the major affects education that Bok and the AAC&U do not discuss, and that will not be raised by reports made from a major departmental perspective. Departments, where the majority of majors are housed, are likely to focus on the need for depth in their field, and the need for specialized training as a component of a liberal education, whereas from the National Leadership Council perspective, there is need for a much stronger focus on breadth.

We believe that the push for depth over breadth by disciplinary scholars is to be expected; it comes from a passion for their field; to push too much breadth on a major within a disciplinary field will likely dampen the passion. For example, a Shakespeare scholar will likely find it hard to be passionate about teaching freshman composition, and a classical game theory scholar will likely find it hard to be passionate about teaching principles of economics as a broad-reaching interdisciplinary consideration of broad themes.[4] We also argue that because breadth is not usually associated with research passion by disciplinary specialists, and because the college is a collection of disciplinary specialists, breadth gets short-changed; it is interpreted as "superficial." Who is going to support superficial learning?

We believe that equating "breadth" with "superficial" is incorrect. Breadth to us involves the nature of questions asked. Breadth involves asking questions that likely have no answers – it involves asking what might be called "big think" questions that often question the foundation of the disciplinary analysis and transcend disciplines. Depth involves asking smaller questions that possibly can be answered – it involves what might be called "little think" questions.

Disciplinary researchers often don't deal with big think questions, not because these questions are not important, but rather because, given current tools, there is small likelihood that additional research on these questions will add to society's understanding of them. Put simply, questions and areas of study have two dimensions – a research dimension and a teaching dimension. Research questions are ones where there is a reasonable hope of adding to our understanding by studying the questions. Teaching questions that instill a passion for learning are often questions for which there is little likelihood of adding to our understanding, but which provide a base of understanding of past thinking. The disciplinary nature of graduate education, and of undergraduate college faculties, leads to an emphasis on "research questions," which tend to be narrow and in depth, and a de-emphasis on "teaching questions," which tend to involve more breadth.

In his recent book *Education's End*, Andrew Kronman (2007) captured our interpretation of breadth when he argued that what has been lost in college education is the part that directed students toward addressing unanswerable questions. Kronman suggests, for example, that questions involving the meaning of life are unanswerable. The "meaning of life" is, in our view, a teaching question. As economists, questions that contemplate the meaning of life are far beyond our expertise, but economics has its own set of teaching questions. These include questions such as whether capitalism or socialism is preferred, what the appropriate structure of the economy is, whether the market alienates individuals from their true selves, should one accept consumer sovereignty, and do statistical significance tests appropriately measure significance. These "big think" questions are ones that are worthwhile to teach, but are generally no longer included in the economics major because they don't fit the disciplinary research focus of the profession. In our view, that is a loss, since struggling with these "big think" questions helps provoke a passion for learning in students, and hence can be a catalyst for the student to go more deeply into those areas. Teaching "little think" questions too often involves uncritical acceptance of assumptions upon which the research is built.

In our view, what has too often been removed from the economics major, and from much of modern college education, is the consideration of such "big think" or teaching questions. Removing such questions has reduced the catalyst aspect of college education, and has thus hurt the provision of a liberal education. It is the loss of that catalyst aspect of breadth questions that, in our view, explains employers' somewhat paradoxical support of liberal education with more breadth and less depth. Employers are looking for inquisitive students who have a passion for learning, not ones who have learned specific skills. They prefer general skills such as critical thinking, quantitative, and communication skills. In other words they want a liberally educated student.

GRADUATE EDUCATION AND AN UNDERGRADUATE LIBERAL EDUCATION

A primary reason why a focus on breadth has receded within the undergraduate college curriculum is the nature of graduate education and the graduate degrees required of undergraduate professors that create narrowly based researchers. Modern graduate education (in economics at least) focuses on producing researchers, not teachers. It succeeds in what it sets out to do; it produces passionate researchers. These researchers can also be teachers, but generally the teaching passion is not for addressing broad unanswerable or big think questions; instead it is a passion to answer smaller research questions that fit the particular disciplinary nature of their study. Given the admission process to graduate school, which selects individuals with the greatest potential to develop into future researchers, not future teachers, graduates of the typical US graduate programs are neither likely to see the teaching of issues of breadth as appropriate, nor have they been trained to teach such issues, even if they do see them as important.

It is not only their training that drives professors away from big think questions; it is also the incentives they face. Specifically, because the department is the intellectual home of professors it determines the training he or she has received, motivates the nature of his or her research, and plays a key role in his or her advancement. The department provides the incentive structures that drive a professor's behaviors. It is those incentive structures that are central to how education works and plays out. A professor's department home determines the way in which he or she frames what is meant by a liberal education both within the major and at the institution.

Appointments that are truly transdisciplinary, rather than department based, provide quite different incentives for research and for teaching. For example, if one had a social science department that housed all social scientists, and that made recommendations on promotion and tenure, rather than individual social science disciplines making such recommendations, the undergraduate social science major would likely have quite different characteristics than the combination of the individual social sciences majors have now. What this means is that the department and major structure of higher education go far beyond whether the specific majors are contributing their fair share of courses or training to liberal education; that structure determines the way in which professors frame what is meant by a liberal education.

From our perspective, many of the problems pointed out by Bok and the AAC&U about colleges failing to provide a liberal education are inherent in the current departmental structure of colleges and universities. Without changing those structures, there is little hope of significantly changing the current situation, and in fact, it is not even clear whether one would want to do so. While the departments may recognize a need for breadth at one level of the student's education, faculty who see themselves primarily as belonging to a specific discipline or department will naturally give greater weight to their own contributions to that education, and emphasize arguments for depth as a necessary part of a liberal education.

Simply adding "breadth" courses within the major, or even outside the major, will not, in our view, solve the problem. Because of the catalyst nature of education, when one tries to have "breadth" courses taught by individuals whose disciplinary training is in depth, the attempt often falls short, unless one is lucky enough to find professors whose interests transcend their disciplinary training. The passion for the course is not there. Thus, the attempts to create courses of breadth, such as freshman seminars, and the introductory courses in economics often do not solve the problem because they are taught by faculty whose incentives are to structure the introductory courses for their majors, and who often have not been specifically trained in the broad-based skills that freshman seminars are designed to convey. In reality, introductory and interdisciplinary courses taught by disciplinary-trained researchers are too often seen by professors as obligations that they must teach, rather than as the courses they want to teach, and hence the courses are not taught with the same passion as the upper-level courses. When the passion and excitement isn't there, the course does not provide the catalyst to further learning that is the key to a liberal education.

What we are arguing is that the current institutional structure of graduate and undergraduate education channels the passion of professors toward upper-level courses and to students planning to go on in their discipline, and away from courses that involve breadth. Ironically, education in the major becomes a type of vocational education, where the vocation being taught is the "research college/university professor" vocation. The focus and the teaching passion of professors are on preparing students to be future researchers and specialists in their field, not on teaching courses that introduce the excitement of discovery to those non-specializing students who simply wish to understand the field. When the disciplinary major is the center of tenure and promotion decisions, the incentives facing the professors are to provide the best training from the disciplinary major's perspective, not the best training from a liberal education perspective.

GENERAL EDUCATION AND DISCIPLINES

Discussions of college education were once framed in terms of the educational process being divided into two components: general education and majors, with general education being provided in the first two years, and the major being the focus of the last two years. That may have been the structure of college education at one point in time, but it no longer is. At most colleges, majors have increased in importance, and many require students to start their major in their first year or at the latest in their sophomore year. There are few if any general education courses taught by professors devoted to teaching general education. General education courses are now provided by departments and are often seen as a draw on the teaching resources of the major, not as the foundation for a liberal education. The point is that the major's structure embedded within current college and university structures not only influences the major; it also significantly influences the actual provision of general education. The current structure of colleges leads to what is often called a tragedy of the commons, in which the large majority of the faculty is not directly concerned with achieving the overall goals of a liberal education, as those goals are a tangential element of the disciplinary major.

The issue is the following – people follow their incentives, and if one's primary home is in a department discipline, that is where one's energy is going to be focused. The department discipline determines research, it determines goals; it determines what one wants to teach, and what one is allowed to teach. At research-oriented liberal arts schools and research universities this is especially important since research tends to be discipline-specific, and discipline-specific research has a strong tendency to become more and more specialized. Faculty within disciplines judge themselves by disciplinary standards and feel enormous pressure to prepare students to succeed in their discipline, not to succeed in a broader environment. People are best at training students to do what they themselves do.

Because of discipline-specific incentives, all too often, instead of the major serving to strengthen liberal education by providing depth in one area, the undergraduate major training has a tendency to become vocational – to prepare students for graduate school. It channels the passion for learning to a small group of future researchers and professors. Providing a liberal education, and instilling a passion for learning in undergraduate students who do not want to go on to graduate school becomes a secondary goal of teaching, and is incorporated only to the degree it fits the needs of the departmental major. Thus, in our view, the structure of universities with disciplinary majors being the center of the intellectual life influences the way in which colleges meet the goals of a liberal education well beyond the actual courses offered in the major.

The disconnect between the major and liberal arts goals has become greater over time because the department within which disciplinary majors are housed has become more and more central to professors' research focus and interests. Disciplinary majors become increasingly entrenched, as the power bases for individual disciplines are reinforced by faculty training and institutional structure, and the power base for general education shrinks. In a setting where all faculty homes are within individual disciplines, the general education aspect of the college curriculum shrinks, as it has already done, and students with generalist interests are not provided with the catalyst for further learning and engagement, despite continual attempts by colleges and universities to achieve that end.

An example of what we mean is in freshman seminars, which were instituted to achieve a greater focus on communication and integrative skills, as well as to provide students with more intimate contact with faculty early on in their education. While some professors do quite well in these courses, their success is generally not due to their graduate training, because their training often does not match the training they are providing students. For example, math, science, and economics professors have little training in general writing and communication skills, but in their freshman seminars they are expected to teach these skills. Individuals becoming economists are not selected for their ability to write (students entering into economics PhD programs have a mean 772 Quantitative GRE score, and a mean 562 English score).[5] If economics professors succeed in instilling a passion for learning during the freshman seminar, it is due to their high level of intelligence, commitment to the ideals of such courses, and the fact that they can draw on training beyond what they get in graduate school. It is not due to the training they received in graduate school.

Now all this does not mean that undergraduate programs are devoid of professors committed to liberal education ideals; the top liberal arts schools and other highly ranked institutions are able to find professors who have broader interests. Just as the college major is only a part of an undergraduate's education, so too is graduate training only a part of a graduate student's education. Individuals with broad interests make it into graduate school and some make it through; others develop those broad interests afterwards. But those with the most passion for undergraduate teaching are unlikely to make it into a top graduate program in economics. In part this is because the training that top graduate programs offer is not attractive to these potential graduate students, but even more so it is because that is not the type of student that graduate programs are looking for; training students to be good teachers is not what graduate programs in economics see as their goal. In economics, if a student puts on his or her graduate school application to a top school that he or she wants to pursue teaching economics, he or she is unlikely to get accepted. At most top graduate schools students who want to become teachers know that they should keep that desire quiet (Colander, 2007). At lower-ranked graduate schools, the focus on training researchers as opposed to teachers is less pronounced, but it still exists, in part because these programs are staffed by graduates of the top programs. A culture of research dominates and there is little differentiation across programs (Krueger et al., 1991).

Another example of the difficulties that the departmental structure of majors presents for furthering liberal education can be seen in the "Great Books" approach that a number of schools used in the 1950s and 1960s. These "contemporary civilization" and "general humanities" courses were seen as forming the core of the freshman experience for students. But these programs faded away in part because of the difficulty in staffing them, in part because there was no political support for them as the majors gained importance and strength, and in part from a failure of administrators to truly support the program. For most discipline-based faculty, accepting a position teaching in these programs significantly reduced his or her research productivity since teaching the wide range of literature pulled him or her away from his or her discipline. Yet it is individuals in their discipline who have the greatest influence on decisions associated with tenure and promotion.

The idealized conception of these "Great Books" courses was that their content would cover a broad range of topics while the approach to the course would be grounded in the skills instructors were trained to master in their PhD program; the reality was that the material was taught more and more superficially, as the content of these "Great Books" was no longer part of graduate training in the specific disciplines. Today, an economist teaching in such a program would not, most likely, have any exposure to these texts in graduate school. This is true even for texts representing his or her own field, since the writings of economists such as Adam Smith, John Stuart Mill, and J.M. Keynes, or any past economist, are rarely taught in graduate economics programs. When faculty teaching core integrative courses such as contemporary civilization come from specific disciplines that do not emphasize or reward generalist research or thinking, it is highly unlikely that they have relevant training. PhD economists today get little training in the development of economic ideas, and thus, while they may be able to teach such a course, their ability to advance core goals of the course is not one based on what they learned in graduate school. That leads to little focus on literature in undergraduate training of economics. In the survey of undergraduate economics majors, only 38 percent said that they learned about economic literature in the major, by far the lowest percentage of any of the alternatives presented to them (Jones et al., Chapter 22, this volume).

What we are saying is that the current structure of graduate school works at cross-purposes with the goals of a liberal education. Put bluntly, if one wants to achieve a liberal education, one needs some body of the professorate who have a substantial commitment to that liberal education, not to a specific discipline or major. This would involve a substantial change not only in undergraduate education, but also in graduate education, and will not be an easy change to make.

There are, of course, structural changes in institutions that will generate changes in incentives. For example, if professors are hired into majors that include multiple disciplines rather than into a single disciplinary major, they will be forced to balance the competing forces of the various disciplines. Alternatively, if tenure and promotion decisions were made by broader committees reflecting diverse approaches to research, rather than the current situation at many schools where such broader committees simply ratify department decisions, then multidisciplinary research, which is more consistent with generalist research and "big think" questions that transcend a single discipline, would get more focus. In reality such changes are difficult to make, and often, even when institutions hire into multidisciplinary majors, represented disciplines simply bargain for rights over individual positions, with one discipline getting one hire in exchange for another discipline getting another. Only if institutional changes occur, leading to changes in incentives that become part of the underlying culture of the institutions, so that we have individuals committed to teaching liberal education courses, and committed to doing research that directly fits with liberal education goals, will these interdisciplinary courses be sustainable, because only then will the goals of liberal education mesh with the incentives facing the professorate teaching them.

As should be apparent, our view is that the problem of the relationship of the major to liberal education goes far beyond the structure of the major and the specific courses included as part of that structure. It goes to the specialized discipline structure of graduate education in the US, and its emphasis on turning out cutting-edge researchers and not undergraduate professors. Disciplinary research of the professorate tends to focus on increasingly specialized knowledge, which in turn drives the teaching desires of the professorate. As the individual disciplines, and hence majors based in those disciplines, become more and more specialized, the professorship becomes increasingly made up of a collection of specialists who are trained to do cutting-edge research, but who are tasked with teaching students who are far from the cutting edge of research.

In graduate training one wants, and needs, to develop these specialists, both because such students are very bright and can advance the field, and because they are the ones who can most appropriately teach future specialist researchers. But it takes a certain type of specialist – one whose interests go far beyond their specialty and who is committed to maintaining and conveying a broader vision of their field than specialist researchers generally have – to be simultaneously able to excel at teaching undergraduates and other non-specialists in addition to graduate students. As graduate school study becomes more and more specialized and more and more focused on preparing researchers, not teachers, and as research outlets become more and more specialized, the research focus and the teaching focus of the professorate pull harder and harder in different directions.

We will see these problems in microcosm in our discussion of the economics major, but in our view the problems that we discuss within economics are simply part of this larger problem. Graduate education is not designed to create future professors of undergraduates; it is designed to create cutting-edge researchers who teach undergraduates as a sideline. The process becomes self-reinforcing. Individuals who have the background, proclivity, and skills most appropriate to research are selected into graduate programs, and, when there, learn skills that are appropriate to researchers. They then become professors, and are most passionate about teaching students interested in, and courses related to their research. Focus on broader goals of a liberal education is given lower priority. The research-question-oriented professors encourage those students with the most interest in, and ability for, specializing to continue on to graduate school, resulting in the subsequent generations of professors even more highly focused on specialized disciplinary research and less trained or interested in the broader liberal educational goals.

This leads us to the proposition that if one wants the goals of a liberal education to be the focus of undergraduate education, one needs a set of professors whose research goals and whose teaching interests are in line with the broader questions that liberal arts programs focus on, and less on the specialized research that characterizes most disciplinary research. This means that their home base at the university (the one that has most power in determining tenure and promotion) must be larger than a specific discipline, or be a department that highly values generalist and interdisciplinary work. It also means that their primary research and teaching will not be cutting-edge disciplinary work, but instead be more integrative research that cuts disciplinary boundaries and asks bigger, and probably unanswerable, questions than can be asked in cutting-edge research.

The ACC&U states that general education is 50 percent of the importance of a college education. If this is indeed the case, then in order to create a faculty whose incentives for teaching and research match those values, 50 percent of the professorate need to have their training, and their disciplinary home, in a department or interdisciplinary program that highly values such integrative work and teaching. In economics that is far from the case.

One implication of the above analysis is that for some portion of the professorship, the research focus of undergraduate professors needs to differ from the research focus of graduate professors if the teaching incentives are to match the liberal education focus that Bok calls for. Undergraduate professors' research agenda cannot be just "graduate school lite" research, as it often is. Rather, their research is likely to employ different methods and tools, considering more speculative issues that cannot be considered in cutting-edge research, and be more easily transferable to the classroom. We are not arguing that undergraduate professors must be polymaths who can do it all. We are simply arguing that, in reality, there are trade-offs that must be made and currently the structure of universities and research liberal arts colleges lean more toward a graduate research focus than to an undergraduate research focus.

Consider the following example from economics. Marx considered alienation created by the market as a central problem of Western societies; Hayek argued that the market was necessary to preserve individual freedom; and Alfred Marshall argued that activities determined wants and thus wants could not be considered as primitives in economic analysis. Such issues are all highly relevant for students to consider as they are studying economics in a liberal arts setting, but they are not questions that are actively part of cutting-edge research, which instead generally focuses on narrower questions resolvable with statistical analysis, or on highly theoretical questions that go beyond the level of undergraduate students.

While the above discussion has presented these issues in terms of research-focused institutions, they are equally relevant for non-research-focused colleges. Given that the graduate school training professors currently receive is reflective of promoting cutting-edge, graduate-relevant, research, even if the hiring colleges do not have a strong research focus they must choose from a pool of applicants that reflects this focus. Hence, the graduate school training focus drives what *all* future faculty are most interested in because that focus reflects the training they have received.

Were we not viewing ourselves as consultants, but rather as representatives of the economics major, we would not be advocating major changes in the structure of both graduate and undergraduate education as suggested above. Professors who define themselves and their research within a department, as the large majority do, will not support, and indeed will argue vigorously against, such changes. Our reason for raising these issues is simply to point out that the issues of the major's relation to a liberal education goes far beyond the structure and content of the major. They are intricately connected to the disciplinary structure of colleges and universities, and with the research focus and nature of modern graduate education.

THE GOALS OF THE ECONOMICS MAJOR

Let us now turn to the economics major and its goals. The economics major is one of the most important majors in the liberal arts curriculum, at many liberal arts schools accounting for 20 percent or more of graduating seniors. (The economics major is much smaller at schools with a business program.) The major encompasses both technical aspects drawn from mathematics and natural sciences, and humanistic aspects related to history, philosophy, literature, political science, and public policy. Thus, in some ways, the problems in the economics major relating to a liberal education are a microcosm of the problems of the undergraduate program and a liberal education.

In terms of the goals that Bok sets out, economics neglects the development of certain skills of a liberal education that it could, and once did, include. Specifically, moral reasoning, while it was a part of economics education in earlier times, it is no longer a focus of economics today. Similarly, teaching students about "living with diversity" and, depending on how it is interpreted, providing "breadth of interest" are not specific goals of the economics major. But as we stated above, all aspects of a liberal education need not be integrated into any specific major, although aspects of economics can be seen as fitting into those goals.

The same holds true for "skills" training. Economists are not especially known for their communication skills, and receive little training in writing or communication in graduate school, so it is unlikely that the economics major will be effective in achieving these goals. A survey of undergraduate economics majors[6] found that only 28 percent of economics students said that economics was highly successful in teaching communication skills. Similarly, economists' critical thinking training takes a specialized mode and tends to be more focused on technical issues and analytics than on an understanding of how to arrive at a reasoned judgment, including all aspects of a problem.[7] For example, in a recent book, Duncan Foley (2006) has criticized economists for essentially teaching economic theology rather than reasoned economics. In the Jones et al. survey (Chapter 22, this volume) only 21 percent of economics majors saw economics as highly successful at teaching moral reasoning.

Probably the clearest statement of the goals of the economics major can be found in Siegfried et al. (1991b), who reviewed both the purpose and structure of the undergraduate major. The central phrase and goal that emerged from this report, "thinking like an economist," was recognized then as encompassing many of the goals of liberal education, including deductive reasoning skills, decision-making techniques, understanding complex relationships, creativity, and acquiring and using knowledge that cuts across disciplinary boundaries. That report helped to establish, or at least codify, the general structure for the undergraduate economics major that almost all economics departments currently follow.

THINKING LIKE AN ECONOMIST AND THINKING LIKE A LIBERALLY EDUCATED PERSON

Economists have come to specify the goal of the major as teaching students to think like an economist. This is a relatively non-controversial goal in that it allows each professor to think of the training that they provide as essentially getting the student to think like him or herself. The goal has been pushed further by some who favor teaching a set of proficiencies. Hansen (2006a) argues that the goal of the economics major should be to teach students to "act like an economist," which suggests that "instructors want students to be able to demonstrate at various levels their ability to perform the various proficiencies, culminating at graduation with their ability to demonstrate mastery of every one of the proficiencies" (p. 7). Almost everyone would agree that proficiencies should ground what is taught; where the disagreement tends to be is in how broadly or narrowly these proficiencies are to be defined. Should they be reflective of liberal arts goals such as being able to read, critically analyze, and write effectively, or should they be reflective of more narrow economics major skills such as understanding opportunity cost, being able to run regressions and interpret "t" statistics, and explain the connection between money supply and inflation?

Precisely what thinking like an economist means changes over time, mirroring changes in an economist's training. Through the 1960s both graduate and undergraduate economics training was focused on broad-based skills that integrated critical thinking, historical knowledge, and statistical skills. Since then, graduate economics training has become more technical, more and more reliant on mathematics and statistics. Initially, there were debates within the economics field about this change, but those debates have died out and technical mathematics and statistical training won out. Today the reality is that graduate training in economics is a highly technical field, and anyone who is not comfortable in higher-level mathematics and statistics is not advised to continue on in graduate work in economics. The focus on general economic problem-solving in a broad setting – a focus that characterized economics training through the 1960s – is much less than it was before, and thus the professorate has more training in making important technical inputs into policy analysis, than it has at developing a policy question within a broader framework. Graduate training is designed to develop skills of technical expertise, not to focus on policy design or the moral philosophy aspect of policy. In graduate economic programs, students learn to translate problems into formal models, and to empirically study those problems using high-level statistical techniques. They get little training in non-formal policy analysis or in synthesizing a broad range of literatures and approaches.

To the degree that thinking like an economist is now associated with the narrower, more technical proficiencies of the modern approach rather than the broader proficiencies of the earlier approach does not mean that the economics major does not contribute to a liberal education; it simply means that the economics major fulfills a slightly different aspect of the liberal education than it previously did. This is apparent in the economics major's role in contributing to the goal of providing training in moral reasoning. The typical economics professor receives little training in guiding students through moral reasoning or civic engagement activities, and his or her interests have been highly narrowed into those sets of problems that are susceptible to formal modeling and statistical testing, and less so to questions of policy that involve complicated ethical or moral issues or what might be called tragic questions (Nusbaum, 2000). So, today, as a result of their increased technical training and reduced broad-based training, the economics professorate contributes more to the quantitative literacy goal of a liberal education, and less to the moral reasoning goal.

This suggests that what it means to "think like an economist" has evolved from what it was 10 or 20 years ago. The training that undergraduates get within the economics major in "thinking like an economist" is more specialized than it previously was, and that specialization is likely to increase in the next decade. In our view "thinking like an economist" is no longer sufficient to provide what Bok has in mind when he argues for a liberal education. As part of a broader liberal education, the economics major can play an important role, but that role is changing to be more like the role that the sciences and math currently play, leaving students to round out their skill development through other components of their education.

The argument that the economics major is becoming more technical and specialized needs to be kept in perspective. Relative to history, English, or the other social sciences, economics is indeed technical and specialized, although the same pressures for specialization are at work in those other fields as well. Relative to the undergraduate science majors the economics major is non-technical and general. These differences across majors are revealed through student perceptions of their associated level of difficulty. For example, in the Jones et al. survey (Chapter 22, this volume) 37 percent of economics majors considered economics hard; less than 3 percent considered sociology hard, and 80 percent considered chemistry and physics hard. The economics major also typically has far fewer required courses than the science majors, and, unlike most natural science majors, is still designed to be taken by students who do not intend to continue their education in economics beyond graduation.

The reason why economics has found this balance of difficulty and course requirements, we suspect, is that, because of its connections to business, the undergraduate economics major has to satisfy two constituencies: a very small group who will go on in their formal study of economics (for which the economics professorate is trained to teach), and a much larger (generalist) group who view the economics major either as a stepping stone to business and public policy, or simply as a foundation for a strong liberal arts education. Integrating the needs of these two groups is a major problem for undergraduate economics faculty, and the decisions they make on how to meet the needs of these two groups will significantly influence the nature of the economics major in the future.

In terms of numbers, it seems clear that the second group – those perceiving economics as a stepping stone, not planning to go on for further study – is the largest. In the Jones et al. survey (Chapter 22, this volume), while 10 percent of the majors reported considering going on to graduate school, less than 2 percent of all economics majors actually do go on to do a graduate PhD in economics, and an even smaller percentage complete it. But the professor's interest and focus often tends toward this much smaller group. Current graduate training in economics is focused on preparing researchers who have a narrow research focus, and who avoid asking big think questions and so the graduates who will constitute the future of the economics profession will naturally want to train majors in the manner in which they have been trained. This leads them to design the major and focus their passion on the courses that prepare undergraduates to go on to graduate school, as the natural sciences have already done, and to devote less time and passion to "generalist" courses.

Some programs deal with the dual constituency by creating two separate tracks in the major. The mathematical or economic science track is appropriate for those going on to graduate school in economics and those interested in using economics to get a quantitative liberal arts foundation. That group probably makes up about 20–40 percent of the current economics majors. The other track is a more general economics track that is more relevant to applied policy and provides a combined humanistic/quantitative liberal arts foundation.[8] Other programs leave the two constituencies integrated, and attempt to design a single approach to the major that caters to both groups. Regardless of the program format, however, economics majors are being populated with more and more technical course offerings as younger, more technically trained, economists replace older, more generalist trained, economists. This means that the economics major is becoming less and less appropriate for the students interested in business and public policy, or for those interested in a combined humanistic/quantitative liberal arts foundation, and more appropriate to students going into graduate economics and interested in a quantitative liberal arts foundation.

Economics faculty are teaching students to think like an economist, but it is not clear that "thinking like an economist" is the appropriate final educational goal for these generalist students. The goal for them is not so much to be able to think and act like an economist, since a large majority of them are not becoming economists, but instead to be *familiar with* the reasoning tools that are consistent with the economic way of thinking, and to use those tools when appropriate. The goal of a liberal arts education is to teach students to think like a "liberally educated person." Ideally, when students finish their major, they would know the broad outlines of the economic method, and have some knowledge of the technical tools that economists use, and when it is appropriate to use them. They would understand how the economic way of thinking, when combined with other ways of thinking, can lead to a reasoned solution to a problem. They would not think that the economic way of thinking is the only right way of thinking and they would be knowledgeable about what a "scientific" way of thinking is and what a "humanist" way of thinking is.

Graduate work in economics and non-technical undergraduate programs designed for the generalist students who want to use economics, not to become an economist, come close to existing in "different worlds." Undergraduate education in economics features fairly simple graphical models, and relatively simple data analysis, while graduate work features high-level math and statistics. In a self-study of graduate schools commissioned by the AEA, Hansen (1991) found that "academic economics and graduate training have become increasingly preoccupied with formalism and technique, to the exclusion of studying real-world problems and issues" (p. 1086).

We find it telling that the ACC&U criticisms of the major mentioned earlier:

> the major in most colleges is little more than a gathering of courses taken in the department, lacking structure and depth, as is often the case in the humanities, or emphasizing content to the neglect of the essential style of inquiry on which the content is based, as is too frequently true in the natural and physical sciences (p. 46)

did not refer to the social sciences. We think that it is quite right in not referring to economics, because economics suffers from neither of the problems it mentions. In fact, the undergraduate economics major as a whole has found a better balance between the depth and breadth than majors in the sciences or in the humanities. That balance is, however, precarious because there is a strong push for the economics major to become

more technical and better preparation for graduate school. Professors
naturally have a proclivity to structure their curriculum so that it creates
students in the professor's image.

CHANGES TO CONSIDER

As should be clear from the above discussion our view is that the type of
changes necessary to make the economics major significantly more liberal-
education-friendly go far beyond the structure and content of the undergraduate major. If one is truly serious about providing a liberal education
to undergraduates, one must address both the institutional structure of
graduate schools and the disciplinary structure of undergraduate institutions. The chances of such sweeping changes being made are similar to
the chances of pigs flying. Nonetheless, we discuss some changes that
have potential to increase the desire of those who teach undergraduates
to better reflect a liberal education perspective and provide them with
appropriate skills to achieve this goal.

We want to make it clear that we are not arguing that these changes
need to be mandated for the economics major to be a successful program.
We believe that the current structure of the economics major is providing
important skills to its graduates and any changes imposed on colleges
from the top down are likely to make the economics major worse, not
better. In our view, the economics major is doing a better job providing a
balanced major than most of the natural sciences, which too often become
vocational majors directed at preparing students for graduate school and
use their gateway courses as hurdles that only true pre-professional students choose to make their way through. Similarly, the economics major
does a better job at integrating the quantitative and statistical tools, which
are more and more becoming foundational liberal arts tools, than most of
the other social sciences. But we also believe that the major is not providing the context for the ideas it presents, and the discussion of big think
issues that are necessary for a true liberal education.

Given the current structure of graduate economics education, we are
not sure that it can. As we stated above, in our view, instructor passion is
more important than course content. It is for that reason that we believe
that change in the major, if it is to occur in a positive manner, must occur
from the *bottom up*, reflecting faculty and student characteristics of the
particular institution, with individual colleges and departments choosing
the direction they want to go. For example, a liberal arts program without
a business program may well want to offer a quite differently structured major than what a liberal arts program with a business program

offers. Similarly, a program heavily endowed with historians of economic thought might want to offer a rather different program than one with primarily game theorists or econometricians. There is room for much positive variation within the economics major; there is no one size fits all. Our hope in this report is not to say that there is a single set of "best practices." We believe there are a variety of best practices and that the economics major can take many different forms within current institutional structures. We put the following proposals forward with that multitude of best practices view – our hope is to stimulate discussion that may lead to bottom-up change, not to impose any top-down change.

Before we list some suggested changes, let us add one final caveat. Any restructuring of incentives of the professorate needs to be institution- and discipline-specific. Each specific institution and discipline has different problems, issues, and goals they need to balance. But there are some similarities among types; for example, graduate institutions have the problem of integrating the content associated with graduate teaching with undergraduate teaching, and integrating the members of the department devoted to undergraduate teaching with those devoted to graduate teaching. The problems of research liberal arts schools, where research plays an increasingly important role in the evaluation and promotion of professors, and where faculty have reduced teaching loads that reflect that focus, differs from those of other colleges, at which research plays a smaller component in evaluation of faculty, and from programs within large universities. Similarly, the problems in different disciplines, such as math or English, are likely to differ from those in economics. Our focus here is on the economics discipline within research liberal arts colleges. We hope that some of the ideas carry over to other institutional settings and disciplines, but we do not claim that they do.

Potential Structural Changes

Increase the number of professors whose training is designed to promote good teaching of undergraduates, not to promote research

Graduate school training in disciplines is, by design, specialized, and primarily designed to provide professors with the tools they need to do research. Post-graduation teaching at a liberal arts school as a goal is not encouraged, and is not supported by the training offered (Colander, 2007). While a professor teaching undergraduates would gain by receiving training in the broad outlines of the debates that led to modern economics, such training has been almost eliminated throughout all top-ranked graduate programs. It is simply not what they are designed to do. The implication is that future professors are currently not trained to participate more fully in the development of a liberal education. PhD programs create specialists not well versed in broader ideas within their field, or in the philosophies of other related disciplines and in how economics might relate to those disciplines.

This is not to say that such professors do not exist in economics; they do, but they have acquired that training on their own, exploring interests that may actually have been seeded during their own undergraduate training, not at graduate school. Once obtaining a position at the research liberal arts school, the incentives continue to work against such training. The disciplinary research of those teaching in undergraduate institutions mirrors that faced by graduate school researchers, and is almost inevitably highly specialized.

Changing the training provided by graduate schools is unlikely, since the research pull in graduate departments runs totally counter to providing a more liberal-education-focused training. However, research liberal arts colleges can impact the incentives associated with training at graduate schools by instituting specific requirements for faculty teaching general education courses such as freshman seminars, or broad overview courses. For example, college administrations could require any faculty member hired with the expectation of teaching in general education courses to have covered specific areas in their graduate training. Alternatively, liberal arts schools could agree to provide interview preferences to those graduating from institutions who have invested in more liberal-education-focused training. The hope is that such hiring requirements would feed back to graduate schools, and some of these graduate schools would choose to add such courses or even to specialize in training students for that undergraduate teaching niche.

Schools might also consider creating a dedicated departmental home for those who teach liberal education courses. An example of what we mean might be the social studies department at Harvard. The motivation for this type of structure is that the departmental home of a professor significantly influences his or her interests, both in research and teaching. Currently, we have very few professors at research liberal arts colleges whose primary interest is in more general liberal education, rather than in a specific field. By creating a broad-based "liberal arts or social studies" department whose focus is on liberal studies and that staffs the general education freshman seminars and possibly the general capstone courses at the end of a student's college experience, one would significantly change the nature of education at research liberal arts colleges. Faculty commitment to the liberal education ideals would be enhanced by the incentives associated with positions in a general liberal education department. The existence of these dedicated positions would encourage faculty to focus their energies on integration, breadth of ideas, and specific skills such as critical thinking and communication. Initially, the professors for these liberal education departments could come from existing faculty, who have on their own developed such broad interests, and from newly set up programs, but ultimately it would likely be staffed by those earning degrees from dedicated graduate programs in the liberal arts.

Require all undergraduate teachers to have completed specific courses before they are allowed to teach at the undergraduate level
The push for research specialization throughout graduate training is especially apparent in economics. Integrative aspects of education that almost all would agree are good preparation for teaching in an undergraduate liberal arts environment have been pushed out of graduate training to make room for more technical training. This is evidenced by the reduced emphasis on economic history, history of economic thought, and institutions throughout graduate economic training. Were these courses required, or strongly suggested, as appropriate training for professors seeking employment at liberal arts colleges we suspect that some graduate programs would reinstitute them.

A corollary to this proposal is to allow anyone who has successfully completed a set of graduate-level courses deemed necessary for teaching the associated undergraduate course within the major to be permitted to teach that course. Developing a course by course specification of appropriate background courses necessary for teaching general education core courses in economics (and analogously in other fields as well) would encourage a new cohort of faculty to enter the professorate. Since graduate school is preparing researchers, not teachers, course-specific training, rather than the PhD degree, could be a much more efficient way of organizing the teaching qualifications for particular introductory courses. Since these courses make up a large portion of the enrollment in economics courses, having alternative qualifications for these courses would create a cadre of instructors trained in, and excited by "big think" issues and would be a more efficient method than the current PhD qualification.

Require certification for undergraduate teaching separate from a research-oriented PhD training
Graduate economics programs are dedicated to exposing students to cutting-edge research and developing their research skills. Success is measured by the number of articles published and the prestige of the journals in which they appear. No similar measure of success currently exists for teaching.

In order to ensure that faculty are prepared to participate in the education of young minds, a certification of teaching could be required. Faculty entering the profession and having undergraduate teaching responsibilities would be required to submit a teaching portfolio that includes a statement of teaching philosophy, examples of classroom practices and student work, and course evaluations.

More and more institutions are creating non-tenure-track lecturer or clinical professor positions with heavy teaching responsibilities including course work, advising of TAs, and conducting regional teaching conferences. Little traditional research is expected. Much of the drive for these positions comes from increasing pressure to cover a greater number of courses and to demonstrate to the administration a commitment to teaching. Institutions hiring for such positions might be expected to require certification reflecting appropriate training for these positions.

Create a program developed by liberal arts schools that provides training relevant to undergraduate teaching
A consortium of liberal arts schools could establish a post-doc program that would have an intensive one-month training followed by a one-year placement at a liberal arts school where the graduate student would be mentored in teaching methods and assigned directed readings, or take part in consortium workshops, as well as co-teach a course each semester. The program could be designed as a post-doc or a separate master's program, and could include a combination of discipline-specific and cross-disciplinary studies that provide opportunities to participate in the integration of knowledge and skill development. It could also provide some focus on alternative teaching methods.

Create opportunities for re-education of faculty further along in their careers in preparation for participating in liberal education
This program would allow faculty who have primarily focused on highly specific research, to obtain further education (or demonstrate such self-acquired skills through testing) that certifies them in content most appropriate to a liberal education. One would expect that faculty interested in this program would shift their activities from a specialized to a more general research focus complementing associated changes in teaching responsibilities.

Create opportunities for successful professionals to return to the classroom and share their skills with undergraduates
Programs designed to prepare professionals to teach specific under-graduate courses would tap into an underutilized educational resource that is a natural complement to enhancing the liberal education skills

of undergraduates. Such a program would allow practitioners who are further along in their careers to achieve a certification demonstrating their qualification to teach specific general education courses at the undergraduate level. This program could be developed in conjunction with an executive in residence program where the former executives both teach and learn at the same time.

Develop an alternative ranking system for research productivity that gives greater weight to liberal education research rather than "discipline-specific" research

Measurements of research output are becoming more and more predominant in the process of identifying and rewarding productive faculty in research-oriented liberal arts colleges. Ranking systems currently in place were originally designed to aid in the ranking of graduate programs and therefore focus on technical research in the specific field, providing little weight to generalist or transdisciplinary research. For example, in the standard economics rankings writing a popular book does not even count as a publication, since only journal articles are counted, and an article in *Science* receives no weight as it is outside the bounds of the discipline. Because reward systems are based on these ranking systems, the resultant incentives play a large role in guiding a professor's research. If the ranking system changes, so will the focus on and nature of research. Once such a ranking system for research expected from those teaching at undergraduate programs was developed, it could be used to rate graduate programs for their preparation of professors with such abilities. This rating system would be developed and implemented by the very institutions that it is intended to serve, liberal arts colleges.

Divide the undergraduate economics major into an economic science major and an economic policy major

As described above, much of economics graduate training is highly specialized, devoted to creating economic scientists in the same way that natural science graduate programs are devoted to creating natural scientists. Neither is designed to train students in applying policy or the associated broader moral philosophy aspects, yet this is where a majority of the students' interests reside. The natural sciences solve some of this disconnect by having a separate engineering component; those students going into applied work participate in the engineering branch rather than natural science branch. The teachers are different and the curriculum is different for each branch. As a result, the natural sciences tend to have a very small undergraduate major, which is devoted to preparing students for graduate school. One obviously missing component from the current design of the science major is the policy branch, where the training would be geared to understanding and evaluating science policy.

The economics major has no engineering branch, nor does it have a separate policy branch. It typically combines everything together into a single major. However, there are some schools (Claremont, Princeton) that separate the major into an economic science technical branch, and an economic policy branch. It might even be possible to create distinct departments providing different training for students and potentially requiring different qualifications of their professors.[9] Providing two distinct majors provides better training opportunities for those who are interested in continuing on to graduate school and those who are better suited to applied, policy-oriented or teaching-oriented training.

Create a pre-professional major for students whose interests are only tangentially linked to economics

Because science and math majors at liberal arts programs are geared to preparing students to enter graduate schools, they tend to have fewer majors who have multiple career path options. Furthermore, few liberal art institutions have public policy or business schools, leading many students at liberal arts schools to gravitate toward economics as the closest viable major. While economics reasoning is certainly an important part of the training that a student needs for business or public policy, it clearly is only a part. A preferable training for these students is a curriculum consistent with broad liberal education goals.

Having students choose the economics major as a path to business creates problems both for economics departments (which have students taking economics who are not directly interested in economics) and for students (because they are not getting the business and public policy background they desire and need). One possibility is for liberal arts schools to create pre-public policy and pre-business tracks, the curriculum of which would be designed in collaboration with business and public policy leaders. The goal of this proposal is to provide students with a better alternative, a curriculum that includes depth in business-related courses, such as accounting, finance, and management, and the liberal arts breadth they need, including more computer science, ethics, humanities, math, and philosophy courses. Students who complete this program will be awarded a pre-professional certificate at graduation, which they can put on their resumé. Ideally, this program would be taken as an alternative to a major.

While the proposal is called a pre-professional program in that it meets the needs of the students going on to professions in business and public policy, it is not a vocational program in the sense that an undergraduate business or public policy program would be. Businesses don't want that; they want liberally educated students. Thus, the program takes advantage of the emerging consensus that the vocational needs of business and public policy are best achieved by providing students with a traditional liberal education. (See discussion in the LEAP report.[10])

PEDAGOGY AND A LIBERAL EDUCATION

We now turn to a set of complementary issues – those related to pedagogical practices – and discuss how improvements in pedagogy can improve the fit between the economics major and a liberal education. For all the same reasons that the *content* of graduate economics education is not designed for future undergraduate professors, *pedagogical* considerations receive little focus. Teaching receives little respect. Graduate students are rarely provided sufficient preparation for teaching during their graduate school training. This lack of preparation has been documented by Stock and Hansen (2004), who surveyed two cohorts of graduate students (1996, 2001) to determine the degree of (mis)match between proficiencies and skills emphasized in graduate school and those needed for academic careers. They found that a disconnect exists between what students learn and the skills they need on the job, especially with respect to proficiencies of applying economic theory to real-world problems, understanding economic institutions and history, and understanding the history of economic ideas (p. 270). The lack of training professors have in these areas is also apparent to undergraduate students. Jones et al. (Chapter 22, this volume) found that 63 percent of students identified "add more discussion of real-world issues" as the change in the major they would like most. This was far and away the largest percentage associated with any suggested change. Additional shortcomings of graduate teacher training identified by Stock and Hansen include the fact that over one-third of students they surveyed (44 percent in 1996 and 33 percent in 2001 cohorts) reported too little emphasis on developing teaching skills in their graduate program and that skills such as application, communication, and instruction are under-valued at the graduate school level as compared with their jobs (p. 270). About 70 percent of students they surveyed listed instruction as the least important skill for success in their graduate program, whereas only 29–39 percent made the same statement about this skill in their current job.

Walstad and Becker (2003) surveyed chairs of economic departments to investigate preparation for teaching that students received. They found that about 60 percent of graduate students are involved in some form of teaching activities: about 12 percent of graduate students teach their own courses; about 28 percent lead their own recitation sections; and about 20 percent assist professors with their own courses (p. 450). Preparation for these activities varies widely, ranging from taking preparation courses with graduate credit (25 percent), participating in non-credit programs (50 percent), providing assistance for faculty with courses (50 percent), passing comprehensive exams (25 percent), or passing an English-language proficiency exam in the case of international students (80 percent) (p. 451). Over 60 percent of responding department chairs believed that the preparation for teaching that they provided their graduate students was good or very good (p. 453).

That view of adequate preparation was less likely to be shared by students. In a survey of graduate students in the US, McGoldrick et al. (forthcoming) found that 40 percent of those teaching their own courses claim to have received no preparation for doing so.

The picture that these studies provide is consistent with the anecdotal evidence that abounds. When asked about the importance of teaching versus research in promotion decisions at major universities, one hears that practice dictates 90 to 95 percent of the decision based on research output. The perception is that as long as you are not a truly horrendous teacher, research is what counts. In economics departments at research liberal arts schools, which many of the top liberal arts schools now consider themselves, research is considered to be at least as important as teaching in tenure and promotion decisions. Even at lower-ranked undergraduate liberal arts programs, research is gaining in importance. The reality is that we have a professorate who enter academia in economics with far less preparation for the teaching component of their job than for the research component, and with the content of what they learn determined not by what they will be teaching, but by what content would best prepare them to be a researcher. This means that as long as graduate programs maintain their current practices, new PhDs in economics need additional support in teaching after they join established departments, and they also need to learn the content relevant to undergraduates on their own.[11] For example, a macroeconomics teacher coming in to teach undergraduate macro theory will likely be asked to teach the IS/LM model that he or she has no training in, and convey an understanding of monetary and fiscal institutions that were only mentioned tangentially in his or her graduate courses.

The problem of preparation for teaching has been recognized, and some of the most prestigious institutions in the country are now making a vocal commitment to the importance of teaching. For example, in a recently released report from the Harvard Task Force on Undergraduate Teaching (2007), the problem was seriously considered. They found that the problem regarding the role of teaching did not reside with individual faculty, but rather in the incentives of the institution. Rather than rewarding good teaching, "cutting-edge academic research is what FAS [Harvard Faculty of Arts and Sciences] celebrates and most consistently rewards."[12] In our view, even this courageous report underestimates the difficulties caused by the almost single-minded focus on training researchers, not teachers in economics. Graduate content is determined by its relevance for research, not its relevance for teaching. The lack of training in content relevant for teaching undergraduates is not considered a problem by most economics graduate programs, which see their job solely as training researchers, not teachers.

A number of reasons can be offered as explanations of why teaching is not valued as highly as research. Foremost is the fact that teaching tends to be a private activity, the assessment of which is often generated solely by the audience of students (through standard evaluations). Research, on the other hand, is an incrementally more public process beginning with collaboration of co-authors, continuing through the presentation at conferences, the review process upon submission to a journal, and finally the publication of a paper. Academic debates that occur via published comments or papers that build off of the original work are the basis for continued public dialogue. The public nature extends to the issue of academic prestige, measured by the ranking of journals in which peer-reviewed research appears. Finally, few external resources exist to support the development of pedagogical practices, whereas prestigious granting agencies provide significant support for innovative research.

THE STRUCTURE AND CONTENT OF THE ECONOMICS MAJOR

At most schools, the undergraduate economics major almost always includes one or two introductory courses (usually called principles of microeconomics and macroeconomics), intermediate theory courses in both microeconomics and macroeconomics, one or two quantitative methods courses covering basic statistics, regression models and estimation techniques, a few elective upper-level "field" courses, and ideally a senior seminar or capstone course that includes an extensive research and writing component. Often, there is a calculus requirement, but that requirement is often designed more as an analytic filter for who can major in economics than as an actual needed requirement.

The introductory and intermediate microeconomics courses concentrate on presenting a constrained optimization model in either a geometric or calculus format. The introductory and intermediate macroeconomics

courses concentrate on presenting geometric AS/AD and IS/LM models
that are useful for policy discussions, but which have little formal foundations. This coverage is quite different than what is covered in graduate
schools, where the presentation is much more technical, concentrating on
set theory and game theory in microeconomics, and dynamic stochastic
optimal control theory in macro. Little of the training in the core micro
or macro courses in graduate school relates to what is taught in undergraduate school. (In the statistics sequence, the concordance is better.)
No training in where the ideas came from and how they evolved, which
would be highly relevant for generalist students, is provided to students in
graduate school, and that lack of training is filtering down to teaching in
undergraduate programs.

   The senior course requirements are more common at liberal arts schools,
and in fact at some large public universities these courses are not offered,
or are offered only for honors students. Most economics departments
and faculty would agree that more extensive senior experience courses
are desirable, and that a writing component in the earlier theory and field
courses would enhance student skills. Class sizes are often very large even
in upper division field courses in economics, however – especially at large,
public universities, which means that achieving such goals would involve
significant commitments of additional teaching resources for already
pressured departments.

   While the current structure of the undergraduate economics major
remains appropriate for generalists, there is pressure for change, since new
professors coming in have a natural tendency to want to teach what they
have learned. Over time we expect undergraduate programs in economics to become increasingly technical and focused on preparing students
for graduate school, as graduate training becomes more technical, and as
newly minted PhDs advance into the majority at undergraduate programs.
Eventually all undergraduate economics programs reflect the graduate
economics programs that train the undergraduate teachers. People teach
what they learn.

PEDAGOGICAL PRACTICES IN THE MAJOR

Given the interdependency of structure and content and the current disconnect between graduate and undergraduate content, economic educational
reform at the undergraduate level has often focused on delivery. Research
in economic education has also documented the way in which economics
faculty interact with students in the classroom, and how that differs from
common practice in other fields. Economics teaching across all institution

types makes little use of interactive pedagogy as economics instructors spend roughly 83 percent of available class time lecturing (Becker and Watts, 2001, 2008). While innovative programs are under way to address underutilization of innovative teaching strategies (such as the NSF-funded Teaching Innovations Program[13]), these programs are limited to pedagogical techniques and do not explore the connection to broader goals such as promoting critical thinking and greater engagement by students in their undergraduate course work – enhancing skills that will serve the students throughout their lives. But such programs help get professors focused on teaching, and thus serve a useful role.

Improving Pedagogical Practices

Because of the political difficulties of instituting any structural changes such as those discussed above, much of the pressure to improve teaching at the undergraduate level has focused on modifications of course structure and pedagogy. These are changes that individual professors, departments, and colleges can implement on their own. We strongly believe that these changes should continue, and be expanded. We briefly survey some of the changes that have been made, and offer additional suggestions. Again, we begin with a qualification. The details and implementation of each proposal put forth is entirely dependent on the context in which it is considered. For example, introductory and senior-level courses are likely to differ across institutions because the expected outcomes and cognitive development of the target audiences differ.

Content and skills
Almost all principles students do not continue with a major in economics. For this generalist group of students, if economics is to be meaningful it has to be highly "practical," focusing more on "big think" questions as linked to broader liberal education goals. The economic skills we teach should reflect this practical need and courses should provide context for those skills. Furthermore, students who do choose to major in economics should be required to demonstrate their acquired skills, reflecting the highly practical way in which they will use economics, not in ways that they will never replicate once they leave the classroom. To achieve this end, departments should consider a number of possible changes in the major:

Revise introductory course content   Nowhere in the economics curriculum is the depth versus breadth issue more prevalent than in the principles courses. Principles textbooks, with few exceptions, are structured after the Samuelsonian texts of the 1950s. Not only do they not incorporate the latest advances in economic theory and modeling, they often do not even mention them except in boxed features. It is as if introductory economics is being taught in a time warp. Thus, serious consideration needs to be given to the content of the principles course, how it ties into what is now taught in graduate school, and how it ties to a liberal education. Questions need to be answered such as: is the principles course meant to give students a sense of the empirical nature of much of applied micro today? Or is it designed to teach students economic precepts – policy views that are based on a set of value judgments that are based on classical liberalism. Or is it designed to teach economic science – focusing on understanding the functioning of the economy more so than policy? Or is it providing students with an overview of issues being debated in economics, such as how behavioral economics is changing the nature of economic theory, or how evolutionary game theory is changing the way in which economic issues are framed? Or is it designed to teach what used to be called political economy, in which it provides the broader reasoning for policies favored by most economists today?

Currently the texts seem to be attempting to provide a mixture of all these, but often not making it clear what precisely they are doing. Specifically, they do not distinguish between scientific theorems with which no serious economist would disagree, and economic policy precepts, on which significant debate exists. The economic way of thinking incorporates both but the two foci are quite different and need to be distinguished.

What makes deciding what should be taught in the principles course even harder is that the economic way of thinking is changing. It is more inductive than previously; it uses laboratory, natural, and field experiments to test assumptions and models, and is based more on game theory and strategic reasoning than on deductive calculus subject to strict agent rationality assumptions.

We are not arguing that all these new approaches should be taught to students, but since all these approaches are part of the modern economic way of thinking, it would seem that the issues they raise should be presented if the "economic way of thinking" is actually the focus of the introductory courses. Today, the economic way of thinking has become much more the "scientific way of thinking" than it was in the past. How much of this can be presented to students is debatable, but it needs to be considered.

Some work has been done on the issue of what should be taught in the principles course. For example, Salemi and Siegfried (1999) reviewed the goals of the economics major and suggested a greater emphasis on economic education as general education through a redesign of introductory economics courses. Their work challenges instructors to reconsider the degree to which skill development is limited to preparation for the major and thus neglects the need for both breadth and depth of understanding and application skills consistent with the goals of the general education curriculum. Additionally, they call for more emphasis on the general knowledge proficiencies identified by Hansen (1986), greater use of non-lecture teaching techniques, and more research on important economic education questions such as how students learn.

Enhance the use of context and application   Economic models presented at the undergraduate level are not meant to be an accurate portrayal of either the current state of the discipline or of reality. The complexity of the subject matter of economics and the limited training of undergraduate students in the increasingly complex disciplinary mathematical and statistical tools necessitates the presentation of highly simplified models. These models often lose the richness of modern economic analysis. The associated oversimplified abstract modeling can leave students questioning the practicality of the problem-solving skills these models help to develop. We believe principles students should be given some sense of what modern economic reasoning and analysis is, and training in how limited the models they are being taught are so that the models are understood contextually. Recent research into "how people learn" provides important insights into the importance of context (Bransford et al., 2000). Deep learners know when knowledge can be transferred and can transfer knowledge from one context to another. Deep learners "(a) have a deep foundation of factual knowledge, (b) understand facts and ideas in the context of a conceptual framework, and (c) organize knowledge in the ways that facilitate retrieval and application" (p. 16). Reconnecting economic analysis to the lives that students currently lead and the issues they will face after college is one method of overcoming the abstract nature of the models taught in under-graduate courses. Enhanced use of context and application promote critical thinking, problem-solving, and lifelong learning, all goals associated with liberal education.

Integrate skills and content across courses   Although the major is structured as a set of building blocks that encourages greater sophistication of analysis as students progress, little explicit integration of skills or content is promoted. Opportunities for integration also extend beyond courses in the major, as interdisciplinary courses attest. Skills and content integration provide additional points at which students can be engaged with economic concepts, enhancing the liberal education component of the learning experience. Deep learning, or learning for understanding, necessitates critical thinking skills, integration of knowledge over time and subjects, theoretical application to practical situations and higher-order skills of analysis and synthesis (Entwistle, 1981; Ramsden, 1992; Biggs, 1999; Prosser and Trigwell, 1999)

Implement summative and formative assessment of skill acquisition   Current pressures on higher education suggest that demand for formal assessment processes within the major is likely in the not too distant future. While the well-defined hierarchical structure provides scaffolding for building skills throughout the major, few departments have a formal mechanism in place to determine the degree to which they are successful in developing those skills. Departments need to explicitly identify skills that graduating majors should possess and link each course within the major to the development of those skills. Furthermore, departments should include assessment components that explicitly link the economics major to skills of a liberal education.

   Because of the private nature of teaching, faculty are likely to resist formal assessment of individual courses. Developing assessment procedures at the end of the major would minimize this resistance. Designation of a senior-level course (or series of courses) that explicitly incorporates exercises that assess the degree to which each student has acquired the skills of the major is one possible solution. Results from this assessment could then be used to revise the underlying curriculum.

Pedagogical practices
It is not only content that determines how much passion for learning is generated through a course; it is also the utilized pedagogical practices. In economics few graduate students receive any training in pedagogy, or in the mechanics of teaching. This, we believe is a mistake, and all students who will become teachers should be given some introduction into the latest pedagogical research and practice. Even if they do not adopt them, the presentation of those ideas to graduate students will signal that teaching is important.

Improve classroom dynamics   The dominant pedagogical practice in economics remains the lecture method; in some cases for some people, this method can be highly effective; for others, it can be sterile. Whatever method one uses, studies in economics and higher education have shown that students learn and retain more when engaged throughout the learning process.[14] Except for superb lecturers, lectures seldom fully engage students, and thus most professors should consider teaching methods that lead to student participation in activities that use the information being taught rather than those that simply organize it.

Encourage pedagogical experimentation Because most lectures do not fully engage students, faculty should be provided the appropriate incentives to expand their teaching techniques beyond the lecture. Ideally, faculty should be pluralistic in their use of teaching strategies. Since incorporating new techniques is not without risk, and they have not been introduced to modern pedagogical insights in graduate school, faculty need an incentive to take pedagogical risks. We believe that summer support should be provided for faculty motivated to make significant revisions in their teaching methods. Decreasing the perceived cost could be achieved by allowing faculty to remove teaching evaluations from merit and promotion decisions for a semester in which they are experimenting with alternative approaches. Faculty should be encouraged to document their experiences and provide supplemental support materials that can be used to provide evidence of excellence in teaching in addition to the standard teaching evaluations.

Engage in the conversation of best practice In order to encourage scholars to dedicate significant resources to enhancing their pedagogical practices, departmental funds should be allocated to encourage participation in the conversation of best teaching practices.

Engagement could be encouraged through the development of a seminar series that highlights pedagogical research on implementation processes and learning outcomes associated with alternative pedagogical practices. Minimal funds could be used to hold a once-a-month lunchtime forum on teaching, the leader of which would rotate through the department. Such forums would be used to keep faculty abreast of current pedagogical research and demonstrate particular pedagogical exercises (such as experiments, cooperative learning, and so on). To launch the yearly seminar series, a prominent expert in economic education could be invited to give a "state of the field" address.

Alternatively, funds can be used to send faculty to workshops (economics and general education) with the requirement that faculty hold a seminar on campus summarizing what they have learned.

Develop and promote the teaching commons Graduate school in a discipline develops and promotes a research commons that often defines a professor. If teaching is to be accorded the importance it deserves, then one needs a means to develop a similar "teaching commons." A teaching commons is "a conceptual space in which communities of educators committed to inquiry and innovation come together to exchange ideas about teaching and learning and use them to meet the challenges of educating students."[15] As such, the commons can act as a public clearinghouse of detailed examples of teaching techniques. Because the commons is intended to be an exchange of ideas, it does not require that shared pedagogical examples include a rigorous proof of learning as would journal publications; rather, documented examples need to provide, through an organized framework, detailed descriptions of learning objectives and instructional environment in addition to a description of the activity. The openness of the commons encourages others to join the conversation through posting reflections on and adaptations of such exercises. Increasing the awareness of alternative pedagogical practices through detailed exercises in a common accessible location lowers the cost of adaptation and increases the probability of incorporating such methods.

Creating institutional value

Create more economic education positions at teaching-oriented colleges Institutions serious about their commitment to undergraduate teaching should demonstrate this by creating a full faculty position dedicated to teaching. A professor who focuses on teaching is no less important to a university than a professor who focuses on research. Economics professors who focus on teaching can be expected to do research but that research is more likely to focus on economic education. Besides doing research on economic education, such professors would attend national workshops (economic-specific and interdisciplinary), conduct seminars for their department and other departments on teaching, and help develop assessments of learning tools. Instituting similar positions across departments would provide a cohort capable of developing or enhancing existing teaching resource centers.

Institute a system for which excellence in teaching creates institutional value Colleges and universities now almost totally base their comparative rank on research output. This is counterproductive. Colleges and universities who include excellence in teaching in their mission statements should be ranked on the degree to which they are successful in achieving that, and a ranking of colleges and universities on both should be provided. A consistent teaching ranking system needs to be developed, one that ranks teachers at schools, possibly based on portfolios and outside visitations. The development of such a system will not be easy and will be far from perfect, problems also faced with existing rankings based on research. But simply having such a system in existence, and publicizing it, will help make teaching a more prominent and, in practice as opposed to in theory, an evaluated component of professors' jobs across all institutions. If teaching is 50 percent of a professor's job, then 50 percent of the determination of whether that professor is successful should be based on teaching.

CONCLUSION

Let us conclude our discussion by reiterating the caveat that we have continually expressed. Education is a personal process, involving a connection between the professor and the student. That connection comes about best when the professor is teaching what he or she is passionate about.

Thus, professors should retain their property rights over what is taught and how it is taught. Reports, or mandates from above telling professors to do something different than they want to do will remove the passion and thus undermine the catalyst role of education, which in our view is central to enhancing economic education in ways that are consistent with the liberal education perspective. We believe it is better to have the "wrong" content taught passionately than the "right" content taught perfunctorily. It is this perspective that has driven so much of this report and its focus on broader questions of institutional structure rather than on specific disciplinary content. The content of what is taught will, and should, be determined by the individual professors and schools. Ideally, however, one would want the "right" content taught passionately, and if one's goal is a liberally educated student, given the current structure of graduate schools and universities, that is not going to happen, because content taught with passion will be research driven, not teaching driven. Only major institutional change at both the graduate training level and the undergraduate institutional level will affect that.

In the absence of such major institutional change, marginal improvements can be made by modifying incentives and institutions to give more emphasis to pedagogy and teaching. While there is no one set of "best practices" in economics pedagogy that make it suitable for a liberal education, there are better practices and worse practices, and discussion of such practices should be an important part of the discussion at any college or university. University administrations that have not created an atmosphere that makes such discussions central have failed in an important part of their job.

The bottom line of this report is that much more discussion is needed about the focus of content taught in economics, and how that content is taught if the economics major is to make the best contribution it can to a liberal education. We don't know what that "best contribution" is, and believe that there are many ways that departments can contribute, some of which may seem contradictory. We strongly believe that positive change in any discipline does not come from the top down; it comes from the bottom up, and major change builds on initiatives of individual schools. That is why the goal of this report is to open up a conversation rather than come up with a set of specific recommendations. Our descriptions of structural and micro-oriented changes are offered simply as a starting place for these conversations. We recognize that there are many roles that the economics major can play in contributing to a liberal education, and thus there are many structures of the major that will promote this objective. But the best ones will not develop out of bottom-up discussion unless departments are concerned about the major and have incentives to see that it is contributing in the best way possible. We hope this report helps generates that concern.

NOTES

1. For a detailed description of each of these skills, see Appendix A, AAC&U (2007).
2. See http://www.aacu.org/advocacy/leap/documents/GlobalCentury_final.pdf for a report from the National Leadership Council that spells out the vision behind the Teagle initiative on liberal education (accessed 17 April 2009).
3. The discussion in this section is not specific to economics. In writing it we considered ourselves as economic consultants to the National Leadership Council, not as representatives of the economics major. What that means is that in this section we provide the economic approach to the issue of liberal education; namely, we attempt to describe the opposing foci using our tools as economists rather than as faculty participants in the major. Thus, the arguments we make in this section are not specific to the economics major, but are for all majors, and our use of economics is simply as a case study.
4. There are, of course, exceptions; we agree, some scholars have a passion for all aspects of learning and teaching. But they tend to be exceptions, not the rule.
5. Siegfried and Stock (2007).
6. Jones et al. (Chapter 22, this volume).
7. J.N. Keynes in a famous book on economic method (Keynes, 1891) distinguished the two by calling one the science of economics and the other the art of economics.
8. The size of these groups differs with different institutional settings. For example, schools with undergraduate business programs have more students directly interested in economics than schools without such programs.
9. The natural science "solution" to this problem has left a void in liberal arts education. Far too few students major in science at liberal arts schools than would be desirable because the programs are designed for those going on to graduate school, not for individuals interested in science as a background or a vocation. Thus, they do a great job for a small number of students. As training in economics becomes more like training in the natural sciences, it will likely follow the same route.
10. See http://www.aacu.org/advocacy/leap/documents/GlobalCentury_final.pdf for a report from the National Leadership Council. In that report the National Leadership Council points out that "employers are urging more – and better – liberal education, not less." They quote Robert T. Jones (President, Education Workforce Policy) "Employers do not want, and have not advocated for, students prepared for narrow workforce specialties" (accessed 17 April 2009).
11. Recall that the macro-level recommendations address changes associated with teacher preparation in graduate schools.
12. "A Compact to Enhance Teaching and Learning at Harvard," p. 6, http://www.auburn.edu/academic/other/biggio/resources/TeachingAndLearningAtHarvard.pdf (accessed 17 April 2009).
13. http://www.vanderbilt.edu/AEA/AEACEE/TIP/TIP.htm (accessed 17 April 2009).

14. See, for example, Johnston et al. (2000).
15. Huber and Hutchings (2007). "Building the Teaching Commons. The Carnegie Foundation for the Advancement of Teaching," http://www.carnegiefoundation.org/perspectives/sub.asp?key=245&subkey=800 (accessed 17 April 2009).

PART 2

Challenging the content: what do we teach?

2. Teaching students to "think about the economy"

Joseph Persky

David Colander and KimMarie McGoldrick's "The economics major as part of a liberal education" does us all a major service by articulating a clear and forceful case for reducing the hold of "departmentalism" on liberal arts majors in general and economics majors in particular. At the core of their well-thought-out program is the proposal to train and employ a cadre of "liberal arts economists" as opposed to "department economists." This program gives us an explicit and constructive counterpoint to current practice. Precisely because it makes its case so clearly, Colander and McGoldrick's essay has already stimulated considerable debate. My own sense is that they have very correctly identified the problem as one of "narrowness," but have gone too far in suggesting something of a caste system for a brave new world of liberal arts economics.

As suggested in the report, our colleagues in other fields have rightly accused economists of a narrowness in outlook. Often this narrowness is coupled with exaggerated claims to scientific rigor and pretensions to mathematical precision. This narrowness can easily take on the coloration of ideological bias. For the most part, scholars in sociology, political science, and history are more than willing to acknowledge that economic motivations lie behind much individual activity, economic divisions lie behind much political activity, and economic interests pervade history. Philosophers recognize that in approaching ethics they must wrestle with the often socially useful consequences of economic self-interest and greed. Scientists know that science and technological change have major economic consequences. And those in humanities are deeply aware that literature and creative arts often deal with economic themes. The possibilities for a natural, unforced, interaction between economics and the other liberal arts departments are manifest. So where's the problem? The Colander-McGoldrick report argues that economists exposed to standard graduate education have become narrow, because they must specialize to survive in the world of research. The big problems are unsolvable, and economists have simply retreated to the minutiae. While there is undoubtedly some truth to this view, I doubt that the pressures of specialization are any more severe in economics than in many other academic disciplines. It is not that economists refuse to engage in "big think." Just the opposite. A considerable majority of economists regard these big problems as fully resolved.

Economics departments in a highly speculative move have raised one heavily assumption-laden theoretical structure (the model of perfect competition among maximizing economic agents) to the centerpiece of their discourse. This focus on perfect competition easily migrates into ideological territory (for example, support for minimum government interference, free trade, hostility to unions). But one might hold all these ideological positions and reasonably recognize that the model of perfect competition just doesn't have the scientific legs to carry the role it is awarded in the economics curriculum. Most markets, now and in the past, simply aren't very close to the competitive model. While that model is of some interest as a policy benchmark and as intellectual history, it hardly deserves the time and energy we spend on it, time and energy that distract us from teaching economics. Acknowledging this problem would in a very natural way generate a more liberal-arts-friendly curriculum. Focusing on the range of real-world market structures would logically require a more extensive institutional exploration of the industries of the US, opening up potential ties to history and engineering departments among others. Recognizing that labor markets are complex and require a range of institutional supports ties us closer to sociology, psychology, and history. The meaning of personal choice in a social setting more rich than the competitive model immediately suggests trade-offs that challenge us to understand more deeply the ethics of the philosophers. These moves all make undergraduate economics richer and more interesting. It is well worth giving up an unscientific ideological consistency in favor of this richer brew.

But how do we "free" undergraduate economics from this narrowness? I don't think creating a new caste of liberal arts economists answers the central question. Something important has been left out of graduate economics education in the United States. PhD candidates are taught to "think like economists," but not what the economy looks like. Economics becomes not a subject to be studied with many tools, but a small set of tools forced to fit any problem. Historical and institutional materials have been largely removed from the graduate curriculum. This is an unfortunate and destructive development. Economists rightly value their efforts at rigor and discipline. But it is foolish and self-defeating to achieve those at the cost of abandoning realism.

An appropriate response to this narrowness is to reintroduce courses in economic history, intellectual history, and institutional structures into the graduate curriculum; indeed, to make them required in the education of

PhD's. Such a proposal might be most easily implemented if coupled with a reduction of fields of concentration or specialization from the currently common figure of two to just one. Alternatively, a modest expansion of course work at the graduate level by one semester would manage the same reform. Convincing three or four of the major economics departments of the soundness of this reform would very likely be enough to guarantee its wide acceptance. While such moves are hardly a cure-all they would move us a long way toward more liberal-arts-friendly undergraduate departments. The point is not to create a special class of liberal-arts-oriented economists, because "serious economists" have become something else. Rather, the point is to reassert the foundations of the discipline in liberal arts. Ideally, a teacher of economics should be enmeshed in both the realities of the economy and his or her research agenda. And if this is the goal, departments must reward both broad scholarship in the classroom and research achievements in the profession.

A major benefit of reintroducing this range of courses into the graduate curriculum will be the considerable expansion of the group of first-rate economists doing research on economic history, history of economic thought, and economic institutions. This expansion can only strengthen that broader perspective within economic departments at all levels.

At the same time I am somewhat more optimistic than Colander and McGoldrick as to the basic structure of the economics major. In particular, I am not convinced that a liberal arts education is at odds with a "deep" approach to a major. The tradition of liberal arts education in the US (excepting only a few experiments such as St. Johns) has always acknowledged a major as an integral component to the curriculum. While liberal education emphasizes the importance of gaining a familiarity with a range of intellectual skills (of "learning how to think"), it has also asserted the importance of seeing how such tools can be applied in depth, and of gaining a critical capacity in at least one field. For some liberal arts students their major, reasonably enough, becomes a form of pre-professional or even professional training. But more will ultimately choose a field only loosely related to (or even unrelated to) their major. Undeniably this latter group will generally have to do a bit of catching up as they switch their primary interest. Conceivably, such students might have benefited from a broader smorgasbord of courses from which to explore their interests. But it seems to me that such a comment misses the key motivation behind having majors in a liberal arts curriculum. That motivation is to introduce students to something approaching deep thinking in or deep applications of at least one field. The major begins to involve students in the processes by which people actually use their brains (reason, deduction, induction, inspiration, and so on) to generate new knowledge. If there were worlds and time enough it might be preferable to have two or three majors so as to more fully sample the range of intellectual activities. But to claim a liberal education, a student should at least have an experience of one such field. From this vantage point I doubt that the tension between specialized and general education is nearly as sharp as suggested in the essay. The point of the major is not so much that the facts, skills, and tools learned will last forever, but rather to experience as close as is practical the feel of the real thing. In this light, economics majors should probably attempt to master some basic college mathematics and statistics. Not because (or at least not primarily because) they might go on to graduate school, but rather because over the last century, mathematics and statistics have become the favored language of a majority of economists. How could one really get an introduction to the products of deep economic thinking without being able to read at least a bit of the language?

Taking this line of thought, I am not terribly sympathetic to the proposal to divide the major into three parts. As to the division between "economic science" and "economic policy" this seems unnecessary. Much of the desired effect can easily be achieved by good undergraduate advising. Students actually interested in proceeding to graduate school in economics are best served not by courses in "economic science," but rather by extending their mathematical education well beyond the foundation courses. Taking the equivalent of a minor is probably a minimum as preparation. At the same time, this expansion of mathematical training will strengthen, not undermine a student's appreciation of the liberal arts. A sophisticated exposure to concepts such as proof, probability, and mathematical spaces cannot help but open rich perspectives on the world around us.

Again, the proposal for a pre-professional major also strikes me as a bit of overkill. There is nothing wrong with economics departments in liberal arts schools adding elective courses in such fields as finance and personnel economics. The question is not so much renaming the major as achieving appropriate funding for a broad range of electives. However, for students who really want a business school degree, the liberal arts economics department is probably not the right place for them.

These are my major concerns with the Colander and McGoldrick report. I have emphasized here my differences with the report and not the considerable areas of agreement. For example, the report's suggestions concerning training our future teachers in teaching strike me as eminently reasonable. Putting newly minted PhD's into the classroom with little experience and no serious preparation seems close to negligent. Similarly, the pedagogical proposals in the report are quite strong and long overdue.

In summary, the economics major will do well to move away from training undergraduates to "think like economists" and instead invite them to "think about the economy." In the long run, this move requires a modest but serious expansion of graduate education. To achieve such an expansion, graduate departments will have to reallocate their own resources and, where possible, obtain resources from outside to facilitate the transition. Those interested in preserving the broader liberal arts tradition in economics would do better to support such additions to the graduate programs of mainstream departments, rather than seek to establish a new tier of degrees, which will inevitably be seen as "second best."

3. The economics major as illiberal education

Stephen A. Marglin

David Colander and KimMarie McGoldrick perform a valuable service in the thoughtful way they address the problem of the balance between specialization and general education. I agree with the major thrust of the Teagle Foundation draft report, that the economics major, and other majors as well, do not adequately serve the purposes of a liberal education. And I think the report is right on the money in arguing that the organizational problem is one of incentives. I am perhaps a bit less sanguine than the report's authors about the possibility of changing those incentives. Presumably the authors intend their recommendations for the deans and faculties of individual colleges and universities. But reform in one institution may not be practical in a culture in which prestige and power are determined largely within academic disciplines.

This said, I think there are some issues that, if not peculiar to economics, deserve emphasis in the context of the economics major. I will ruffle few feathers by asserting that a primary goal of a liberal education ought to be to learn to think critically. But my next proposition will perhaps be less agreeable: that the economics major subverts this goal. At best it teaches students to think like economists; it does not teach students the limits of thinking like an economist.

One might object that this is someone else's concern. A liberal arts education is more than the major, and thinking like an economist is challenged in other disciplines, in other courses, in bull sessions far removed from the classroom setting. The Anglo-American legal system supposes that Truth emerges from the confrontation of alternative truths. So in the marketplace of ideas, economics offers one perspective to be tested against others, and Truth will emerge from a healthy competition among alternative points of view. I would take issue with this view of the law, and with this view of a liberal arts education.

I think we owe our students both instruction in thinking like an economist *and* a critical perspective on this type of thinking. Historically, room for critical thinking in economics has been limited by a commitment to the market. If all we cared about was describing the world, we could easily forego much of the framework that I find problematic. Take the most basic tools of economic analysis, demand and supply. If we did not care about drawing conclusions about *how well* markets work, as distinct from *how* markets actually work, we would not have to base demand and supply in the choices made by rational, calculating, self-interested individuals. We could start instead directly from demand and supply themselves, as elementary concepts. But we do not take demand and supply as primitives because it would then be impossible to argue that – subject to some fine and not so fine print – a system of markets maximizes welfare. In short, thinking like an economist has facilitated the celebration of the market, indeed thinking like an economist is essential to the logic of the economist's case for the market.*

Surely I exaggerate. Economics progresses through self-criticism. This *must* rub off on students. Yes, there *is* dissent and disagreement in economics. Harry Truman is said to have longed for a one-armed economist – an economist who was not constantly hedging his bets with "on the one hand . . ., on the other hand . . . ." And dissent and disagreement are not limited to policy. Indeed, economics provides the basis for searching self-criticism: if you take seriously the fine print on the warranty that mainstream economics provides for the market, your celebration of the market is likely to be rather subdued, or at least nuanced. Nor is the fine print accessible only to the priests, to people steeped in many years of graduate training. Most elementary texts discuss a variety of structural assumptions that must be satisfied if markets are to produce desirable outcomes.

Take "externalities," the unintended by-products of an exchange that fall on third parties. If Mr *A* gives Ms *B* heroin in exchange for sex, the economist will have a relatively easy time showing why this trade might be undesirable despite the wishes of the two participants. Providing heroin to *B* contributes to an addiction, and *B* might in the future rob or kill in order to satisfy her craving. The effects on *B*'s victims, externalities of the original transaction, would swamp the benefits that *A* and *B* derive from the original exchange.

The claim that the market reduces waste to a minimum requires not just any system of markets, but a system of *competitive* markets, a system of markets in which there are so many players that no single agent has any economic power. Prostitution, especially where it is illegal, hardly fits the model of the competitive market.

The normative claims for the market also preclude information asymmetries. It is not that agents have to be fully informed, but, even on the narrowest efficiency grounds, the market can be improved upon in situations where some agents know more about the goods and services on offer than do other agents. Presumably both prostitutes and their clients know much more about their own health, and specifically whether they are carriers of sexually transmitted diseases, than they know about each other's health. But again, information asymmetries are hardly peculiar to sex markets.

(I would make a very different case for the market: the virtue of the market is not that it provides an analog computer for registering the rationally calculated plans of producers and consumers, but rather, that it allows, indeed compels, us to act on hunch, intuition, and feeling. Markets allow us to bring to bear knowledge that is *not* the product of rational deliberation.)

There are thus many arguments against a market in sexual services based on a critique that is not only purely internal to the discipline, but a standard part of every elementary text. And in this respect the only peculiarity of prostitution is that the externalities may be more important, the monopoly element more pronounced, and the consequences of asymmetric information more serious than in other markets.

So why do we need to look for other critiques? My answer is that the internal critique based on structural problems of markets does not question the *logic* of markets. It looks instead to making markets work better. Externalities? Internalize the externalities by creating new rights and claims and new markets in which these rights and claims are traded. If the problem is heroin addiction, legalize this and other hard drugs to bring street prices down to a level that eliminates the incentive for crime. Too few sellers? Open up the market by legalizing prostitution and perhaps by propaganda to reduce the stigma associated with the sex trade. Information asymmetries? Introduce regulations to insure full disclosure of all relevant information about one's health status, at least with respect to potentially lethal infections like HIV. In short, create new markets to solve the problems of markets.

But markets have negative social consequences that are not made right by making markets work better. For example, markets undermine community. Markets, based on voluntary, instrumental, opportunistic relationships, are diametrically opposed to the long-term commitments and obligations that characterize community. By promoting market relationships, economics undermines reciprocity, altruism, and mutual obligation, and therewith the necessity of community. Economics, by justifying the expansion of markets, leads inexorably to the weakening of community.

To critically evaluate this assertion we have to look at the assumptions that economists make about economic agents themselves: that agents rationally calculate their individual self-interest in ever more consumption, free of ties to any community save the community of the nation. Are these "foundational" assumptions universals? Or do they – as I would argue – characterize a particular culture, the culture of the Modern West? If the second, what makes the Modern West distinctive? How well do they characterize us; that is, how modern are we? Do we wish to be modern? Should we? Is our cultural model one we should be actively trying to export? These questions, I submit, should be addressed within the economics major.

There are at least three other critiques with which economics should engage: a distributional critique, macroeconomics as critique, and an ecological critique. Take the distributional critique: it is well understood that the sense in which markets maximize welfare, even on economists' own terms, is quite limited. The most that can be claimed on the basis of the two welfare theorems is that markets minimize waste. And once the limitations of lump-sum transfers are recognized, the virtue of minimizing waste loses any compelling quality it might have in a world of frictionless transfers. Yet the prejudice of the profession is evident in the language in which taxation is discussed. The emphasis is on the "deadweight" losses that accompany taxation, not on the distributive gains (or losses) that accompany taxation.

Macroeconomics as critique is a bit more surprising, but if we go back a bit in time it makes sense. Keynes intended *The General Theory* (1936) as critique, and so it was understood until the fundamental critique was diluted into various forms of sand-in-the-wheels, short-run frictions that need not trouble us in evaluating the fundamental message of economics that markets are good for people. I suppose it makes me a fundamentalist of a different sort to believe, as I do, that the message of Keynes – that aggregate demand matters – is valid in the long run as well as in the short run, and that this constitutes a basic critique of standard economics.

The ecological critique raises questions about how we as a society should behave under conditions of radical uncertainty. Like the name Keynes, the very name radical uncertainty has a somewhat archaic ring since it has long been fashionable to blur the Knightian distinction that puts risk and uncertainty into separate categories. Archaic or not, how we react to radical uncertainty of the kind inherent in, say, global warming is the basic divide between the economic and other approaches to the great ecological questions of our day.

This hardly exhausts the list of possible critiques. For example, Catholic social teaching of the lineage of *Rerum Novarum*, the 1891 encyclical that called for a third way between the market and socialism. Or Marx. Or Veblen. Or Galbraith.

There remain the questions of how and when to integrate a discussion of the limits of economic thinking into the economics major. There is much to be said for a stand-alone course devoted to critiques, but I would emphasize the need for this course to be integrated into the core of the major rather than being offered as simply one alternative in a grab-bag of electives. And this leaves out the large number of students outside the major, whose only exposure to economics may be the elementary course. So there is a case to be made for building the critique into the teaching of economics from the get-go.

NOTE

* As in the leading elementary text: "[C]an the [hypothetical] social planner raise total economic well-being by increasing or decreasing the quantity of [a] good [relative to the amount which the market would provide]?" The question is quickly disposed of: "The answer is no" (Mankiw, 2004, p. 149). Or more formally, in the two welfare theorems relating competitive equilibrium and Pareto optimality.

4. Moral reasoning in economics*

Jonathan B. Wight

The Teagle discussion analyzes why economics teachers have become overly narrow in their pedagogical perspectives, thus pulling back from fully supporting the liberal arts agenda. In Chapter 1, Colander and McGoldrick (p. 6) observe that the generalist approach that excites students by asking "big think" questions across disciplinary boundaries fails to generate new knowledge, while the narrow "little think" questions that *can* be answered often fail to develop the critical thinking skills necessary for liberal education. As one example, the authors cite the decline of moral reasoning in economics, which was once center stage in Adam Smith's analysis of society. Since the rise of positivism in the late nineteenth century, moral reasoning has become an intellectual casualty.

Virtually all major public policy problems cross disciplinary boundaries however, and raise substantial normative questions. If a key goal of the liberal arts is to prepare students to make reasoned judgments about complex issues, economics educators cannot sit on the sidelines and expect that this will happen magically. Teachers play an important role in defining the questions and discerning the methods for arriving at answers. A liberal arts focus in economics would ensure that students grapple with ethical dilemmas informed by a variety of approaches and competing ethical frameworks. Moral discourse is an important way for students to scrutinize their own unstated beliefs and to develop a deeper appreciation for the benefits (and the limitations) of economic theory. Without it, we may be training technocrats skilled in techniques but not prepared to be business or community leaders – who will certainly have to navigate moral minefields.

The contribution of this discussion is to point out that a liberal education requires critical thinking skills that are only partially addressed by traditional methods in economics. What it means to "think like an economist" contains a hefty dose of implicit ethical judgment – which in a liberal arts setting should be examined and debated as a way of integrating economics with its sister disciplines in philosophy, political science, and other fields. This comment deals with two areas of potential controversy – welfare analysis and alternative moral frameworks.

WELFARE ANALYSIS IS NOT PURE SCIENCE

If economics is a science, why should economists and their students know or care about ethics? The answer has three parts: first, students are implicitly using ethical frameworks and theories in carrying out positive research whether they are conscious of it or not. To progress, science requires shared moral norms and positive economics entails acceptance of these ethical ideals. Second, having students pursue the "little think" questions in research often involves an uncritical acceptance of the ethical assumptions and worldview upon which the research is built (Colander and McGoldrick, Chapter 1, this volume, p. 6; Kuhn, 1962). Third, many students (and faculty) are unaware that efficiency and Pareto optimality are ethical constructs. Critical thinking about cost/benefit requires going outside this comfort zone. This last point is the most troubling, because if "efficiency" is viewed simply as a "fact" instead of an evaluative concept, this creates intellectual blinders for students attempting to cross disciplinary boundaries (as we hope they would do in a liberal arts setting). I note below, for example, that economics students and public health students will likely have opposing views of what is meant by efficiency – which is understandable only if the concept is properly understood as part of normative discourse.

Economic efficiency is often portrayed as a positive concept however, because "welfare" can be defined and quantitatively measured through consumer and producer triangles. Few principles textbooks adequately address the point that welfare economics was developed as a branch of normative economics and that its offspring of economic efficiency is equally an ethical proposition: it is constructed on the basis of choosing a worthy normative goal. As the history of thought fades from graduate school requirements, fewer teachers understand the evolution of welfare theory and the issues that arise for public policy analysis.

Here is a quick thought experiment to bring out the normative character of economic efficiency. Assign students the role of doctors engaged in an emergency medical triage (the ranking of patients for treatment based on medical severity and/or survivability). Tell the student-doctors that each patient needs an antibiotic to survive and that there are more patients than doses of antibiotic available. In this short-run emergency, the supply of antibiotic is perfectly inelastic. Some gravely ill patients will likely die even if given the antibiotic. Ask the student-doctors: "How would you decide to allocate the scarce antibiotic?" (Answer: doctors would probably want to allocate serum so as to be efficient at "saving the most lives," which means giving doses of antibiotic to those whose survivability is most enhanced.) Next ask the student-doctors, "What would you do if many of the patients most likely to die without antibiotics were children?" (Answer: many doctors would now change their allocation so as to be efficient at "saving the most life-years-extended," which means factoring in not only expected survival but expected years lived after survival.) Finally, ask the student-doctors to consider what would happen if antibiotics were allocated not by triage, but rather sold to the highest bidder so as to satisfy individual consumer preferences in the market. (Answer: economic efficiency is achieved, but probably fewer lives would be saved since triage was ignored.)

This exercise makes clear to students that there are a multitude of notions of "efficiency," and each serves a different normative master. Economists use a particular ethical norm as their implicit "baggage" – the definition and choice of dominant goal ("economic welfare") – by which the economic system is evaluated. The economic view is most certainly defensible, but not on positive grounds; it relies upon a series of restrictive normative arguments. This economic baggage should be subject to scrutiny and discussion in the classroom. You would not let someone on a plane without checking the contents of their carry-on, and economics education should be no different. We should unpack and examine the ethical framework that informs the standard economic approach. For a complete discussion of these issues, see Hausman and McPherson (2006).

Textbooks set the context for much classroom discussion, and most textbook authors have followed the trend of preparing students for narrow specialization rather than liberal learning. In the most recent edition of Frank and Bernanke (2009), the authors illustrate some of the problems relating to the discussion of efficiency. First, the authors carefully note that "efficiency is not the only goal" of an economic system and that an efficient outcome is not the same thing as a "good" outcome. But they go on to state – as if it were a scientific fact rather than a normative argument – that, "efficiency should be the first goal." The authors base this claim on the assertion that being economically efficient "enables us to achieve all our other goals to the fullest possible extent" (p. 179). This implies that static efficiency in the short run is *in fact* the only "good" outcome because there is an alchemic process that can best turn it into any other desirable outcome. As we demonstrated in the triage case, however, this is not always possible. Achieving economic efficiency often comes at the expense of other measures of efficiency, such as saving the most lives or life-years extended.

Even if the economic welfare approach (satisfying consumer preferences) does not save the most lives in the short run, students should discern that allowing patients to bid up the price of antibiotics could lead to more serum (and better serum) being produced in the long run. Hence, more lives might be saved over time by allowing competitive markets to work. This is an insightful point, and students should consider the structure of it: the economic goal has suddenly shifted from *static* efficiency to *dynamic* efficiency. Our attention turns away from satisfying consumer preferences in *this* market, and towards satisfying preferences in some undefined *future* time period. Do future consumers have moral standing (for example, should their preferences count)? What is the correct time horizon for making this analysis? And how should we discount future lives gained versus the present lives lost? One distinction between classical and Austrian economists on the one hand, and modern neo-classical economists on the other, is the differing attention provided to dynamic versus static efficiency (Blaug, 2001). These are thorny ethical issues in addition to scientific questions, and students will confront similar problems in a variety of policy areas and classes.

In summary, economics teachers can make a strong case for appraising policies on the basis of static efficiency, but this requires an evaluative framework that is substantially different from classical economics and from other consequentialist approaches (such as classical utilitarian or rule-utilitarian approaches). *Non*-consequentialist modes of analysis might also be helpful in some cases (Frank, 2000). We turn briefly to this topic.

ALTERNATIVE ETHICAL FRAMEWORKS

The analysis of public policy goes deeper than simply choosing normative goals within a consequentialist framework. The reason for this is that sometimes *process* matters, and "the ends do not justify the means" as exemplified in Kantian and religious ethics. My experience is that many students adopt duty-, rights-, and religious-based arguments either consciously or unconsciously. Students encounter Kantian ethics in a variety of non-economics classes, and they are taught the categorical imperative that no person should be used as a means to another's end. Students thus justify the Living Wage movement based on a belief in the inherent dignity and equality of every person, rather than an analysis of outcomes produced by such a policy. Religious rules and duties (such as the Ten Commandments) also shape the social landscape and their "rightness" is said to derive from divine law. Some students support market interventions like price controls because of intrinsic religious or other norms against price gouging and usury.

In addition to rules and duties, virtue ethics is an increasingly popular moral theory that students will encounter in philosophy and business ethics classes. Virtue ethics deals with understanding and shaping the intentions and preferences of the economic agent. Students are thoroughly familiar with this approach because proper socialization usually entailed parents and other mentors highlighting virtuous conducts and enforcing habits they would like their children to internalize. For most economists, intentions and preferences are exogenous to our models and not within the scope of public policy choices. Yet current policy debates may raise notions of personal responsibility, self-control, and civic virtues (for example, in welfare reform, in tax compliance, in voting, and ultimatum game behaviors).

Rather than dismissing non-economic perspectives, teachers should engage students in critical thinking exercises about non-consequentialist ethical approaches. This creates openings for discussion between classes in economics and political science, philosophy, religion, and other areas where rights, duties, and virtue ethics often dominate the discourse. It is also important that faculties in those disciplines abandon the caricature of *Homo economicus* and develop a deeper appreciation for consequentialist thinking in economics and the ethical justification for markets that derive from it. To promote these ends, I briefly outline in class and in a handout the three main ethical approaches (consequences, duties/rules, and virtues). I tell students that economics can contribute important insights to the analysis of consequences, but that some public policy situations may require them to analyze and judge alternative ethical frameworks supported with relevant arguments. While economists are not experts in moral theory, that in itself is an insufficient reason for ignoring the topic. Critical thinking would require grappling with alternative ethical frameworks because they are ubiquitously intertwined with public policy choices and with the lives our students lead outside of economics classes.

CONCLUSION

Preparing students for complex decision-making may require reintegrating a basic understanding of how economists construct measures of welfare, how moral agents actually behave in markets, and how science relies upon virtuous norms and normative arguments. The Teagle report rightly laments the neglect of moral reasoning in economics because its absence in the classroom limits critical thinking and ultimately debases the liberal arts experience. If economic concepts were successfully integrated into a liberal arts setting, students "would not think that the economic way of thinking is the only right way of thinking" and they would be knowledgeable about alternative ways of thinking (Colander and McGoldrick, Chapter 1, this volume, p. 19). A liberal arts education would reveal the economic way of thinking in its historical and ethical context, providing linkages to other disciplines. It is always challenging for teachers to take on something new, and moral discourse may be a particularly troubling add-on for economists. My own experience is that the marginal costs of introducing ethics are quite low when normative discourse is addressed in small doses over many days (examples can be found in Wight and Morton, 2007). Like most teaching, repetition is needed for students to develop competency. The marginal benefits of addressing moral inquiry are quite large, however, because the study of economics adds more to the students' liberal arts experience when its practice is synergistic with, and complementary to, other social sciences and humanities.

NOTE

*   Erik Craft, KimMarie McGoldrick, Robert Frank, and Justin Weiss provided valuable
     comments; conclusions remain the author's. This discussion draws on a forthcoming
     essay (Wight, 2009).

5. Thinking for yourself, like an economist

Robert F. Garnett

David Colander and KimMarie McGoldrick's call for a liberal arts revision of the economics major is timely and compelling. It coincides with the increasing prominence of the undergraduate major as a locus of liberal learning (AAC&U, 2006). It feeds economic educators' growing demands for pedagogies and curricula that promote critical inquiry (Ferber, 1999; Earl, 2000; Feiner, 2003; Fullbrook, 2003; Underwood, 2004; Becker, 2007; Groenewegen, 2007). It invites renewed reflection on why even high-achieving majors have difficulty applying economic knowledge to real-life personal, professional, and public problems (Katz and Becker, 1999; Salemi and Siegfried, 1999; Hansen et al., 2002). And it acknowledges structural impediments to its own proposed reforms, such as the chronic mismatch between the intellectual skills developed in economics PhD programs and those required for effective undergraduate teaching (Colander and McGoldrick, Chapter 1 this volume, pp. 9–12).

Colander and McGoldrick offer no facile prescriptions. Rather, they pose an evocative question: how can the economics major contribute more effectively to the goals of liberal education?

In this short essay, I seek to add breadth and force to Colander and McGoldrick's intervention by highlighting one of its unstated premises: the value of intellectual freedom. This concept plays a crucial role in their argument, such as their criticism of the current major for "not providing the context for the ideas it presents" (ibid., p. 20) and for placing undue emphasis on formal models that "too often involve uncritical acceptance of assumptions" (ibid., p. 6). Yet Colander and McGoldrick never articulate the ethical principle underlying these complaints: the idea that college-level economic educators have an academic duty – derived from the Socratic tradition of liberal education and from the US tradition of academic freedom – to cultivate their students' capacities for intellectual autonomy and judgment (AAUP, 1915, 1967; Strike, 1982; Nussbaum, 1997; Finkel, 2000; Ellerman, 2005; AAC&U, 2006).

This silence in Colander and McGoldrick's argument vitiates their case for a liberal arts overhaul of the economics major. They miss the chance to leverage the philosophical liberalism of Adam Smith ([1759] 1976), John Stuart Mill ([1859] 1956), Friedrich Hayek ([1945] 1948), George Shackle (1953), Amartya Sen (1999), and many others. Also, without recourse to a Smith/Mill/Hayek/Shackle/Sen notion of intellectual freedom, Colander and McGoldrick's indictment of prevailing economic education becomes unbalanced, focusing too much on how to increase students' desire ("passion") to learn economics while neglecting the equally salient problem of how to enhance students' *capacity* to learn – their effective freedom to think for themselves, to reach reasoned conclusions in the face of analytical, empirical, or normative uncertainties. Most importantly, they provide no normatively satisfactory answer to the skeptical colleague's question: "Why should we care about the goals of liberal education?" Colander and McGoldrick's best answer is that 98 percent of our students do not wish to pursue PhD-level study in economics and would be better served by a curriculum that enabled them to "think like liberally educated persons" rather than to "think like economists," as the latter is currently defined (ibid., pp. 16–20). But this only begs the question: "Why is it *our* job to enable our students to 'think like liberally educated persons'?"

In search of better answers, I turn to two complementary literatures: the broad post-Smithian tradition of economic thought in which the value of intellectual freedom is clearly recognized and the post-Perry literature on critical thinking in economic education. The intersection of these two literatures is germane to the present discussion since each links liberal education to intellectual development, both definitionally and causally: as part of what intellectual development is, and as an important part of what creates and sustains intellectual development (Sen, 1999, p. xii).

LIBERAL ECONOMISTS FOR INTELLECTUAL FREEDOM

In his *Theory of Moral Sentiments* ([1759] 1976), Adam Smith describes intellectual and moral autonomy as an important form of human self-mastery: the capacity to judge one's own conduct in dialogue with one's impartial spectator (Harpham, 2000). "We endeavor to examine our own conduct as we imagine any other fair and impartial spectator would examine it" (Smith [1759] 1976, p. 110). "It is only by consulting this judge within, that we can ever see what relates to ourselves in its proper shape and dimensions; or that we can ever make any proper comparison between our own interests and those of other people" (ibid., p. 134). When Smith speaks of human autonomy, he envisions a socially embedded individual, a person who gains the capacity to "think for himself" via ongoing social interaction and moral dialogue "in the great school of self-command" (ibid., p. 146). Smith's emphasis on human judgment is rare among modern moral philosophers (Griswold, 1999, p. 180). Philosopher Samuel Fleischacker (1999) suggests that Smith regarded the "freedom to judge" as an elemental form of human freedom. Smith, on Fleischacker's reading, "construes freedom above all as that which enables one to judge for oneself – unlike a child, who requires others to judge for her, who requires tutelage" (Fleischacker, 1999, p. 4).

Smith's emphasis on intellectual autonomy is characteristic of modern economics at large. Mill highlights the intellectual liberty of the individual in his vision of public discourse as a marketplace of ideas (Mill [1859] 1956, pp. 26–78). It is similarly visible in Hayek's subjectivist theory of knowledge and learning (Hayek [1945] 1948), particularly his emphasis on the individual appropriation of information via "learned and skillful judgment" (Lavoie, 1995; Boettke, 2002), and in Sen's insistence that intellectual freedom – the substantive ability to exercise one's reasoned agency as an autonomous thinker – ranks among the essential human capabilities (Sen, 1999). Shackle links all of these themes in his eloquent account of the liberal educator's mission:

> The first task of the University teacher of any liberal art is surely to persuade his students that the most important things he will put before them are questions and not answers. He is going to put up for them a scaffolding, and leave them to build within it. He has to persuade them that they have not come to the University to learn as it were by heart things which are already hard-and-fast and cut-and-dried, but to watch and perhaps help in a process, the driving of a causeway which will be made gradually firmer by the traffic of many minds. (Shackle, 1953, p. 18)

Though none of these thinkers is an education theorist and few speak of academic freedom per se, all show commitments to human freedom in the realm of ideas that are profoundly intertwined with their commitments to human freedom in the economic domain. They also offer keen insights into the perennial challenge of liberal education, namely: how to provide "autonomy-respecting help" that helps students learn to think for themselves while minimizing the "unhelpful help" that overrides or undercuts a person's capacity for learning and self-direction (Ellerman, 2005).

CRITICAL THINKING FOR UNDERGRADUATE ECONOMIC EDUCATION

Within contemporary economic education, these liberal visions of learning and teaching are championed by advocates of critical thinking (Fels,

1974; Moseley et al., 1991; Shackelford, 1992; Feiner and Roberts, 1995; Ferber, 1999; Colander, 2001; Feiner, 2003; Knoedler and Underwood, 2003; and Becker, 2007, among others). The term "critical thinking" is potentially problematic in this context since many economists "believe that the analytical nature of most economics courses inherently teaches students to think critically" (Borg and Borg, 2001, p. 20). Yet within the economic education literature, critical thinking is clearly distinguished from analytical thinking and its analogues, such as complex correct thinking: "the thinking required to solve problems where there is a single right answer and the teacher has taught the students 'the way' to find that answer" (Nelson, 1997, p. 62). Genuine critical thinking is characterized by (1) reflexivity – a commitment to "question our own purposes, evidence, conclusions, implications, and point of view with the same vigor as we question those of others" (Paul and Elder, 2001, p. 2); and (2) judgment – the art of "making judgments in the context of uncertainty" (Borg and Borg, 2001, p. 20). The latter coincides with the "contextual relativism" stage in the Perry/Nelson intellectual development scheme (Perry, 1970; Nelson, 1997) in which learners move beyond a relativistic view of truth by learning to employ disciplinary criteria to judge the relative value of competing ideas.

Defined in this way, critical thinking both requires and generates intellectual autonomy, "the ability and responsibility of individuals to make independent intellectual choices" (Thoma, 1993, p. 128). On the Perry/ Nelson ladder of intellectual development, learners are propelled to each new stage by the realization that ideas they once regarded as certain are actually uncertain. With each successive layer of uncertainty comes a new opportunity (or burden, depending upon one's perspective) to think for oneself. As Smith, Sen, and other philosophical liberals would surely emphasize, such autonomy is an achievement, not a natural state. It must be cultivated (Earl, 2000).

THINKING LIKE AN ECONOMIST, REVISITED

As teachers of a liberal arts subject, it is our job (individually and as departments) to respect and develop our students' capacities to think for themselves. To fail to develop our students' autonomy as economic thinkers is to leave them ill prepared to "grapple successfully with uncertainty, complexity, and conflicting perspectives and [to] still take stands that are based on evidence, analysis and compassion and are deeply centered in values" and thus "poorly prepared to deal with personal and professional decisions and with the major issues of our times" (Nelson, 1997, p. 71).

For the intellectual heirs of Smith, Mill, Shackle, Hayek, and Sen, this is surely an unacceptable outcome.

Economic educators have long known that liberal education is under-provided by standard undergraduate courses and curricula. These problems were flagged two decades ago by Colander and McGoldrick's predecessor, the Siegfried et al. (1991b) report on the economics major in the liberal arts, which concluded that the economics major tended to undercut students' intellectual autonomy:

> If we really want to foster independent thought and critical thought by our students, we need to demonstrate open-minded, self-critical thinking. Teaching whatever paradigm we choose as "the truth" does not help. . . . When enthusiasm crosses the fine line dividing it from dogmatism and when economic models are [presented] as self-evident truths, debate is stifled and learning is sacrificed. (Siegfried et al., 1991b, p. 212)

The criticisms of Siegfried et al. never gained much traction, in part because the energies of economists who might otherwise have been mobilized to reform the undergraduate major were divided along the familiar fault lines of our profession. The breadth and strength of professional support for such reforms was further eroded by a failure to articulate the central values on which all would-be reformers agree, first and foremost the value of intellectual freedom.

I applaud Colander and McGoldrick's instigation of a fresh, inclusive conversation about how to increase the educational value of the economics major. However, I urge participants on all sides to remember their shared commitment, as economists and academics, to the liberal project of intellectual freedom. Regardless of analytical or ideological orientation, intellectual autonomy is a value that all economists hold dear. The constructive possibilities for this new conversation will be greatly enhanced by highlighting this philosophical common ground.

One can imagine, for example, a rich and fruitful dialogue – on the terrain of intellectual freedom – between a Colander/McGoldrick enthusiast and a mainline economic educator who favors a "less is more" rethinking of standard textbooks and courses (for example, Hansen et al., 2002). The former sees critical thinking (broadly defined) as the proper goal of the economics major, whereas the latter is committed to the received goal of teaching students to "think like economists." But both seek to increase students' intellectual autonomy: one via Perry/Nelson critical thinking, the other by making more space in introductory and intermediate economics courses for students to actively acquire – that is, to make their own – the knowledge of how to apply theoretical concepts to messy, real-life situations.

A key question would then become: "How *do* economists think?" How do we ourselves adjudicate among competing arguments? And how might we employ this self-knowledge as a pedagogical tool? Craig Nelson (1989) argues that our students' capacity for higher-order thinking is greatly enhanced when they see their professor as "an individual striving, like the students, to interpret a complex and uncertain world" rather than an inscrutable "sage on stage":

> Although lectures require much prior thinking, it may seem to the students as if professors spontaneously think the way we lecture, as if "real" thinking is beyond the students' reach. This impact can be softened by exploring new ideas as they emerge during class and by noting how our views have changed: the mistakes and other factors that led to changes, the alternatives we explored and rejected, and the changes we are now considering. (Nelson, 1989, p. 24)

By candidly revealing the grounds of our own thinking – how we ourselves have combined theory, evidence, values (professional and personal), and other prior assumptions to reach reasoned conclusions about complex or controversial questions – we give students a concrete model of how to think critically within our discipline. Faculty too can benefit from this activity, especially instructors who find it difficult to "raise their assumptions to an explicit level for acknowledgement and examination" or those who are "unaware of the values and beliefs that are implicit in their approach to a subject" (Ehrlich and Colby, 2004, p. 38).

As the Colander/McGoldrick conversation proceeds, we and our colleagues would do well to resist the either/or logic of Borg and Borg's claim that "teaching our students to 'think like economists' does not teach them to think critically" (2001, p. 24). *Pace* Bartlett and Feiner (1992), we should not *reject* the goal of thinking like an economist. We should instead unpack, rethink, and rearticulate this pregnant phrase so that it more accurately conveys the multiplicity of ways in which one can reasonably think as an economist, as well as a meta-economic understanding of the nature and limits of economic knowledge (and of human knowledge in general). Doing so would give economics educators a chance to re-examine what we deem to be the chief educational goal(s) of the economics major, and whether or not "helping our students to acquire the intellectual means to think for themselves as economists" is or should be among them. We might also rediscover the liberal impulse that inspired the goal of "thinking like an economist" in the first place.

6. Teaching economics students as if they are geniuses

James Wible

In the comments that follow, I will present a line of thought supporting a broadening of the conceptual framework of the undergraduate economics major in a liberal arts college or university. The argument is that a more broadly focused major would be of great value to the vast majority of students enrolled in economics classes. The current undergraduate curriculum in economics has many strengths, but it also exhibits some inadequacies. Furthermore, some of these deficiencies can be expressed from an economic perspective. The main point is that undergraduates in economics classes should be taught as if they were going to be geniuses in some field or career other than economics. To not do so implies that most of our students are being educated for a career they will never enter. As an economist, my conclusion is that the current pedagogical practices in economics seem to be inefficient and highly wasteful.

Before making more specific comments, I would like to comment on the historic relevance of a liberal arts perspective, not just in liberal arts colleges, but also in liberal arts universities. The reason for this is the largely US experience of the large state university. US liberal arts colleges have origins in many respects similar to their European counterparts. US colleges were often started by religious founders or denominations to further the education of those who would become the leaders of society – lawyers, doctors, ministers, and businesspeople. Given this educational mission, good teaching was considered more important than research in most US colleges in the nineteenth century. Liberal arts universities had a different beginning. In 1863, Congress passed the Morrill Act, which gave land or the proceeds of vast tracts of land to the states for creating colleges or universities that are now known as "land grant" universities. The mission of these land grant institutions was to educate students not only in the agricultural and mechanical disciplines, but also in the liberal arts. Congress recognized a broadly educated citizenry was essential for the viability and survival of the nation. Consequently, more than a century later, the US has many large liberal arts universities. Every large and medium-sized state university considers a liberal education a cornerstone of its educational mission. Of course, the large liberal arts university has a somewhat different production function for higher education than liberal arts colleges. Many classes are much larger and faculty are expected to be somewhat more heavily engaged in research. Because of the sheer number of students in economics majors and classes in large liberal arts universities, the recommendations of this commission for a conceptually broader economics major are especially relevant to the liberal arts university and not just to the well-known and prestigious liberal arts colleges in the US.

INEFFICIENCIES AND INADEQUACIES OF THE PRESENT ECONOMICS CURRICULUM

In almost anonymous settings when I have met former college students at the mall, the golf course, or the grocery store, about nine out of ten tell me that economics was among the least favorite of all of their college classes. Then when I identify myself as a professional economist, usually there is a mutually pleasant exchange of words. An underlying sense of embarrassment is often defused with some humor. There are exceptions of course. Some students do well in economics and it has been central to the success of their careers. These students seem to realize that economics has some cachet as a difficult major with a broad array of applications. Students also realize that many potential employers value economics students as among the more talented college graduates in the job applicant pool.

Throughout my career as an academic economist, I have wondered if we could do a better job in the classroom, especially with students who will not become economists in the future. I would love to hear more often that an economics class was the best class that a student had taken – not just from a few of the better students, but from almost everyone who had taken that class. This is not a reflection on my colleagues or their teaching abilities, since several of them have won major teaching awards. But their classes like mine are constrained by the need to prepare our students for courses at the next level of the economics curriculum. Principles of economics classes need to prepare students for intermediate theory and the intermediate theory classes need to prepare them for advanced electives and perhaps graduate or professional school. However, few of my students go to graduate school in economics. Most of them go to business or law school or enter the world of business or finance directly. Quite recently, undergraduate economics has apparently become "the pre-professional major" on US campuses for many career paths. Also, like every other academic economist, I have witnessed the mathematical arms race in the profession. Every generation or so, the profession escalates the level and complexity of its mathematical and quantitative tools. This mathematical arms race has become so significant that I often tell my graduate students that they are the rocket scientists of the social world. The mathematics that was used to optimize the flow of resources during World War II and that put astronauts on the moon has been adapted for the latest versions of dynamic economic theory.[1] The research tool kit of the economist is unsurpassed on most US university campuses. In a very real sense from a research tools perspective, economics may be the envy of not just all of the social sciences but the natural sciences as well.

The economics profession's success as an analytical science has come at a high price. The relevance of course content is increasingly constrained by the time and resources needed to get the students to more advanced levels of theory and econometrics. What this means is that the big picture view of economics that attracted so much student interest in the past seems to have receded into the background. Actually the intellectual picture of economics is much more complex that this. Metaphors of wide and deep or broad and narrow do not do justice to the strengths and weakness of economics as a scientific discipline. Somewhat paradoxically economics is both more universal and more limited at the same time. Let me explain. One of the intellectual dimensions of economics that has interested me for more than three decades is its claims to universality. Its key assumptions of rationality and competition in the face of scarcity can be used to construct an all-encompassing mechanistic conceptual framework. That conceptual framework can be used to try to explain almost every type of ordered or patterned human phenomena. This is the paradigm of rationality within a general equilibrium framework in which market, partial, and individual equilibria also can be nested. Regardless of its realism and scientific status, either the micro or the macro versions of general equilibrium present a real intellectual challenge to the college student. Most of them have never seen a conceptual system of such breadth, depth, and rigor. General equilibrium theory is probably the best model of systemic interrelatedness that most college students will ever see. It certainly equals conceptions of systemic interrelatedness that college students may see in other disciplines such as physics and biology. Among the social sciences, general equilibrium theory in economics is almost unchallenged as an intellectually rigorous model of complexly interrelated social phenomena.

Even if an undergraduate student somehow manages to miss the undergraduate versions of general equilibrium in either intermediate theory course, the economists that most students encounter tend to be among the more analytically rigorous minds encountered in the academic world. This is especially the case when compared with academics in the humanities and other social sciences. The social process of acquiring the analytical tool kit of the economist in graduate school leads to young economists with exceptional analytical talents. Again, this analytical capability of the discipline is surely an attribute that most economics departments bring to their respective universities, their students, and especially their undergraduate majors.

If exceptional emphasis on analytical tools and concepts is the strength of the modern undergraduate curriculum in economics, it may also be a weakness. Going as far back as John Stuart Mill and Stanley Jevons, economists have recognized that analytical tools are quite limited. Those who founded consumer economics in utility theory knew that they were portraying a narrow view of the human being. They were creating a theory of human choice in so far as humanity was concerned with the material conditions of life and scarcity. But human life is far more encompassing than economic aspects of life. Economists founding utility theory also tended to interpret economic theory as related more to lower than higher mental processes. Utilitarianism in the hands of most of the founders was a theory of simpler rather than complexly conceptualized behaviors on the part of the decision-makers in the economy. They viewed simpler human behaviors such as consumption as ubiquitous. Simple, but universal human behaviors were to be the subject matter of the new science of economics. Human actions of economic agents inspired by complex processes of abstraction and conceptualization were left to the domain of cognitive psychology known as associationism. More recently, economists have been unclear to what extent they view economic agents as being motivated by relatively simple or extremely complex processes of human cognition. For example, expectations of agents, as J.M. Keynes dealt with them in the *General Theory* in 1936 during the Great Depression were intended to be theoretical concepts allowing for high levels of complex abstraction on the part of agents in the economy. The picture with regard to the more recent macro theory of rational expectations coupled with an assumption of highly competitive markets is not so clear. Perhaps the most logical interpretation of rational expectations is to regard it as a version of economywide behaviorism applied in the form of a new macro theory. However, other interpretations would seem to require agents as smart as the most empirically informed scientific economists assuming that economists can be taken as a model of human rational agents at their highest levels of complexity.

But this is precisely the issue in question. To what extent do economists and the discipline of economics represent the most creative human processes at their highest levels of complexity? It should be obvious that the majority of the most creative people in the world are not economists.

Certainly the best economists might be included in that group without prejudice. However, much of life in its fullest capacities transcends economic and material concerns. Consider, for example, the concept of opportunity cost. Opportunity cost is one of the greatest lessons that college teachers of economics give their students. Life is full of choices with alternatives and constraints. The alternatives not chosen are the true measure of how things could be different. Now many non-economist academics have either not learned or forgotten this lesson. Too many university committees are populated by faculty who have difficulty ranking alternatives. In the academic universe, all intellectual contributions are considered equally valuable. Yet there are many settings in life where opportunity cost should be operating in the background rather than at a conscious level. For example, a great musician might have been a gifted historian or orator. So the logic of opportunity cost is relevant to understanding the great musician's career choice. However, once the career is selected, opportunity cost might have a different relevance. Consider a concert performance. Logical choices about career, the allocation of time, and financial resources supporting the performance would be useful to a limited degree. Also, the choice of repertoire needs to be made and ultimately suppressed once the artist takes the concert stage. But, if taken more seriously, an obsession with economic ideas could simply clutter and ruin an artistic performance. For instance, one could imagine a brilliant solo pianist who after taking a class in economics continuously focused on opportunity cost. Every note played by a concert pianist in a performance could have been different. If Beethoven's Emperor Concerto is being played, one could imagine a note-by-note tug of war with another concerto, say Rachmaninoff's No. 1. The opportunity cost of playing the next note from the Beethoven concerto is not playing the next note of the Rachmaninoff piece. Surely everyone, including the brilliant economist, would realize that a high level of creative performance might mean forgetting about an active conceptualization of economic constraints and opportunity costs, at least for a few hours.

TEACH THEM LIKE THEY ARE GENIUSES

The case of the performing artist is just an example of one type of creative person who will not become an economist. One could add others: the great scientist, the novelist, the physicist, the politician, the athlete, the doctor, the psychologist, and many others. In the extreme, one could ask the question of how economics should be taught to creative geniuses who will not become economists. Indeed this is an economic question. If the time and talents of the creative genius are scarce, how much knowledge of economics is optimal beyond well-organized personal finances and an awareness of the basic institutions of the economy? The opportunity cost of greater awareness of economic dimensions in life and work in most cases is less time to be creative in the other non-economic domains of life. Too much knowledge and preoccupation with economics and scarcity could mean less time and resources for processes of discovery and innovation in every other area of human creativity than economics. Professionals who deal with some important aspect of the economy would be an exception to the preceding comments. Lawyers, bankers, and businesspeople may benefit from knowing more economics than those in other walks of life for obvious reasons. Again, they may benefit from a different conceptualization and presentation than future economists who are going to acquire the research tool kit of professional economics.

There may be an alternative to teaching undergraduate students as if they were on a career path to graduate-level economics. The alternative would be to teach them as though they would become creative geniuses in other walks of life. One of the marvels of the economy and its sub-systems is that they mostly work without most people in the economy paying much attention to them. Certainly there is a sub-category of economics, business, and related professionals who do nothing but make the economy work for everyone else. In the US economy, we produce something less than 1000 new PhDs in economics every year. About half of them are foreign students and many of them return to their native countries. Judging by the number of jobs categorized as "economists" from the Bureau of Labor Statistics, there are 13 000 economists in an economy of nearly 150 million workers. The point of all of this is the following. Is it not really an economic virtue that so few people in society pay so much explicit attention to resource allocation and budget constraints? One of the successes of the economics profession is that so few economists and financial professionals are needed to make the economy run so well. Most people making significant creative contributions to society simply do not need to have a highly complex awareness of the economy that rivals that of the professional economist. This frees them to invest their creative minds, talents, and time in all of those other endeavors of human life that make things better for all of us. The more efficient economics and related professions are in organizing and streamlining economic and financial affairs, the less everyone needs to pay attention to economic and financial matters.

Suppose that we imagine a thought experiment posed like that of John Rawls in his *Theory of Justice* (1971). Rawls imagined thinking about the good society from behind a hypothetical veil of ignorance. Suppose that we knew the categories of professions that would occur in a good society but did not know which individuals would fill those professions. Now take this thought experiment to the level of the freshman economics class. Suppose you were asked to teach a class of geniuses who would eventually take the lead in several major professions. In a class of 45 suppose you were given five students going into nine highly creative professions, but not economics. The question is, would you teach them any differently than how economics is taught now? Of the 45 brilliant undergraduates, suppose that five would become leading surgeons, five would become leading scientists, five would make important literary contributions, five would become the best lawyers of their generation, five would come to lead their religious denominations, five would become renowned performing artists, five would become top academics in disciplines other than economics, five would rise to be heads of state, and five would become CEOs of the most successful companies in the country. Again, remember that not one of our geniuses is headed into graduate school and a career in economics. Faced with such a class, one would imagine that economics might be presented differently. Also, enough economics needs to be presented to let them become intelligent citizens of society and public affairs. Certainly the logic of economic processes, institutions, and decisions would get presented. However, a qualitative presentation providing informative overviews of vast stretches of the economy might take precedence over more complicated puzzles and minutiae requiring ever advanced levels of mathematics and statistics.

The argument being presented is that it may make a great deal of economic sense to teach the average undergraduate economics student as if she or he would become a creative genius. This stands in sharp contrast to assuming that every student in the classroom might be a potential scientific economist. What the economy needs most is for people to optimize their innovative talents. This may mean teaching them very differently. Teaching them as though they all could become future economists could be a huge waste. Creative people in every walk of life focus on the next major innovations in their domains of life and work. Such innovations transcend the marginalist mind set of the well-trained analytical economist. Creative minds typically are focused on path-breaking contributions and being first to do something in their profession or their business. Shouldn't economics be taught with these considerations in mind?

BIG PICTURE CONTRASTS BETWEEN UNDERGRADUATE AND GRADUATE ECONOMICS

While there are many good reasons for taking a broad liberal arts perspective in economics, there are some big picture issues that need to be mentioned. There is simply not enough space to do anything more than mention these issues here. With regard to the current economics major, there are many strengths to the dominant approach and the most powerful departments of economics in the country no doubt may favor the continuation of the intellectual and pedagogical status quo. However, the reforms recommended in the main report could be of great benefit to the various categories of students enrolled in economics classes throughout the nation.

One issue that has bothered me for years is the scientific mind set that seems prevalent in many economics texts and probably presented in many undergraduate classes. When the student enrolls in physics, astronomy, biology, sociology, psychology, and probably many other disciplines there is more of a shared mind set about the nature of science and the world and how the sciences fit together. But when they come to economics, the student enters a scientific universe quite different than what they find in many other disciplines. Economics is quite isolated in an intellectual sense. Students are taught to "think like economists" whatever that may mean.[2] Broadly speaking, I would describe the conception of science shared by many disciplines as a conception of evolutionary complexity. The various sciences deal with differing systems and sub-systems of our universe and our society. These varying systems are layered, nested, and semi-autonomous. This permits disciplinary specialization and a sense of the complementarity of the various natural sciences, the social sciences, and the humanities with one another. Where systems of complexity are found to overlap, interdisciplinary or new approaches are needed to study new scientific and social problems. The point is that there is no widely agreed upon big picture view of the economy that shares the big picture principles of the other scientific disciplines. In many respects, economics has become an intellectually isolated profession with conceptual structures that significantly limit how we teach our students.[3]

There is another dimension to the lack of a clear conception of science and economic science within economics. Most economists espouse a form of scientific agnosticism especially at the more advanced levels of research and graduate education. At the most advanced levels, economists will tell you they don't know whether economics really deals with the real world and the real institutions and processes of the economy. If you press economists hard enough they will tell you they don't know whether economic models have any fundamental sense of validity. They are just tools of professional inquiry and nothing more. This is clearly a form of scientific agnosticism. The formal name for this attitude is instrumentalism. Instrumentalism is the idea that broad intellectual questions about whether science, mathematics, and economics are really informative cannot be answered. Instead, science may be nothing more than an array of models that have proven to be successful using the most up-to-date criteria of empirical or scientific validity. Additionally, if a student asks whether the patterns implied by the equations of a model have any counterpart in real patterns among the real people, economic systems, and institutions of the economy, graduate professors have mostly been inclined to give the instrumentalist response. As long as the models predict well, they serve as scientific instruments guiding the inquiry of specialists and nothing more. Moreover, the graduate student's question does not need to be answered and should not be answered because it diverts attention and resources from progress in scientific research. This is a pedagogy of small rather than big concepts. In the short run, such responses may be needed so that economists don't become bogged down in unanswerable philosophical questions. It may be that an instrumentally minded economic researcher may discover something unusual and surprising. But in the long run, someone needs to make comprehensive sense of what it is that economists are doing. Do the tools and theories of graduate-level economics ever amount to anything and imply some grand picture of the economic universe? A conception of science and economic science like that of evolutionary complexity may be such an array of big ideas that allows greater conceptual synthesis and integration of the many disparate contributions to economics over the past two centuries. Economic science, like the economy, is a mix of unfolding quantitatively and qualitatively describable patterns of economic activity. Such patterns certainly occur at various levels of aggregation, nesting, and layering, and they would seem to require both quantitative and qualitative methods of inquiry.

Coming back to liberal arts education, the contrast between the intellectual mind set of the graduate and undergraduate classrooms could not be more stark. At the undergraduate level, even though there may be problems with the curriculum, the relevance and realism of many principles and elective classes in economics is quite apparent. In many classes, instructors may transcend the confines of the formal curriculum and teach a course conveying an integrative vision of markets, institutions, and the history of important sectors and layers of the economic activity. At the undergraduate level, economists typically give the impression they know a lot about the economic processes of our world. They convey a big picture view of the economy, the discipline of economics, and their significance to society in the undergraduate classroom. Things are different at the graduate level where the emphasis is on mathematical models, sophisticated modeling techniques, and instrumentalist economic agnosticism. The contrast with disciplines such as physics and astronomy is startling. In economics, graduate students rarely if ever are given a big picture synthesis of graduate-level economics. Hardly anyone ventures to explain why graduate economic education in economics is so dominated by highly technical mathematical and quantitative modeling and whether the formal research methods of the discipline ever really tell us anything informative about the economic world we inhabit. Instead, nearly every graduate instructor falls back on an instrumentalist economic agnosticism mentioned above. The problem then becomes how the new PhD in economics trained with the small picture mind set of the standard highly technical graduate program can enter the undergraduate liberal arts classroom and convey an integrated big picture view of economics. Of course most newly minted doctoral students cannot do this, so their first years in the liberal arts classroom may be quite erratic and difficult for teacher and students.[4] The alternative is to implement many of the suggestions outlined in Chapter 1 of this book.

CONCLUSIONS

One of the most significant challenges now facing liberal arts colleges and universities is the increasing intellectual incongruity between undergraduate and graduate-level economics. Most undergraduates need a critically-minded, pluralistic, big picture synthesis of the economy and the most important economic questions facing society. In contrast, most graduate students are taught a small picture conceptual approach to the research questions of their chosen fields of advanced study. Consequently, few graduate students are adequately prepared to enter the undergraduate classroom of the liberal arts college or university. That is why many of the reforms advocated in the report need to be given serious consideration. One reform being proposed is special programs aimed at preparing doctoral students to be better classroom teachers of economics at the undergraduate level. This is an excellent proposal. At my own university such an option is already available. Economics graduate students may elect to take the equivalent of a supplemental doctoral field in the teaching of college-level economics.[5] This college teaching program provides graduate classes, seminars, and supervised teaching experiences for advanced doctoral students. Participation has significantly increased the teaching capabilities of our graduates.

NOTES

1.   On my campus, there is significant research on space programs. Our graduate students in economics are now as well trained in applied mathematics as any of the physicists or engineers on campus.

2. In the nineteenth century, Simon Newcomb (a prominent astronomer and mathematician) thought that economists ought to be taught to think like scientists. This view is most clearly stated in his 1886 article in *Science*.
3. But the issue of an adequate conception of economic science is much more problematic than the previous comments would suggest. While the natural and social sciences have come to terms with the theory of evolution, economics has not. This is no doubt due to the peculiar history of evolutionary ideas in economics. Those who first tried to make economic sense of evolutionary ideas, the American Institutionalists such as Thorstein Veblen, favored an analysis of broad cultural patterns and mind sets. Most intitutionalists saw no role for mathematical theory and statistical tools in economics. Later, another group of evolutionary thinkers best epitomized by F.A. Hayek, also opposed the development of the analytical tool kit of economics with sophisticated applications of mathematics and econometrics. Over the past 70 years, economics has come to be dominated by a mostly non-evolutionary school typically known as neo-classical economics. Neo-classical economists have seemingly taken up the evolutionary critiques of mainstream economics and reciprocated with a contrasting position. Their position seems to be that mainstream economics is better off being scientific and mechanistic than evolutionary and qualitative. Unfortunately, if one becomes aware of conceptions of science in other disciplines, this is a false dichotomy. Economics can be both analytical and evolutionary. Rich quantitative and qualitative concepts are needed in economics. Mathematical and statistical techniques as applied on the scientific side of economics somehow seem to be informative in the economy in which we live. But analytical knowledge can be qualitatively generalized as well. The latest research on scientific inquiry seems to suggest that quantitative knowledge is embedded within the qualitative theoretical and conceptual systems that most scientists rarely address. What undergraduate economics needs most in my view is a conceptual framework of evolutionary complexity so that economics can be taught in an intellectually and scientifically coherent way, so that economics can be conceptually and qualitatively generalized, and so that the subject matter of economics can be related to conceptions of science in other scientific disciplines.
4. As a practical matter, the agnosticism of the instrumentally minded economist could be tempered with a whiff of realism. Economists have battled for decades over the issue of realism and opposing conceptions of realism. It would be inappropriate to bring back every piece of conflict over realism. However, an evolutionary realism that recognizes significant patterns of connections among individuals in the economy and that such patterns of connections constitute systems and sub-systems of the economy would be a step in the right direction. There really are real patterns of economic connections in the economy. There are such entities as monetary systems, financial markets, factor markets, production systems, distribution systems, systems of taxation and subsidy, educational institutions, and systems and processes for providing health care, and so on. Economic systems and sub-systems and individuals within those systems engage in mostly stable patterns of conduct. Rigidly stable systems of conduct can be modeled quantitatively. Less rigidly stable systems may have sequential patterns of conduct that can be modeled qualitatively. Economists can study these systems and sub-systems of economic processes. Many of the systems of the economy could be improved with sequences of perhaps thousands of marginal changes over a significant period of time. In my estimation, these are the types of changes that the economist's tool kit are best able to appraise. Other systems and sub-systems may require wholesale change requiring an appraisal of very different, alternative future states of those systems. In contrast, wholesale changes are among the most difficult for economists because their analytical focus tends to be so narrow.
5. More general information about the University of New Hampshire's Cognate in College Teaching can be found online at: http://www.gradschool.unh.edu/catalog/programs/coll_teach.html (accessed 20 April 2009). Also, a description of the cognate in the department of economics can be found at http://www.gradschool.unh.edu/catalog/programs/econ.html (accessed 20 April 2009). The discipline of psychology has adopted the UNH teaching program as one of four recommended by the American Psychological Association.

7. The role of depth in a liberal education

Benjamin M. Friedman

The issues raised by the Teagle Foundation report in Chapter 1 are serious ones, well worth engagement. The report articulates well the point of view it advances. It certainly spurred my thinking.

Each of us, I suppose, comes at these questions from a particular point of view. We're shaped by the experience of the institutions at which we've served, our observations of our fellow faculty members alongside whom we've worked, and – most of all, I think – the students we've taught. Some members of this group will have taught at several different institutions, and perhaps even at several different kinds of institutions (research universities, liberal arts colleges, and so on). I've taught at only one, and so my views are perhaps somewhat parochial. Every institution of higher education is idiosyncratic, the one I know surely no less so than others.

That said, I'm skeptical of the approach taken in the report and dubious of many of its recommendations. The chief matter at issue in this regard is the role of a student's major, whether it be economics or biology or French literature, in his or her liberal education. Too much of the report seems to be based on the view that the typical student somehow isn't going to take courses outside his or her major. Hence the burden of achieving what we want students to get from a liberal education – breadth of thought, freedom of inquiry, exposure not just to different perspectives on a single issue but to entirely different ways of thinking about the world – rests on the major to provide. More specifically, if an economics student is going to get a liberal education, it's up to the economics curriculum to provide it. (I wondered whether the authors would mount this same ambition if the major in question were mathematics. Or Sanskrit.)

I've always thought of a liberal education, at the college/university level, as combining some aspects of breadth with some aspects of depth. Economics, probably less so than physics but more so than history, say, or English, can provide a student with the experience of learning about something in depth because the subject is vertical as well as horizontal. In other words, economics is both a subject area and a discipline.

In saying that economics is a subject area I mean that there are certain phenomena – unemployment, inflation, trade imbalances, budget deficits, to name just a few that naturally occur to a macroeconomist – and also certain questions – why are some countries richer than others? how important is education, relative to physical investment, in fostering development? do rising incomes always bring worse pollution? – that are immediately recognizable as objects of economic study and inquiry. This is not to say, of course, that others (sociologists, political scientists, historians, for example) can't or don't usefully think about these matters too. But no one is surprised that economists study these phenomena and ask these questions, and many people look first to economists to address them.

Importantly, however, economics is also a discipline in the sense that it offers a specific intellectual apparatus, a way of looking at, and analyzing, human behavior. The underlying idea of scarcity, and the consequent need for choice, have motivated the development of a conception of behavior that we formally conceive as constrained optimization, or informally as simply doing the best one can do, under the circumstances one confronts, to achieve one's aims when a large part of the point is that those aims can't all be achieved at once. To be sure, not all of economics has to be done in this way (much of what I personally do isn't). And, in the other direction, one can rightly complain that some economists naively apply the apparatus of constrained optimization with little sense of context, meaning little sense of what the relevant objectives and constraints are (and often with little common sense as well), and it is easy enough to caricature the outcome of their endeavors. But this intellectual apparatus is nonetheless what explicitly or implicitly supports much of the thinking that economists do. And it is a sign of how central to economics this intellectual apparatus is that many economists apply it to phenomena and questions that no one would immediately think of as falling within the purview of economics if they were analyzed differently. (To cite one concrete example, in my own department several graduate students have recently written dissertations on the gerrymandering of election districts. Why is their work something economists would recognize as economics? Because they explicitly model the constrained optimization problem being solved by the various political actors involved.)

One consequence of the fact that economics is in part a discipline, in this sense of having a recognizable intellectual apparatus at its core, is that students learn the subject cumulatively – again, probably less so than in physics but more so than in English literature. The usual progression is first to learn basic principles and concepts (what's a price? a demand curve?), then to develop the behavioral theory at an "intermediate" level, then to use the concepts and the theory as a supporting framework for

studying the various phenomena and questions about the world that interest economists as well as many people who aren't. If all this is done right,
it provides the sense of intellectual building.

I think understanding how that building works is an important *part* of
a liberal education. No one would claim that economics is the only discipline that can convey it, but surely economics is on the list of those that
can do the job. But at the same time, no one should think that gaining this
sense of intellectual building, and along the way learning something about
the substance of the various phenomena and questions to which economists apply our particular intellectual apparatus, constitutes the *whole* of a
liberal education. Students don't devote their entire undergraduate experience to taking courses within their major, nor should they. And, at least at
most institutions, there are principles to guide the part of their education
that takes place outside of the major.

Hence the major in any subject has a very important contribution to
make toward a student's liberal education, but it should not be expected
to carry the full burden. In light of what I think the role of the major to
be in this process – to repeat, providing the element of depth, of vertical
learning in the sense of cumulation, of acquiring a discipline in the sense
of an intellectual apparatus that one can apply to new questions that
come up long after one has left one's college or university behind – I think
economics provides opportunities as great as just about any subject and
greater than lots of them. How to enhance this process, to make this contribution more effective, is what I think is worth considering in an analysis
of the economics major in relation to a liberal education. I certainly don't
understand the report's claim that all this is somehow "inconsistent" with
the goals of a liberal education.

I have some more specific reservations about the report as well:

1. I'm skeptical about the value of reshaping economics departments and
    economics teaching along lines explicitly conceived as "general educa-
    tion." The idea brings to mind the movement to train and certify high
    school teachers in "education" but not in the subjects they're going to
    teach. It also isn't sufficient for this purpose (still less for the proposed
    alternative departmental rankings) to assume that everyone is going
    to share the same presumptions about what "general education" is
    supposed to mean for this purpose. Even within my own institution,
    well-meaning people debate such ideas vigorously. Gaining agreement
    across a broader spectrum is surely more challenging still.
2. I understand why people trained in "general education" (if we can
    agree on what this is to mean) may well have a large role to play in
    teaching introductory courses like freshman seminars. But why also

in "capstone" experiences? Here my view may be especially parochial, but at my institution the "capstone" experience in the economics major is writing a senior thesis. Isn't this activity, in most cases, better done under the supervision of an experienced specialist researcher?

3. Perhaps another parochial viewpoint: I was surprised at the concern expressed that the economics major is currently designed mostly to train undergraduates to go on to graduate school in economics. At my institution we're well aware that fewer than 10 percent of our undergraduate majors do that. Indeed, the great majority – even sometimes including the ones who graduate summa cum laude – aren't qualified to do so because we haven't given them the technical training they'd need to survive the first year of most PhD programs. We expect them to go on to careers in law, business, journalism, any of dozens of different pursuits, and we teach most of the undergraduate courses we offer accordingly. In parallel, I was startled by the idea that the economics major is becoming "less and less appropriate" for students interested in public policy. My sense, instead, is that with the trends of recent years in the teaching of disciplines that once were fine training for such interests – political science, sociology, anthropology – economics has become all the more attractive as a major for students interested either in careers bearing on public policy or simply in becoming informed citizens of a modern democracy.

In conclusion: while I believe that the report raises some provocative issues, I am not convinced that it has appropriately captured the sense of the major that I have from my perspective.

PART 3

Changing the way we teach economics

8. Using pedagogical change to improve student learning in the economics major

Scott Simkins and Mark Maier

We argue here – in support of the recommendations put forth in the Teagle Report in Chapter 1 – that well-designed pedagogical innovations can have a significant impact on the type of student learning that occurs in the economics major. Further, we believe that these changes in student learning are likely to narrow the gap between twenty-first-century liberal education goals and those undergirding the curricula of most undergraduate economics majors. In this response we summarize ways in which pedagogical changes in economics education can achieve both the learning goals of the economics major and those of a liberal education. In addition, we offer suggestions about how those pedagogical changes might be implemented, including discussion of a web-based teaching and learning portal for economists currently being developed as part of a new National Science Foundation-funded project.

USING PEDAGOGICAL CHANGE TO BRIDGE THE GAP IN LEARNING OUTCOMES

The goals of liberal education are by definition broad and diffuse and have been traditionally aimed at developing students' critical thinking, analytical reasoning, quantitative analysis, oral and written communication, and moral reasoning skills. Over the last decade national initiatives such as the AAC&U's Greater Expectations and the National Leadership Council's LEAP projects have extended these goals to: "work within complex systems and with diverse groups . . . demonstrate the ability to manage change . . . transform information into knowledge and knowledge into judgment and action," among others (p. xi, *Greater Expectations* report[1]). Clearly, the direction of change in modern liberal education goals is in the direction of developing not only specific academic skills but also the ability to integrate knowledge across disciplines in order to address "big think" questions. By contrast, the Teagle Report authors point out, the educational goals of the economics major have narrowed over time, focusing more and more on technical skills than the ability to address complex social problems, reason critically, or work together in interdisciplinary teams.

So, how can pedagogical change help to bridge this gap? What are the implications for economics instruction if we want students to achieve learning in the major that is consistent with that of a liberally educated student? Our own work exploring and implementing pedagogical innovations in economics, coupled with insights that we have gained from research in the learning sciences and educational research in disciplines outside economics – physics in particular – leads us to believe that we can achieve the goals of both a liberal education and a meaningful economics major through pedagogical change in the discipline.

The starting point for pedagogical innovation in economics education, in our view, are the introductory-level economics courses that provide instruction to as many as 40 percent of undergraduate students in the US and serve as a gateway to the economics major. With economists consistently reporting that they spend more than 80 percent of class time lecturing in these introductory courses, there appears to be a large potential for making significant gains in student learning, especially in areas that are often associated with liberal education goals. Our hope is that once implemented in introductory courses, the pedagogical changes and associated learning gains will begin to "trickle up" to upper-level courses in the major. In fact, the smaller size of upper-level courses makes them perfect laboratories for experimenting with innovative new pedagogies.

LEARNING FROM THE LEARNING SCIENCES AND PHYSICS EDUCATION RESEARCH

To improve teaching and learning in economics, especially in introductory-level courses, economists would do well to heed three key principles summarized in *How People Learn: Brain, Mind, Experience, and School* (Bransford et al., 2000), a seminal educational resource guiding both classroom practice and educational research.[2] According to the learning sciences research summarized in *How People Learn*, to improve student learning educators should:

1. teach subject matter in depth and in a structured manner to promote expert-like (as opposed to novice) thinking;

2.   uncover, understand, and work with students' pre-existing knowledge, including pre- and misconceptions; and
3.   help students become self-monitoring and reflective learners.

Promoting Expert-like Thinking

Most introductory courses in economics are encyclopedic in nature and develop little in-depth understanding of economic thinking, a key learning goal in the economics major. Further, the teaching methods used in these courses often promote surface-level learning that rewards memorization and short-changes both economics majors and non-majors alike. As classroom instructors know, it is very difficult to teach students to "think like an economist" (pp. 16–20, this volume), a process that requires more than lecturing, an occasional homework set, and multiple-choice exams. Both research and classroom experience tell us that higher-order thinking skills are best developed and reinforced through repeated hands-on, interactive, and collaborative learning that encourages students to analyze trends and correlations in economic data, apply economic theory to real-world problems, and evaluate economic policies. In other words, students need to *do* economics, but with developmental guidance that encourages them to order ideas, structure their knowledge, and build confidence in their skills. By providing this "scaffolding," students can then be progressively challenged to develop more complex thinking processes that promote the acquisition of new skills and ideas, but with an underlying framework that makes the learning both deep and durable.

Educational research in science, technology, engineering, and math (STEM) disciplines has identified several teaching techniques that help students think more like experts by requiring students to practice new concepts repeatedly in new situations, an approach identified in learning theory as a precondition for deep and sustained learning. Our research identifies cooperative learning, context-rich problems, and just-in-time teaching, among others, as techniques that offer particular promise in economic education.[3] These pedagogical practices help to develop not only traditional economics learning outcomes but also general critical thinking, analytical reasoning, communication, and teamwork skills that can be applied to "big think" kinds of questions that may not have predetermined answers.

Understanding Students' Pre-existing Knowledge

Research in the learning sciences tells us that providing students with structured opportunities to develop expert-like knowledge and practice

problem-solving skills in a variety of contexts is necessary for improvements in learning. However, to be long-lasting, these pedagogical practices
need to be accompanied by additional teaching strategies aimed at uncovering student pre- and misconceptions – common sense beliefs grounded
in everyday experience, which are often at odds with formal economic
principles.

Traditional economics instruction, with its focus on content acquisition,
pays little attention to the notion of prior student knowledge, resulting
in learning that is often much different than what we think or intended.
Most instructors of introductory courses presume no prior knowledge
of economics concepts or ideas, yet research on learning demonstrates
that students not only bring to the classroom preconceived ideas of how
economics "works" based on their prior experiences, but also that these
preconceptions, however ill-formed, are very difficult to change and often
retard learning. Understanding students' preconceptions and developing
pedagogical techniques to directly address them is critical to improving
learning in economics. Many of us have had the experience of grading an
exam and finding that a number of students have completely missed key
points covered in previous class sessions, even though these same students
attended class each day. We wonder whether these students heard what
we were saying in our lectures. In a sense, it is likely that they didn't – or
rather that they heard something very different from what we were saying
because it was being filtered by a different mental model formed by their
previous life experiences. These mental models often shape and structure
the information students obtain in course lectures in ways different than
what was intended by the instructor. As a consequence, students often
develop an understanding of economics principles that runs counter to
what the instructor is trying to teach.

As research illustrates, even when students score well on traditional
assessments they often revert to their prior understanding, in particular
when asked questions in new contexts. Perhaps the most striking example
of this is illustrated in the video, *A Private Universe*, where Harvard
graduates (and even some faculty members) have difficulty explaining to
an interviewer the causes of the seasons, despite having taken numerous
science courses (Annenberg, 1987[4]). To improve learning in economics we
need to first recognize the deep and enduring conceptions that students
bring to our classrooms, then develop pedagogies designed to change specific misconceptions. In many science disciplines researchers have developed diagnostic tools called "concept inventories" that help to inform
both curricular and pedagogical changes and are then used to test whether
or not student thinking has changed.[5] We believe that the time is ripe for
the development of an economics concept inventory that could be used to

uncover student preconceptions in economics and develop both curricular and pedagogical innovations to address them. Without knowing students' preconceptions we have little understanding about what students are really learning and the durability of that learning.

Developing Self-monitoring and Reflective Learners

The preceding two sections make clear that changing curricula or content is not enough to improve student learning in economics. Without attention to the way the content is taught *and* learned, we are likely to fall short of our learning goals. In addition, learning theory points out that retention and durability of new thinking is increased when students are self-reflective about their learning. Producing self-reflective learners requires instructors to engage students in learning activities that force them to (1) think intentionally and explicitly about their prior beliefs, (2) illustrate how these preconceptions led to contradictions with new knowledge, and (3) explain how they were able to construct a new understanding out of these contradictions. Such complex and introspective tasks require that instructors identify in advance problematic preconceptions and prepare activities, assignments, and assessments that encourage metacognition. This could be as simple as including questions on homework assignments asking students to explain their steps in obtaining specific answers or asking students to submit "muddiest point" questions at the end of a class.[6] More structured pedagogical techniques aimed at improving students' metacognitive skills, initially developed in STEM disciplines, include documented problem-solving and just-in-time teaching. The former asks students to verbally document their problem-solving processes while the latter often includes questions asking students to identify ideas or concepts that are unclear, even after reading the text or an article for class. These techniques not only develop specific economics-related skills but also general problem-solving and self-monitoring skills that are central to a liberal education. In turn, these broad-based skills are critical in developing the ability to transfer knowledge to new problems, in particular the kinds of unstructured economic, social, and environmental problems that characterize the modern world economy.

Summary

The learning sciences research summarized in *How People Learn* provides clear direction on how to improve student learning through intentional pedagogical innovation that pays attention to not only *what* students learn, but *how* they learn. Educational researchers in STEM disciplines, in particular physics education, have used this insight to systematically address student misconceptions, promote metacognition, build a cumulative knowledge base about student learning in physics, and develop more expert-like learning among their students. Economists can learn much from this research, adapting effective pedagogical and curricular innovations developed outside the discipline for use in economics education.

MAKING PEDAGOGICAL INNOVATION AND ADAPTION IN ECONOMICS EASIER – IMPLEMENTING AN ECONOMICS PEDAGOGIC PORTAL

A new project funded by the National Science Foundation – Starting Point: Teaching and Learning Economics (DUE 0817382)[7] – aims to make the process of adopting or adapting new pedagogical techniques easier for instructors. Starting Point[8] is an economics pedagogic portal that will serve as a comprehensive resource for college-level economics instructors interested in exploring new pedagogical techniques for the introductory course. It is based on the successful geoscience pedagogical portal, Starting Point: Teaching Entry Level Geoscience[9] developed at the Science Education Resource Center (SERC) at Carleton College (MN). The project investigators for the Starting Point: Teaching and Learning Economics project (Scott Simkins, North Carolina A&T State University; Mark Maier, Glendale Community College; and KimMarie McGoldrick, University of Richmond) are teaming up with Cathy Manduca, director of the SERC project, to develop a series of online pedagogical modules that will describe and illustrate a variety of pedagogical innovations, many developed outside of economics, that are grounded in the *How People Learn* principles described above. Each module will include multiple examples of how the pedagogy can be incorporated in economics courses. The Starting Point site will both extend and draw from SERC's Pedagogy in Action[10] portal and will initially include the following 16 modules:

Context-rich Problems
Just-in-Time Teaching
Quantitative Writing
Teaching with Cases
Cooperative Learning
Classroom Experiments
Interactive Lectures

Interactive Demonstrations
Undergraduate Research
Interdisciplinary Approaches to
   Teaching
Service Learning
Spreadsheets Across the Curriculum
Documented Problem-solving

Teaching with Computer
    Simulations
Effective use of Personal Response
    Systems

Using Media to Enhance Teaching
    and Learning

Leading economic educators who are experts in the module topics have been identified to develop the pedagogic modules for the Starting Point site. The first modules are scheduled to be available online in fall, 2009. We believe that this economic pedagogic portal will substantially reduce the time cost of adapting new pedagogical innovations for use in introductory economics courses and will help make a wider set of teaching strategies available to economists. In addition, we hope that the portal will lead to greater cross-disciplinary pedagogical fertilization, something that has been lacking in most disciplines. By taking advantage of new insights and results developed across disciplines, faster implementation of effective teaching and learning processes can be achieved.

PEDAGOGICAL CHANGE, INSTITUTIONAL BARRIERS, AND ACCOUNTABILITY FOR LEARNING

As the authors of the Teagle Report point out, there is currently little incentive for changing either the curricular structure or teaching of economics in most universities. However, we disagree with the strong version of the statement on p. 7 that seems to signal defeat in the attempt to bridge the divide between liberal education learning goals and those of the economics major: "Without changing those structures [the departmental structure of universities] there is little hope of significantly changing the current situation [focusing on depth versus breadth], and in fact, it is not even clear whether one would want to do so." Our response so far is more hopeful, pointing out the potential for improving learning – and bridging the gap between liberal education and economics major learning goals – through intentional pedagogical innovation in economics that is centered around learning science and discipline-based educational research.

We believe that broader national trends in higher education provide an additional ray of hope. The economics major, and by extension, the economics department where faculty members "live" and get their professional identity, is not an island in the university, college, or community college. Increasingly, departments are being held accountable for aligning departmental and course learning goals and objectives with those of the university, university systems, or accreditation organizations (disciplinary or geographic). Those goals are often both broader – like those promoted by the AAC&U – and more pragmatic – such as increasing student retention and graduation rates – than the current learning goals and objectives of most economics departments. This push for greater alignment (and accountability for liberal education learning outcomes) in turn provides greater incentives to promote both innovations in classroom teaching and research on economic education.

FINAL THOUGHTS

As we noted at the start, we believe that changes in pedagogy, grounded in learning sciences research and building from pedagogical experimentation in other disciplines, can help improve student learning in economics, both in developing technical skills typically associated with the economics major, and in promoting broader liberal arts skills aimed at addressing "big think" questions. Research and classroom experience show that intentionally focusing on developing expert-like learning, understanding and addressing student preconceptions, and promoting reflective learning among students has the potential to significantly improve student learning in economics and build lifelong learning skills that are transferable beyond the major. In most cases these pedagogical changes can be implemented with little or no reduction in course content coverage while at the same time increasing students' skill levels. That is, they help to make classroom teaching and learning more effective and more efficient. Of course, implementing new pedagogical practices involves an investment of time up front for the instructor, but even here we believe that new educational resources like the Starting Point: Teaching and Learning Economics pedagogic portal will help to greatly reduce both the search and implementation costs by providing a single source for economics pedagogic examples.

NOTES

1. Available at http://www.greaterexpectations.org (accessed 20 April 2009).
2. For example, the National Science Foundation has made the principles outlined in *How People Learn* an integral component of its CCLI (Course, Curriculum, and Laboratory Improvement) research grant program that includes awards for research on economic education. For information on how these principles are being implemented in the classroom, see *How Students Learn: History, Mathematics, and Science in the Classroom* (2005), http://www.nap.edu/catalog.php?record_id=10126 (accessed 20 April 2009).
3. Maier and Simkins (2008) provide a number of examples of pedagogical innovations developed in physics education that can be readily adapted in economics, including context-rich problems, just-in-time teaching (JiTT), interactive lecture demonstrations

(ILDs), and concept tests. For more information on cooperative learning, see Maier et al. (2009). Simkins and Maier (2004) and Simkins and Maier (2009) provide additional details about the adaptability of JiTT pedagogy in economics and its use as an effective teaching and learning tool.

4. http://www.learner.org/resources/series28.html (accessed 20 April 2009).
5. Among the most famous of these is the Force Concept Inventory, initially developed by Halloun and Hestenes (1985) and widely used in physics education research. Additional background information about concept inventories is provided by Richardson (2004) at http://www.aaas.org/publications/books_reports/CCLI/PDFs/02_AER_Richardson. pdf (accessed 20 April 2009). For an extensive list of concept inventories in a variety of fields, see https://engineering.purdue.edu/SCI/workshop/tools.html (accessed 20 April 2009).
6. See Angelo and Cross (1993) on classroom assessment techniques.
7. http://www.nsf.gov/awardsearch/showAward.do?AwardNumber=0817382　　(accessed 20 April 2009).
8. http://serc.carleton.edu/econ/ (accessed 20 April 2009).
9. http://serc.carleton.edu/introgeo/ (accessed 20 April 2009).
10. http://serc.carleton.edu/sp/ (accessed 20 April 2009).

9. Providing incentives for change: evaluating teaching

Ann L. Owen

If the goal of integrating the economics major into a liberal education is to be achieved on a widespread basis, many individual instructors will need to make significant changes. Instructors need to have incentives to make the investment in changing the way they teach their classes and any kind of incentive scheme will necessarily require college administrators to be able to identify those deserving of the rewards. Current methods for evaluating teaching effectiveness typically do not provide information about this aspect of teaching, and this change in emphasis will require a change in the way in which teaching is evaluated at most colleges and universities. Because implementing such a change will likely also involve costs for the institutions, institutions will need to have incentives to incur these costs.

CHANGES TO THE WAYS TEACHING IS EVALUATED

While different institutions may place differing levels of significance on the quality of teaching during tenure, promotion, and salary reviews, common practice weighs student input given through anonymous teaching evaluations heavily in the evaluation of teaching. This is inherently problematic as these kinds of evaluations are, at best, very noisy measures of teaching effectiveness. It is even more troublesome if a substantive evaluation of how the courses an instructor teaches contribute to a liberal education is desirable. Most undergraduate students in the process of this education are not sophisticated enough to make this assessment. Furthermore, they typically take only one course taught by the instructor and are not in a position to evaluate the entire teaching portfolio.

There are several, relatively low-cost changes to the current practice that would allow a better assessment of how individual instructors contribute to the liberal education of their students. A first step in the process is that individual professors should write a brief statement articulating goals for courses, how they relate to the goals of a liberal education, and specific tactics used in courses to achieve these goals. Whenever possible, evidence that these goals were achieved should be weighed heavily in the evaluation of teaching. Although it may not be possible to provide evidence for every goal, examples of student work, class assignments, or comments on student evaluations that address the instructor's course goals might all be used as evidence that these goals were achieved. This statement should be circulated as part of the tenure and promotion materials so that both external and internal reviewers of the record can consider it.

Second, at least one external reviewer used in the tenure and promotion process should focus on the teaching portfolio. These reviewers would be asked to comment on teaching materials, assignments, syllabi and be asked to comment on the extent to which instructors have adopted goals for their teaching consistent with the goals of a liberal education. Adoption of this policy would be a very dramatic departure from current practice and send a strong signal that teaching quality does matter. Note, however, that it could be accomplished by adding one additional reviewer; designating one reviewer to evaluate teaching materials does not have to detract from the evaluation of research. In order to make this external review of teaching materials valuable, institutions would need to give clear guidelines to reviewers regarding the nature of the evaluation. Although some institutions do currently circulate teaching materials to external reviewers, typically no clear guidelines are given. The task of reviewing research is more well-defined and typically consumes the majority of the reviewer's time.

Furthermore, the importance of anonymous teaching evaluations should be reduced. They should be replaced by alternative means of evaluations such as: peer review, letters from students who have taken more than one class with a professor, letters from previous students who have graduated and are out of the college environment, reviews of the nature and quality of assignments given in class, and the personal statement from the instructor mentioned above.

Finally, professional societies, like the American Economics Association, could provide individuals (for a fee) with an evaluation of their teaching materials that could be used as certification of effective teaching for job seekers or job changers. Currently, many graduate students have the ability to obtain some kind of certificate from a teaching and learning center at their university; however, unless an employer is familiar with the specific institution's program, these certificates don't have much signaling value. A more standardized review process based on actual materials used in the classroom could provide some value. In addition, simply the process of collecting and explaining how teaching materials are used in the context of a liberal education could help instructors improve their teaching.

It is important that any changes to teaching evaluation methods do not dictate content and interfere with the instructor's academic freedom. Rather, instructors should be given the flexibility to develop methods appropriate for their discipline that teach the core elements of a liberal education. Of course, teaching has to matter in the evaluation process and this requires institutional change at many colleges and universities. Some ideas for encouraging this change are discussed further below.

INCENTIVES FOR INSTITUTIONS

Relying heavily on student teaching evaluations to evaluate the quality of faculty is the low-cost, least resistance path for college administrators. Under the current system, the students are satisfied because they are essentially able to "vote" for their favorite professor. Tenured faculty have, by virtue of their successful tenure award, fared well under the current system and may be reluctant to change it; while untenured faculty have no authority or power to change the system. Therefore, any change to the status quo is likely to meet resistance. Institutions need to see benefits to undergoing this change.

The report suggests creating a ranking system to create institutional value for improved pedagogy. This type of ranking system might help spur institutional change by establishing a means for outside recognition or accreditation for institutions that use a more substantive teaching evaluation process that examines the extent to which teachers have contributed to students' liberal education. Rankings of institutions could be publicly provided that would indicate how well instructors at each institution (in aggregate) fared. It is critical, however, that before such a ranking system is created, the current teaching evaluation process be improved. Otherwise, these rankings will be superficial and may end up having a larger cost than benefit by misdirecting institutional efforts.

Costs to implementing changes to teaching evaluation could be reduced with the help of accrediting agencies or outside foundations that provide rankings. For example, the accrediting agency or foundation could develop general guidelines and suggestions for changing the way faculty are evaluated. These guidelines could be customized to meet the needs of individual institutions in the process of accreditation.

Thoughtful, but simple processes that give the institution and the instructor flexibility to define their own objectives (within limits) are likely to be the easiest to implement and the least likely to degenerate into an administrative burden with little benefit.

10. Reflections on introductory course structures

Paul W. Grimes

One of the underlying themes of the Teagle Report is the recognition that institutional forces within academe have narrowed and vocationalized the traditional college major. The authors rightfully argue that the vocation in question is that of an academic researcher or specialist within the students' discipline. As a result, students are deprived of a broader understanding of the social context and relevance of their chosen field. Nowhere is this more true than in economics; and it generally begins with students' first exposure to the discipline.

Across the country more than 1 million college students enroll in principles of economics courses each academic year, and their classroom experiences are virtually the same. Whether the course is taken at an elite private college or at a large state-supported research university, students study remarkably similar material from remarkably similar textbooks. Not only are today's introductory textbooks "structured after the Samuelsonian texts of the 1950s," (see pp. 31–2 of the report, Chapter 1, this volume) they are often regarded as commodities by the faculty that teach from them. Pick up any "principles book" and you can be assured that it includes the basic canon of material that makes up 90 percent of the typical "principles course" at a vast majority of US colleges and universities. As a result, textbook adoptions are often not preceded by careful study and consideration by a department's faculty. Today, textbook decisions tend to hinge on matters of convenience ("What did we use last year?") or on which book offers the wider array of (rarely used) ancillary supports ("Is there a supporting website?"). Although this textbook homogenization has led to fewer debates over adoptions, it has also reduced the faculty's discussion about what should be taught in the classroom. And without that discussion, the role of the introductory course is rarely given serious debate.

It was not always so. In the mid-1970s, a small number of economic educators frustrated with maintaining student interest in abstract economic models, introduced the "social issues" approach as an alternative to the traditional principles course sequence. Instead of an introductory micro course being followed by an introductory macro course (or vice versa), they proposed offering a first-semester course built around the study of specific social issues, such as poverty, inflation, protectionism, and so on, through the lens of economics (Leftwich and Sharp, 1974). Instead of teaching economic models and then applying them to the issues, the issues were thoroughly explored first and the economics principles that came to light during this discussion were then developed and taught. (Just the opposite of the way most textbooks present material today.) The proponents of the social issues approach believed that this was a more natural way of learning economics. To calm the fears of those who thought this approach was "too soft," a second-semester course was proposed to cover the "analytics" of traditional micro and macro principles. The social issues format spawned several competing textbooks published by major imprints. Several major universities adopted the social issues approach and followed it for a number of years, but eventually most returned to the traditional two-course sequence.

Why did the social issues approach fail to survive? Based on this author's personal conversations with the recognized originators of the social issues approach, Professors Richard Leftwich and Ansel Sharp (both formerly of Oklahoma State University), the primary reason was the relative time cost that professors bore when teaching a social issues class. It takes substantially more time and effort to teach an effective social issues course as compared with teaching a traditional principles course. Instructors must know the ever-changing landscape of the social issues that provide the platform to deliver the economics content. And it takes significant time and effort to maintain currency across a wide variety of issues. On the other hand, the basic models and theories presented in the traditional principles text evolve slowly over time. After a while, the marginal cost of preparing to teach a traditional principles class drops toward zero while the marginal cost of preparing to teach a social issues course remains relatively high. Given reward structures that rarely reflect student learning outcomes and the pressures of research and service demands on the professorate, it is easy to see why the low-cost approach to teaching introductory economics prevailed. Furthermore, we should recognize that this cost barrier exists not only for the social issues approach, but for any innovative pedagogy that increases the preparation and/or evaluation time for instructors.

Today, the social issues pedagogy survives primarily in niche courses designed for specific groups of non-majors. (Interestingly, several of the textbooks originally written for the social issues course have found these new audiences and are still in print after many updates and new editions. See, for example, Moomaw and Olson, 2007 and Sharp et al., 2008.) The institutionalization of the traditional principles courses is so strong, that even those few schools where the introductory social issues format still survives also offer the principles sequence as an alternative.

It is also important to note that our homogenized principles textbooks support homogenized classroom pedagogy – what Watts and Becker (2008) call "chalk and talk" – old-fashioned lectures accompanied by static diagrams and graphs drawn on blackboards. Although there has been some movement to incorporate more active learning teaching strategies into the classroom, recent surveys indicate that lectures remain the predominate tool used by a wide majority of instructors in the principles courses. (Watts and Becker (2008) report that professors of economics spend about 83 percent of their classroom time lecturing, while classroom experiments and other active learning strategies are used less than 10 percent of the time.) Given that the basic structure of our textbooks was established more than 50 years ago, it is not surprising that lectures still dominate the time students spend in introductory economics courses.

Why are today's introductory courses so standardized? Why do we not see competing course formats and an array of textbooks to accompany them? Undoubtedly, many would answer that it is just too costly to experiment with different approaches and, as noted elsewhere in this volume, the professorate lacks the proper incentives to pursue innovative pedagogy or deviate from the standard canon of material. Clearly, we have become entrenched and comfortable in the way we approach the principles courses.

Perhaps it is possible to find ways to reduce the costs and create incentives for experimentation with new course formats and pedagogies. In the mid-1970s, the innovators of the social issues format were partially motivated by an initiative spearheaded by the American Economic Association's Committee on Economic Education and The Council for Economic Education (then the Joint Council on Economic Education) to "explore alternative approaches to teaching the college introductory economics course" (Welsh, 1974, p. 1). Financial support was provided by the Alfred P. Sloan Foundation and the American Bankers Association. (For details about this nationwide initiative, please see the multiple special issues of the *Journal of Economic Education* published during 1974–75.) Surely, private dollars could be found today to try once again. The need has changed little in the past 30 years; in addition to the arguments put forth for introductory curriculum reform by the authors of the Teagle report in this volume (see pp. 31–3), empirical economic education research suggests that there is much room for improving student outcomes in the traditional principles sequence (Becker, 1997).

Institutional reforms at the local level could also provide greater incentives for the adoption of innovative pedagogical approaches. Academic promotion and tenure policies rarely provide rewards for taking risks in the classroom. (The adoption of institutional ranking systems that explicitly value teaching, such as that proposed by the authors of the Teagle report, would help alleviate this prevalent shortcoming.) In fact, entry-level faculty are often encouraged to "play it safe" in the classroom and to devote their creative energies to research, which is more highly rewarded by the profession. We should note however, that in recent years, some colleges have intentionally put into place reward systems that elevate the importance of high-quality and effective teaching, but these institutions are still the exception and not the rule.

In the 35 years since the introduction of the social issues approach, economic educators have made great advances in understanding how students learn and how to assess that learning. Thus, we may be more successful today at finding viable alternative course formats and accompanying pedagogies. The availability of grant dollars to invest in course experimentation could spark creative efforts and innovation, and modifications of our professional reward systems could create incentives to take the necessary risks. But real and lasting change will require a sustained discipline-wide commitment to effective teaching. That is the larger challenge.

11. Economics and liberal education: why, where, and how

Michael K. Salemi

> The aim of liberal education, however, is not to produce scientists. It seeks to develop free human beings who know how to use their minds and are able to think for themselves. Its primary aim is not the development of professional competence, although a liberal education is indispensible for any intellectual profession. It produces citizens who can exercise their political liberty responsibly. It develops cultivated persons who can use their leisure fruitfully. It is an education for all free men, whether they intend to be scientists or not.
>
> (Adler, "What is Liberal Education?")[1]

> All of this, I think, leads directly to the heart of the matter: that vocational training is training for work or labor; it is specialized rather than general; it is for an extrinsic end; and ultimately it is the education of slaves or workers. And from my point of view it makes no difference whether you say slaves or workers, for you mean that the worker is a man who does nothing but work – a state of affairs which has obtained, by the way, during the whole industrial period, from its beginning almost to our day. Liberal education is education for leisure; it is general in character; it is for an intrinsic and not an extrinsic end; and, as compared with vocational training, which is the education of slaves and workers, liberal education is the education of free men.
>
> (Adler, "Labor, Leisure, and Liberal Education")[2]

The earliest undergraduate reading assignment I can recall is Mortimer Adler's "Labor, Leisure and Liberal, Education." The assignment was made on the first day of a course entitled "Introduction to Education" that was offered to honors students at my college. The course was designed to help students think seriously about the purpose of their education and to make them more intentional about it. The course instructor was Basil O'Leary, a paragon of free and educated men. It is to Mortimer Adler, then, that I return in search of grounding for my comments on the Teagle report.

My comments investigate three issues. First, where should liberal education occur? Ought it reside at the prestigious liberal arts colleges or ought it occur at all sorts of educational institutions including PhD-granting research universities? Second, is economics itself a proper subject for

liberal education? Does economics instruction engage students in sufficiently broad questions or is it stuck in what Colander and McGoldrick
term a "little think" culture (Chapter 1, this volume)? Third, what changes
are necessary so that economics better prepares students to use their
leisure fruitfully?

Liberal education should occur everywhere. It is not the special responsibility of liberal arts colleges. Nor should we expect that liberal arts colleges today do a better job of providing liberal education to their students
than do PhD-granting institutions.

Institutions that offer both graduate and undergraduate education
serve two important student clienteles. Graduate students want training
that will prepare them to succeed in their chosen profession. It would be
hard to describe them as slaves however, since their training will qualify
them for a profession that primarily involves activities that Adler would
describe as leisure.[3] Undergraduate students want a multifaceted experience. They want to improve their minds, prepare for meaningful work,
develop social connections, and enjoy themselves.

Colander and McGoldrick argue that graduate education and liberal
education are not compatible. For example, they write:

> Modern graduate education. . .focuses on producing researchers, not teachers.
> It succeeds in what it sets out to do; it produces passionate researchers. These
> researchers can also be teachers, but generally the teaching passion is not for
> addressing broad unanswerable or big think questions; instead it is a passion
> to answer smaller research questions to fit the particular disciplinary nature of
> their study. (p. 7)

The implication, of course, is that PhD-granting institutions are ill-suited
to provide liberal education to their undergraduate students.

I find this position curious for several reasons. First, individuals who
complete a doctoral program and seek a faculty position at any educational institution are curious people who have chosen a life of the mind.
They have chosen a life of leisure and we should be suspicious of claims
that they are only fit to prepare students to be workers and slaves.

Second, many liberal arts institutions including the most prestigious will
only tenure faculty who have a solid research publication record. Here is
what the section on appointment and tenure of the faculty handbook of
Middlebury College has to say about faculty scholarship:

> Middlebury believes that a faculty actively engaged in scholarship enriches the
> intellectual climate of the College. The mastery of new knowledge or skills,
> including those outside of the faculty member's own discipline, is valued
> as a contribution to the intellectual life of the College; however, the quality

of a faculty member's scholarship is evaluated primarily through his or her published, performed, or executed works. Scholarly achievement that is recognized as of significantly high quality by scholars or artists beyond Middlebury College is a prerequisite for promotion to tenure.

Clearly, the faculty and administrators of Middlebury believe that research productivity is necessary if faculty persons are to make positive contributions to the intellectual life of the college. The quote from the Middlebury handbook tells us that scholarship outside a faculty member's department is valued but that scholarship will be evaluated primarily through the faculty member's published work.[4]

Liberal education, research, and graduate education are complements. A person who completes a PhD, wins a post at a college or university, and continues to publish research findings is better qualified to provide a liberal education for students than someone who completes a doctor of arts degree, reads broadly in the history of economic thought, and publishes rarely. Why? Chief among the many reasons are that productive researchers are better able to distinguish important from unimportant developments in economic science and better able to incorporate important developments into their instructional plans.

Colander and McGoldrick argue that first-year seminars are an attempt to educate students liberally that is hampered by the research mind set of instructors who teach them. The economics department at UNC-Chapel Hill offers five first-year seminars on a rotating basis. Their titles are instructive – Future Shock: Global Economic Trends and Prospects; Current Economic Problems: The Economics of North Carolina; The Root of all Evil? Money as a Cultural, Economic, and Social Institution; The Costs and Benefits of the Drug War; The Entrepreneurial Imagination: Turning Ideas into Reality. None of these five courses satisfies any requirement of the economics major at UNC-CH. The first four courses grew from the research interests of four different faculty persons. The fifth course was developed as part of the Entrepreneurship minor.

I developed the Root-of-all-Evil course myself and drew heavily on literature and issues that I first encountered while writing my PhD dissertation at the University of Minnesota on the German hyperinflation. While working on my dissertation, I learned how to solve expectational difference equations. I also read broadly about Germany and the Treaty of Versailles in order to understand the setting in which the hyperinflation occurred. Researchers are curious people who often look beyond the narrow technical details when they try to answer questions.

Colander and McGoldrick argue that first-year seminars are further hampered by the lack of preparation in writing and communication of instructors. On a regular basis, successful researchers present their findings at seminars and satisfy editors with their wordcraft. Productive researchers supervise graduate dissertations and work hard to help their students express themselves clearly. All of this is pretty good on-the-job training in writing and communication.

Is the economics major, as it currently exists, more like vocational training or more like a component of liberal education? Even allowing for current weaknesses in the economics major curriculum, economics is liberal rather than vocational education. The fact that few economics majors study Marx does not mean that economics is stuck in a little think mind set.

One simple reason that few students read Marx as part of their under-graduate education is that there are better things to read. Economics is about constrained optimization and it is helpful to remember that planning a curriculum or a course within that curriculum is an economic problem. Because contact hours, student study time, faculty preparation time, and educational technology are all scarce resources, instructors must regularly apply the benefit–cost principle to prospective topics, authors, and ideas. So we leave out Marx to make room for Akerlof, Coase, Lucas, and Prescott. And because many of us are active researchers, we are in a better position both to appreciate the importance of new ideas and to figure out how to introduce the essential features of those ideas into our undergraduate courses.

Of its nature, economics is not little think. What happens when a society uses markets to allocate goods and services is a big idea, not a small one. The list of potential demand schedule shifters is a small idea – but a small idea that is necessary to understand a big idea. One of my favorite quotes from a modern economist belongs to Lucas: "Once you start thinking about growth, it's hard to think about anything else."[5] In his *Journal of Economics Perspectives* millennium issue article,[6] Lucas tries to explain the absence in convergence of growth rates across the nations of the world. What could be a more important or a bigger think question?

Is economics instruction stuck in a "little think" culture? Colander and McGoldrick clearly believe so. They say:

> Disciplinary researchers often don't deal with big think questions, not because these questions are not important, but rather because, given current tools, there is small likelihood that additional research in these questions will add to society's understanding of them. . . . Research questions are ones where there is a reasonable hope of adding to our understanding by studying the questions. Teaching questions that instill a passion for learning are often questions for which there is little likelihood of adding to our understanding. . . In our view, what has too often been removed from the economics major. . .is the considera-tion of such "big think" or teaching questions. (pp. 5–6)

At its core, economics is not about the merits of the Paasche and Laspeyres price index. It is about big questions. Can a cap and trade system lower the cost of pollution and carbon abatement programs? Would privatization better preserve national parks and elephant herds than government ownership? Does the imposition of a minimum wage raise the incomes of the poor? Does it raise the natural rate of unemployment? Should the Treasury and the Federal Reserve have bought the mortgage-backed securities that threatened the solvency of financial institutions in 2008? Would failure of those institutions have caused another Great Depression? The bad news may be that too few instructors introduce such ideas into their courses. The good news is that any instructor can remedy this problem without any need for collaboration or any reform in the economics curriculum or the organization of the economics department or its home institution.

Colander and McGoldrick seem to believe that an economics curriculum that studied comparative economic systems would better promote liberal education. I disagree. An economics curriculum founded on neo-classical thought can do an excellent job of promoting liberal education. Here is an example of a way in which neo-classical economics promotes liberal education by bringing to the table a perspective that other disciplines ignore.

Before it is about anything else, economics is about scarcity and opportunity cost. On the first day of my principles course, I ask students whether society has a moral obligation to preserve life despite the cost of doing so and, in particular, whether a wealthy nation like the United States has a moral obligation to provide advanced medical intervention to people from poor nations. It is true that economics does not tell us whether we should answer these questions in the affirmative. It is also true that economics has a lot to say about the consequences of an affirmative answer. The opportunity cost of a $100000 operation for some "poster child patient" may well be mosquito nets for 10000 African children. Helping students understand that "choosing is refusing" is itself a huge contribution to a liberal education. In fact, helping students understand the necessary connection between choosing and refusing will better help students exercise their political liberty in a responsible way than most of the multicultural lessons I can think of.

Finally, what changes are necessary for economics to better promote a liberal education? Here I would like to comment on several of the suggestions put forward by Colander and McGoldrick and then provide a couple of suggestions of my own.

Colander and McGoldrick suggest that appointing faculty to broader organizational units within colleges and universities will promote liberal education. I disagree. Provided that tenure decisions continue to depend heavily on evaluation of published research, the members of a social studies unit will ask the economists whether or not the research is good. In fact, at research universities members of the economics department ask sub-specialists whether the research of a tenure candidate is good. Appointing faculty to broader units will not lead them to write multidisciplinary research papers. They will write what they know, knowing that their college and universities care about their ability to publish and the prestige it conveys.

Colander and McGoldrick suggest that having broader units make tenure and promotion decisions will aid liberal education. Again, I disagree. Currently, at most research universities, the dean of the college of arts and sciences has a college-wide promotion and tenure committee that votes on departmental tenure recommendations and, at many institutions, undertakes a serious review of these cases. The provost is advised by an even more broadly composed committee, which reviews promotion and tenure cases passed to it by the dean's committee.

Colander and McGoldrick also suggest that educational institutions should require, as a condition of employment, that new faculty have completed specific courses, such as history of economic thought, and trained themselves in specific teaching skills. This could work but institutions desiring such specific faculty training should provide it themselves. Before they are hired, graduate students will not be willing to undertake training that will qualify them for a small number of available posts because doing so is unlikely to pass an expected net benefits test. Newly hired faculty will be willing to undertake such training but will regard paying for it as an attempt to lower their wage. Faculty are more likely to respond positively to a program that is paid for by their own institution and helps them gain the skills they need to be successful there.

Finally, as Colander and McGoldrick discuss on pp. 31–2 of the report, economics departments can promote liberal education by reforming the curriculum of the principles of economics course. As I have argued elsewhere,[7] the principles course should be targeted to meet the educational needs of non-major students who never take a course beyond principles, a group that accounts for the great majority of those who enroll in the course. Principles instructors should teach a short list of topics and use recovered course resources to help students apply the basic tools of economics to problems and questions that they will face throughout their lives – not in the workplace but as they exercise their rights as free human beings. Reform of the principles course is, in my view, the single most important step that economics departments can take to promote liberal education. And, departments can take that step with the personnel they have and the culture they currently enjoy.

There are three ways in which colleges and universities can promote liberal education at their institutions that I believe are feasible and do not require a complete remaking of educational culture.

First, colleges and universities that wish to promote liberal education can create term professorships that reward faculty who engage in desired activities. UNC-Chapel Hill has a program that awards five-year Bowman and Gordon Gray Professorships to faculty who have excelled in teaching and research. The professorships provide a salary supplement, a study leave, an annual research and teaching fund, and a one-time grant that the recipient can use to acquire technology or pay for an enrichment experience. Over five years, the professorship provides about $125 000 to the recipient and the recipient's department. The Bowman and Gordon Gray Professorships are highly respected and sought after, which suggests that, at the margin, existing faculty at a research university are willing to respond to incentives to teach well. I think it likely that faculty attracted by the Bowman and Gordon Gray Professorships would also be attracted by term professorships that were attached to particular teaching activities that a college or university believed would promote liberal education.

Second, colleges and universities that wish to promote liberal education can hire and train fixed-term faculty to specialize in the desired teaching activities. If division of labor is the source of all wealth, then it seems reasonable for a department to hire both research and liberal education specialists. A key to the successful working of such an arrangement is a department culture where both research and teaching specialists are respected and where there is an exchange of ideas across groups. At UNC-CH, fixed-term faculty oversee the Fed Challenge, the Undergraduate Economics Club, and the honors thesis program but interact with tenure track faculty in all three of these initiatives.

Third, departments, colleges, and universities can pay for training that helps faculty acquire teaching skills that Colander and McGoldrick rightly believe promote liberal education. In economics, the Committee on Economic Education sponsors the Teaching Innovation Program that helps economics instructors develop interactive teaching skills. Teaching interactively promotes liberal education because it helps students master economic concepts at high levels and teaches them to educate themselves. Teaching students how to educate themselves is preparing them to be free human beings.

Liberal education prepares free human beings for a life of continued education and responsible citizenry. Economics can play a large role in promoting liberal education simply by helping students to appreciate the large questions that neo-classical economics is concerned with and by helping students to understand economics well enough to use it throughout their lives.

NOTES

1. Adler, Mortimer, "What is Liberal Education?," http://www.ditext.com/adler/wle.html (accessed 20 April 2009).
2. Adler, Mortimer (1951), "Labor, Leisure, and Liberal Education," http://www.source-text.com/grammarian/adler2.html (accessed 20 April 2009).
3. Adler distinguishes between "leisure" and "play." Leisure is the hard work of developing one's mind and human spirit and of making contributions to society. Play is amusement, activities that are fun and nothing more.
4. http://www.middlebury.edu/about/handbook/faculty (accessed 20 April 2009).
5. Lucas (1988).
6. Lucas (2000).
7. Hansen et al. (2002).

12. Reinvigorating liberal education with an expected proficiencies approach to the academic major

W. Lee Hansen

Common laments among economics professors include the lack of basic knowledge and skills their students require to learn economics, the narrow focus of students on course grades rather than a deeper understanding of the subject, the difficulty students experience in retaining for any appreciable time what they learned, and the relatively small increase in the knowledge of economics displayed by college seniors who studied economics compared with those who had not done so (Walstad and Allgood, 1999).

This is a familiar and dreary story. Despite efforts over more than a half-century to improve economics instruction led by the American Economic Association Committee on Economic Education, the gains in knowledge acquired in economics courses remain small. Should we be disappointed? Yes. Should we be surprised? Probably not.

What explains this state of affairs? Economics majors are exposed to an abundance of theory, concepts, facts, and information. Yet, they receive little or no experience in how to demonstrate that knowledge while in college and after they graduate (Becker and Watts, 2001; Hansen, 2006b; Schaur et al., 2008). In short, students are stuffed with content knowledge but graduate without knowing how to use that knowledge.

What is to be done? This situation, common to many academic disciplines, has generated calls to reform undergraduate education. Recent well-publicized proposals stress the central importance of strengthening the general education or liberal education component of the undergraduate degree. Yet these proposals say almost nothing about the academic major.

This neglect of the academic major is surprising because of its importance to student learning and the very nature of the baccalaureate degree with its breadth and depth requirements. The central role of the academic major emerges from the Study of Undergraduate Learning (SOUL). It followed a cohort of entering University of Washington college freshmen until they graduated four years later (Beyer et al., 2007). Through extensive interviews and student surveys, the authors focused on seven specific areas of learning: personal growth, understanding and appreciating diversity, critical thinking and problem-solving, writing, quantitative reasoning, information technology and literacy, and general learning. The authors conclude that what and how students advance their learning is filtered through the lenses of particular disciplines (p. 23). Supporting evidence is provided by differences in an array of learning outcomes for students majoring in the arts, business, engineering, humanities, science/math, and social science. The implication of these findings is that efforts to enhance the quality of undergraduate education and increase student learning must pay greater attention to the academic major (the so-called depth requirement) rather than focusing exclusively on the general education or liberal education program of courses (the so-called breadth requirement).

Confusion about the distinction between general education and liberal education needs to be resolved before proceeding. The reason is that the two most prominent proposals for reforming undergraduate education use these terms differently. Former Harvard College President Bok in his book *Our Underachieving Colleges: A Candid Look at How Much Students Learn and Why They Should Be Learning More* (2006) focuses on what he calls general education. It encompasses the entire undergraduate curriculum excluding the academic major (or concentration as it is known at Harvard College). By contrast, the Association of American Colleges & Universities in its recently published report *College Learning for the New Global Century* (AAC&U, 2007) focuses on liberal education, which embraces the whole of the undergraduate curriculum including the major.

For this discussion I relabeled what seem to be the three separate parts of the undergraduate curriculum. The most easily identified part is the major, which is referred to as the academic major. A second important component is represented by a set of required courses, usually completed in the first year of college, that are designed to enhance students' intellectual skills and thus lay the groundwork for academic success in the major and in the other courses students take; this is referred to as general education core skills. The third component is represented by a combination of required and elective courses that expose students to learning in a variety of fields outside their major; this component is described as general education core knowledge. These three categories are sufficient for the purposes of this presentation.[1]

The chapter begins by describing the expected proficiencies approach to the academic major as it applies to economics (Hansen, 1986, 1993a, 1993b, 1998a, 1998b, 2001). It then explores the nature of an expected proficiencies-based undergraduate major and the spread of this approach in undergraduate economics programs. This is followed by a brief discussion of an expected proficiencies approach to the undergraduate degree. The chapter concludes with a review of the problems and possibilities of implementing an expected proficiencies approach in undergraduate education.

EXPECTED PROFICIENCIES IN THE ECONOMICS MAJOR

The failure of periodic campus-wide attempts to enhance the quality of undergraduate education by adopting new undergraduate requirements calls for a different approach. Evidence of this failure comes from continuing efforts to correct mistakes made when the curriculum was last changed. The author's experience with curriculum reform at both the department and campus level reinforces this conclusion. The reason is straightforward: both departments and individual faculty members are skillful at finding ways to avoid bearing the costs of curriculum reform.

An expected proficiencies approach to the undergraduate major would largely circumvent these problems. It would do so by giving greater emphasis to the filtering role of the major in shaping student learning. It would draw on student interest in the major. It would appeal to the strong self-interest of faculty members whose professional allegiance is to their disciplines rather than to undergraduate education and particularly to interdisciplinary courses created to broaden students' intellectual interests. Finally, it would have a strong leveraging potential to improve the intellectual capabilities of students before they enter their academic major.

Fundamental to the expected proficiencies approach is deciding how student learners are expected to be able to demonstrate their learning after they complete their undergraduate degrees, whether it be what they learned in individual courses, sequences of courses, or the major itself. Specifically, the expected proficiencies approach to the major refers to the ability of students immediately after they graduate, and throughout their lives, to demonstrate and subsequently use to good effect the knowledge and skills they acquired in their academic major.

Under this approach, a fundamental difference emerges between what occurs in proficiency-based courses and traditionally organized courses. In traditional courses, the focus is on how well students can display their content knowledge, ultimately, in the course final examination or paper. In proficiencies-based courses, the focus is on what students can do with what they learned, which involves combining their content knowledge and core intellectual skills, both during their college years and, more importantly, after they graduate. Put another way, by emphasizing the importance of mastering the proficiencies, students are encouraged not only to think like an economist but even better to act like an economist.

Lest there be any confusion, the expected proficiencies in the economics major are independent of the content knowledge traditionally taught in economics courses. That is now the case inasmuch as most instruction is not guided by the expected proficiencies. But even if it were so guided, there would be no need to change the content knowledge being taught.

Considerable agreement exists among economists about what should and should not be taught and how it should be taught (Salemi and Siegfried, 1999; Hansen et al., 2002). This is most apparent with respect to the central principles, concepts, and objective knowledge that should be imparted to students enrolled in introductory as well as intermediate and advanced courses in the major.[2] The principal criticism of most economics courses, especially introductory economics courses, is that instructors try to teach too much, as exemplified by the ever-increasing comprehensiveness of economics textbooks. The principal criticism of intermediate and advanced courses in the economics major is that students are taught as if all that counts is reaching the small minority who plan to enroll in graduate economics programs.[3]

These expected proficiencies in the academic major, developed by the author (Hansen, 1986) in the spirit of Bloom's taxonomy of educational objectives (1956), are tailored to the economics major:

1. accessing and organizing existing knowledge;
2. displaying command of existing knowledge;
3. interpreting existing knowledge;
4. interpreting and manipulating quantitative data;
5. applying existing knowledge;
6. creating new knowledge;
7. questing for knowledge and understanding.

These proficiencies have two dimensions. The first is a hierarchy of evermore complex levels of knowledge and understanding that students are expected to demonstrate. The six proficiencies within this category range from the lowest level, which is knowing how to access information, to the highest level, which involves creating new knowledge. The second dimension, represented by the seventh proficiency, is a cross-cutting, all-purpose proficiency that does not fit neatly into this hierarchy. It might best be described as questing for knowledge and understanding. It entails the ability to ask penetrating questions and to engage effectively with others in exploring and discussing economic issues and policies.

These latter abilities are essential to learning, and they are invaluable in testing one's learning while engaged in the very process of learning. These abilities are also essential to life after college, enabling graduates to continue their learning and to become active and informed citizens, voters, consumers, workers, and investors. In these roles, they must be able to understand human behavior and particularly those behaviors influenced to a greater or lesser degree by economic forces.

My concept of expected proficiencies for economics majors emerged as a result of years of teaching and reflection, surveys of recently graduated undergraduate economics majors, discussions with undergraduate focus groups, and the normal feedback received from students in conversations with them and in their course evaluation responses. This information has been supplemented by interviews with a wide range of employers of undergraduate economics majors (in the private, non-profit, federal, state, and local government sectors) about their expectations of what the economics majors they hire can and should be able to do with what they learned. The resulting list of expected proficiencies has been fine-tuned by using it to guide my own teaching and by illuminating suggestions and comments from friends and colleagues.[4]

My updated list of expected proficiencies in the economics major is presented below along with illustrations of how these proficiencies can be demonstrated.

1. *Accessing and organizing existing knowledge*: Retrieve, assemble, and organize information on particular topics and issues in economics. Locate published research in economics and related fields. Track down economic data and data sources. Find information about the generation, construction, and meaning of economic data.
2. *Displaying command of existing knowledge*: Explain key economic theories and concepts, and describe how they can be used. Write a précis or summary of a published journal article. Summarize in a two-minute monologue or a 300-word written statement what is known about the current condition of the economy and the economic outlook. Summarize the principal ideas of an eminent economist; describe the unique contribution of a recent winner of the Nobel Prize in Economic Science. Summarize a current controversy in the economics literature. State succinctly the economic dimensions of a current policy issue.
3. *Interpreting existing knowledge*: Explain and evaluate what economic concepts and principles are used in economic analyses published in articles from daily newspapers and weekly news magazines. Describe how these concepts aid in understanding these analyses. Do the same for non-technical analyses written by economists for general purpose publications. Read and interpret a theoretical analysis, which includes

simple mathematical derivations, reported in an economics journal article.

4. *Interpreting and manipulating quantitative data*: Explain how to understand and interpret numerical data found in published tables such as those in the annual *Economic Report of the President*. Be able to identify patterns and trends in published data such as those found in the *Statistical Abstract of the United States*. Construct tables from already available data to illustrate an economic issue. Describe the relationships among several different quantitative measures (for example, unemployment, prices, and GDP). Explain how to perform and interpret a regression analysis that uses economic data such as might appear in an economics journal article.

5. *Applying existing knowledge*: Prepare an organized, clearly written three-page analysis of a current economic problem. Assess in a four-page paper the costs and benefits of an economic policy proposal. Prepare a two-page decision memorandum for your employer that recommends some action on an economic decision faced by the organization. Write a 600-word op-ed essay on some local economic issue.

6. *Creating new knowledge*: Identify and formulate a question or series of questions about some economic issue that will facilitate its investigation. Synthesize the literature on a topic to determine gaps in our existing knowledge and how those gaps might best be filled. Prepare a five-page proposal describing a potentially useful research project and how that project might be undertaken. Complete a research study with its results contained in a carefully edited 20-page paper or an undergraduate thesis. Engage in a group research project that prepares a detailed research proposal and/or a finished research paper.

7. *Questing for knowledge and understanding*: Demonstrate an understanding of questions that stimulate productive discussion of economic issues and help keep discussions centered on the issue under discussion. Develop a line of questions that probes the meaning or seeks to interpret the meaning of a reading selection written by a well-known economist. Show how a questioning approach can get to the heart of substantive issues by focusing, for example, on the equity and efficiency implications of alternative arrangements, policies, and programs (for example, what are the benefits? What are the costs? How do the benefits and costs compare? Who pays? Who gains?).

Proficiency-based courses change what goes on in the classroom. These courses require moving away from the traditional chalk and talk lecture method of instruction. Doing so means that instruction must be modified to give greater scope to students' intellectual skills, among them close reading, writing, speaking, discussing, reasoning, and thinking. This can be accomplished by giving assignments similar to those used to illustrate the various expected proficiencies.

These assignments give students much-needed practice in mastering the proficiencies. Such practice easily falls into the category of active learning and can take many forms: summarizing and discussing non-textbook reading assignments, completing a variety of writing assignments, making use of quantitative reasoning skills, and applying what is being learned to new problems, issues, and policies. Students can become proficient only through regular guided practice.[5] To the extent that student learning styles differ, the varied learning experiences offered in an expected proficiency-based course play to the differing strengths of students and reduce the advantage to those students who thrive on the chalk and talk approach so prevalent in undergraduate instruction.

Such courses also change the roles of instructors and students. No longer is so much attention directed to course examinations and course grades. For instructors, their efforts shift to helping students develop their mastery of those proficiencies being emphasized in the particular courses they teach. For students, their efforts shift to gaining practice in developing a mastery of the proficiencies by the time they graduate. Instructors continue to concentrate on teaching subject matter or content knowledge, but do so knowing that students must be able to combine their content learning with demonstrations of their mastery of the expected proficiencies. Students continue to concentrate on learning content knowledge but do so recognizing they must be able to use that learning in demonstrating the expected proficiencies. What all of this does is to lengthen the time horizons of both instructors and students, moving them away from individual courses and closer to the academic major as a whole.

For the expected proficiencies approach to succeed, students must be engaged in these learning activities regularly and frequently to give them the practice they need to enhance their proficiencies. The prospects for success will be enhanced to the extent that students have already mastered the basic intellectual skills that are emphasized in the general education core skills courses students take early in their college career. It must be recognized that incorporating these learning activities into individual courses does require some class time to manage, and they may mean that less content knowledge can be covered in any given course. But inasmuch as instructors often cram too much content knowledge into their courses, this reallocation of class time can be beneficial. The reason is simple: proficiencies-oriented learning activities reinforce student mastery of content knowledge as they learn it.[6]

A PROFICIENCIES-BASED UNDERGRADUATE ECONOMICS MAJOR

What would it mean to construct a proficiencies-based undergraduate major using economics as an example? Consider the traditional requirements for graduation (Hansen, 1986). Students must complete the required number of course credit hours, achieve a satisfactory grade-point average, and complete some mixture of courses that enhance their intellectual skills (general education core skill requirement) and broaden their intellectual horizons (general education core knowledge requirement). Typically, the intellectual skills-building courses are taken in the first year or two to equip students to perform well in their subsequent courses.[7]

Key to the effectiveness of a proficiencies-based major is the structuring and sequencing of individual courses as well as a determination of what particular proficiencies are to be emphasized in each of these courses. Building on the general education core skills courses and core knowledge requirements, courses in the major – introductory, intermediate, and advanced – must be coordinated to move students forward toward mastery of these proficiencies. This is no easy task, because the proficiencies cannot be readily separated from one another, they are interrelated and mutually reinforcing. For example, mastery of the proficiency "creating new knowledge" cannot be achieved without building on lower-level proficiencies, such as applying existing knowledge and also interpreting and manipulating quantitative data.

Yet some division of labor is required. For example, introductory courses would give greater emphasis to the first three proficiencies, intermediate courses would focus on proficiencies three, four, and five, and advanced field courses would focus more heavily on proficiencies four, five, and six. Capstone courses embracing research and thesis writing would focus heavily on proficiencies six and seven. It goes without saying that this seventh proficiency would be emphasized through the full range of undergraduate economics courses.

Assessing student mastery of the proficiencies poses an important challenge because there is no simple way of doing this. Ideally, students would be called upon just prior to graduation to demonstrate their mastery of the proficiencies in the major. Such an examination system is employed in only a few liberal arts colleges, those that engage outside faculty members to help assess the learning of their graduating majors. To the extent that students are responsible for their command of both course knowledge and mastery of the proficiencies, course grades could serve, albeit imperfectly, as a measure of mastery of the proficiencies. To ensure that this would be the case, both types of learning would have to be emphasized. In addition, at least some of the examination questions would have to be proficiencies-oriented in what they demand of students. Presently, relatively few courses provide such a balanced emphasis, and hence the typical economics major on graduation day can display at most a modest degree of mastery of the proficiencies.

Some readers may need to be convinced that economics students are really deficient in their mastery of the expected proficiencies. Evidence on this question comes from a spring 2006 survey of senior economics majors at the University of Wisconsin-Madison (Hansen, 2006b). That survey revealed that relatively few courses in the major gave attention to any of these proficiencies, and those that did gave them only moderate attention. The major exception was what might be called capstone courses, among them junior and senior thesis seminars, a research methods seminar, and independent study courses. On average slightly less than 20 percent of the majors rated their mastery of the proficiencies as excellent. At the other end of the spectrum, 25 percent rated their mastery as only fair or poor.[8] Desirable as it might have been, no attempt was made to assess student mastery of the proficiencies. Doing so would have required assembling this large group of seniors and asking them to participate in proficiency-based learning activities and respond to proficiency-based examination questions.

ADOPTION OF THE APPROACH

One criticism of the expected proficiencies approach to the undergraduate major is that whatever its good intentions, it remains largely untried. That is true for two reasons. First, I have had neither the time nor inclination to aggressively market this approach. If instructors wanted to use the approach, they were welcome to do so. Second, this approach has been under constant development and only now am I pulling together the results of my experience with the approach. I developed this approach during the last half of my 40-year teaching career in teaching introductory, interme-diate, and advanced courses in the economics major, and junior-senior thesis seminars. I also experimented with it in graduate-level courses and seminars. Because these courses differed in purpose, content, and level, modifications had to be made in the proficiencies and particularly in the tasks needed to help students demonstrate their mastery of them. I found this approach congenial, my students appreciated the shift in emphasis to that of mastering the expected proficiencies, and student interest and learning improved under this approach.

Interest in the expected proficiencies approach to the major has gradually increased and is now gaining a foothold in economics instruction. The approach first received favorable mention in a report prepared for the Association of American Colleges (the predecessor to AAC&U) Study-in-Depth Project (Siegfried et al., 1991a).[9] Beyond that, various encouraging developments have occurred in implementing the expected proficiencies. Wyrick (1994) published a research and writing guide organized around my 1986 list of expected proficiencies. Salemi and Siegfried (1999) in their assessment of the state of economic education offered four recommendations, the second of which stated that departments should revise their curricula so that majors attain the Hansen proficiencies (p. 358); they also called for an integrated educational process designed to assist students in gaining *all* of the Hansen proficiencies.

The first adoption of the proficiencies approach is reported by Carlson et al. (2002). Since then, other adoptions have been reported, by departments (for example, Grant, 2005; Myers et al., 2008), by individual faculty members in courses for their senior economics majors (McGoldrick, 2008), by faculty members who have communicated informally to the author about how the proficiencies approach is reshaping their programs, and by still other faculty members who are simply emphasizing to their majors the importance of mastering these proficiencies.

A recent survey of economics department chairpersons (Adkins and Newsome, 2006) reveals that 30 percent of them were aware of the Hansen expected proficiencies approach; 15 percent of these departments had implemented related curriculum changes, and another 19 percent were discussing related changes. Other departments and a considerable number of faculty members are moving toward a proficiencies approach by building a curriculum that leads to a capstone or research course (Siegfried, 2001; Colander and Holmes, 2006).

Additional information on the impact of the expected proficiencies approach comes from the early results of an ongoing survey of economics department chairs (Myers et al., 2008). It reveals that departments without formal assessment plans rely more heavily on Hansen's expected proficiencies than do those with formal assessment plans; this is especially true for economics departments on campuses with no business school. This result is not too surprising because formal assessment programs are still in their early stages of development. Business schools are more likely to have already defined their learning outcomes but used different language because they were unacquainted with the language of expected proficiencies.

Informal assessments of student mastery of the expected proficiencies should not be dismissed as lacking in objectivity. Whenever faculty members evaluate student papers or essay answers to examination questions they are exercising their judgment based on their knowledge of economics and their assessment of the ability of students to provide responses that make sense. Informal assessments of students and their knowledge are constantly being made by faculty members even if these assessments are not guided by lists of proficiencies. Based on their experience, faculty members develop their own intuitive sense of mastery rather than relying on an explicit set of guidelines to assess whether students have developed the intellectual skills they will need in parallel with the content knowledge they are acquiring. The suggested lack of objectivity may be off-putting to some readers. Yet judgment is an important part of assessment.

Several models have been reported on how to assess student mastery of the expected proficiencies. Grant (2005) and his colleagues at Linfield have embedded the expected proficiencies in their goals for both the major and minor in economics. As part of their assessment, they conduct a pre- and post-test to check the development of these proficiencies. Students write end-of-semester reflections on how their proficiencies developed in their courses. At the end of a senior capstone course they write a reflective essay about their increased mastery of the proficiencies. That essay forms part of the discussion during an oral interview with several faculty members prior to graduation. Their plan is well articulated, with elaborations on how the proficiencies are assessed and the problems that arise in making these assessments. Their proficiencies approach continues to be fine-tuned as the department ten-year reaccreditation approaches. I should add that the practice of asking students to reflect on their mastery of the proficiencies is a fine way to make students more aware of their learning and more appreciative of what they are learning.

Myers et al. (2008) have also gone to great lengths to incorporate the expected proficiencies in the University of Akron undergraduate major. This is done by individual instructors, who have considerable freedom in what and how they teach. The assessment plan it has devised operates on several levels. It includes formative and summative assessment through the use of student portfolios and a capstone experience for all majors. In addition, exit and alumni surveys are used to gather additional information for their assessment program and to identify strengths and weaknesses in their program while at the same time suggesting ways to overcome these weaknesses.

McGoldrick (2008) takes a quite different approach in her own teaching of the capstone course. The course goal is to promote student skill in acting like economists and builds on the expected proficiencies. The course involves the preparation of a research paper and calls for demonstrating the array of research methods appropriate to the topic under study. The iterative research process involving interaction between students and the instructor provides an introduction to the hierarchy of intellectual skills students must draw on in carrying out their research. A separate anonymous course evaluation questionnaire encourages students to reflect on their learning in ways that go beyond the traditional course evaluation.

A PROFICIENCIES-BASED UNDERGRADUATE DEGREE

Moving to a proficiencies-based undergraduate degree would represent a real departure from existing requirements for such degrees. As a first step, all departments would have to specify the expected proficiencies for their academic majors. More challenging is the task of gaining agreement on the expected proficiencies in the areas of general education core skills and general education core knowledge. Agreement on the first should be easier than the second, because all students will be expected to master a similar set of proficiencies. The same would be true if a college adopted a core curriculum that allowed no choice among courses in satisfying that requirement. If students are given some choice, one would hope that survey courses in, for example, American history, European history, or Far Eastern History, would highlight what it is that historians do and how they do it rather than chronologies of rulers, wars, and the like.

An expected proficiencies-based undergraduate degree program would produce a level of learning well beyond that occurring at most colleges and universities. Specifically, it would require students by the time of graduation to have demonstrated three kinds of expected proficiencies in general education core skills, in general education core knowledge, and in the academic major. But to master the proficiencies in the major, students would first have to master the expected general education proficiencies. In other words, students must begin with a good command over what the AAC&U proposal calls intellectual and practical skills. Recognizing that success in the major is of key importance, students will see more clearly the important link between these intellectual and practical skills developed in general education and the skills required to succeed in the major.

Upon graduation, students will have mastered all three sets of expected proficiencies. Having done so, they would be well prepared to demonstrate a larger set of outcomes expected of baccalaureate degree recipients. These outcomes might embrace the following: equipping students to pursue their own personal and career goals, demonstrating through their thoughts and actions the social benefits society expects of college graduates, and becoming adaptable lifelong learners with sustained intellectual interests.

To fully realize the goals of an expected proficiencies approach, one important link remains to be developed, that between the major and liberal education. An attempt was made to do this back in the early 1990s when the Association of American Colleges (now known as AAC&U) initiated its Study-in-Depth Program to elaborate the academic major and link it more tightly to the undergraduate curriculum it sought to reform (AAC, 1985). Though task forces from a dozen disciplines were organized to rethink their respective academic majors, no assessment of the effect of that effort seems to have been made. The report of the economics task force report was published by the AAC (1990b) and received prominent attention by being published in two prominent economics journals (Siegfried et al., 1991a, 1991b). What impact the economics report had is not at all clear.

In 2006 the Teagle Foundation launched a new but similar effort to improve the connection between the undergraduate major and liberal education. A half-dozen disciplines including economics are being asked to prepare white papers. The purpose is to stimulate a rethinking of the relationship between academic majors and the goals of a liberal education. Under the auspices of the American Economic Association Committee on Economic Education (AEA-CEE), David Colander of Middlebury College and KimMarie McGoldrick of the University of Richmond wrote the report for economics (Chapter 1, this volume). They point out several fundamental conflicts between the goals of the economics major and a liberal education that are not easily resolved. However, they do go on to discuss a series of macro and micro changes that could narrow the gap by giving greater emphasis to the goals of liberal education set out by Bok (2006). Aside from the comments in this volume, whether and how economists will respond to their suggestions remains unknown.

A new force is likely to change the landscape of student learning and may prove to be more important than proposals from within higher education to reform undergraduate education. That is the periodic reaccreditation of colleges and universities. Most pertinent to this discussion is pressure from the Association to Advance Collegiate Schools of Business (AACSB) on business schools and in turn on those economics departments housed in business schools.

The focal point of this pressure is contained in the AACSB accreditation standards and its statement on assurance of learning standards (2008). Three standards are of particular interest. The first two require business schools and presumably their separate departments to provide learning experiences in a variety of general knowledge and skill areas as well as learning experiences in a variety of management-specific knowledge and skills areas. A third standard requires that *each school [must] specif[y] learning goals and demonstrate achievement of learning goals* in the first two standards as well as appropriate discipline-specific knowledge and skills that its students achieve in each undergraduate degree program [Emphasis added]. These standards are now being applied to economics departments in business schools. Similar standards are being applied by regional accrediting associations across the country. In view of the demands for greater accountability and assessment in higher education, it seems likely that in the not too distant future similar learning standards will be in force throughout higher education.

The pressure of reaccreditation is going to force change whether faculty members like it or not. Interestingly, the expected proficiencies approach provides a convenient framework for departments as they seek to develop learning standards and devise ways to measure and assess student learning. Economists in several economics departments housed in business schools have told me that the expected proficiencies approach, often modified to fit local circumstances, has helped them figure out how to develop learning goals and ways of assessing student learning.

ADOPTING AND IMPLEMENTING A PROFICIENCIES-BASED APPROACH

Anyone who has ever served as a college or university faculty member knows the difficulty of not only adopting but also implementing even relatively minor curriculum changes. The challenge is even greater when curriculum reform designed to strengthen liberal education changes how instructors teach and how students learn. Here, in brief, is how the story generally plays out: a campus-wide committee is appointed to study the curriculum. It develops recommendations, holds hearings, and after some months issues its final recommendations. The faculty then takes up the recommendations and may approve them but usually only after important modifications are made, modifications that often weaken the promise of the original recommendations. Whether the resulting curriculum change or reform will make any real difference in student learning is rarely examined. Why, then, would anyone believe that an even bolder plan to rejuvenate undergraduate education, through an expected proficiencies approach to the major, would have any possibility of being implemented?

The barriers are formidable. Economists, for example, will offer the standard economic response to proposals for change, whether in the curriculum, approaches to teaching, or improvements in student learning. They will argue that the costs to faculty members of shifting to a proficiencies approach are too great. Faculty members are already overburdened with demands to produce ever-larger quantities of high-quality research, acceptable teaching, and responsible participation in department and campus life. By contrast, the benefits of change will accrue to students in the form of increased learning. To compensate for the mismatch between who benefits (students) and who bears the cost (faculty members), the incentive structure must be changed to reward faculty members for the increased demands on their time required by the expected proficiencies approach.

At the campus level, general education curriculum reform efforts too often ignore the distribution of the perceived costs and benefits among departments. The burden of costs inevitably falls on those departments, and on individual faculty members in departments, that will be teaching new or revamped freshman/sophomore courses mandated by the curriculum change. Meanwhile, the perceived benefits to the rest of the faculty are regarded as minimal at best. This situation leads to a deadly inertia.

On the positive side, the goals of an expected proficiencies approach should be appealing to three important groups of constituents. One is undergraduate students, who seem to be increasingly focused on how their college degrees can help them obtain and hold good jobs and lead to fulfilling lives, which means more than achieving a high GPA. Another is employers who regularly complain about weaknesses in the academic preparation of the college graduates they interview and often hire. A third is the general public, best represented by college trustees, state legislators, and parents of college students, who have come to expect greater accountability and firmer evidence on student learning in the nation's ever-more expensive colleges and universities. Thus, implementation of an expected proficiencies approach should have strong appeal to both sides of the college graduate labor market, graduating students who seek good jobs and employers who seek good employees who can add value to their enterprises, as well as those who underwrite many of the costs of higher education, namely parents and taxpayers.

Adoption of an expected proficiencies approach shifts the balance of the costs and benefits in a beneficial way. Because the focus is on the academic major, the costs of change fall rather equally on each and every department and, within them, on all departmental faculty members. To the extent that departments take pride in offering a first-rate program of courses in the major, faculty members in these departments are likely to develop a greater interest in what their students are learning. In turn, faculty members will become more interested in how their departments stack up against other departments in helping students master the expected proficiencies in their majors.

This approach to reform also transfers responsibility away from outsiders and administrators, many of whom have had little teaching experience and whose views on reform are frequently discounted by faculty members. Departmental faculties, by contrast, are well equipped to fashion the expected proficiencies in their major and implement them. They know intimately the subject matter content of the major. In addition, they have close contact with their current students, recent graduates, and often with employers who seek to hire their graduating majors. With this additional knowledge, they are better able to develop effective ways for their students to demonstrate mastery of the expected proficiencies, both in the classes they teach and in the major itself.

If faculty members lack such knowledge, they can easily acquire it. One good source is the *Journal of Economic Education*, another is the papers on economic education published in the May issue of the *American Economic Review*, and still another is the teaching workshops regularly offered under the auspices of the American Economic Association Committee on Economic Education. Plus there is a growing body of economists who claim the field of economic education and are available to provide advice to departments as well as to individuals.

Gaining adoption of a proficiencies approach at the department level poses four immediate hurdles. First, this approach requires that instructors invest time and effort in revamping their pedagogy, classroom teaching strategies, and assignments. The key is to find low-cost ways for instructors to implement these changes. Summer funding for course development might be one solution and a less costly one than granting released time during the academic year. To the extent that any substantial number of faculty members incorporate a proficiencies approach in their teaching, the way may be paved for adoption at the department level.

Second, this approach requires departments to adopt a different view on curriculum structure and instruction. Agreement is required on what proficiencies will be emphasized in the sequence of courses in the major, what kinds of demonstrations will be most effective in showing student mastery of the proficiencies, and how mastery of the proficiencies is to be assessed. Accomplishing these changes cannot occur overnight but could be phased in over a several-year period.

Third, this approach requires that academic deans and department chairs take the lead in opening discussion of the proficiencies approach, securing agreement to adopt the expected proficiencies approach, and leading the transition to such an approach. Finally, this approach must be supported by strong campus leadership by both faculties and top-level administrators if it is to succeed.

The bright side of the picture is the chain reaction that may be triggered by implementing an expected proficiencies approach. As individual faculty members and then departments adopt this approach to the major, shortcomings of the general education program will become more evident. Too many students will be found not to have acquired the core intellectual skills or the core content knowledge needed to perform well in the academic major. This realization has the potential to generate strong support across the entire faculty to strengthen general education proficiencies during the first year or two of college. Such a realization in turn will sharpen the focus on the knowledge and skills that must be acquired in the high school years to improve the academic success in college of graduating high school seniors, thus having a still broader and deeper effect on education generally.

The expected proficiencies approach to the academic major provides an attractive alternative to institutional plans that in some cases seek to employ standardized tests to measure and assess undergraduate learning outcomes. The advantage of the approach advocated here is that control of the assessment process remains with the campus and, within the campus, with academic disciplines and departments. What is now called for is leadership by administrators and college faculties to fashion a new approach where control remains within the institution and where the learning outcomes are likely to be most easily and effectively established.

SUMMARY AND CONCLUSIONS

This paper interprets the strong renewed interest in improving undergraduate education as an opportunity to examine the usefulness of an expected proficiencies approach to the undergraduate major and undergraduate education as a whole. Such an approach can revitalize and enrich the undergraduate liberal arts curriculum. This means linking the expected proficiencies in the academic major to the expected proficiencies in general education. This offers practical and relatively low-cost means of effecting change, principally because it builds on existing interests of faculty members in their academic disciplines and in intermediate and advanced courses they offer to their majors. Adoption of this approach will expose the limitations of general education as it is now practiced and in turn the limited content knowledge and intellectual skills students bring with them from high school.

The expected proficiencies approach to the academic major offers what might be viewed as a stealth approach to promote the goals of a liberal-arts-oriented undergraduate education. This less direct approach spreads the costs of change more evenly across the entire faculty. It should also be appealing to department faculties because it builds on the interest and expertise of their own faculty members and the pride they presumably take in producing successful graduating economics majors.

The widespread but seemingly costless strategy of periodically revising first- and second-year course requirements to promote improvements in undergraduate education is unlikely ever to be fully successful. The Bok proposal to improve what it describes as general education, while attractive in many ways, does not make the case for complementary changes in the focal point of undergraduate study, the academic major. The AAC&U proposal with its emphasis on embedding the challenges of globalization within a liberal arts education has considerable appeal but appears to be unduly complex and difficult to implement. How its several dimensions can be translated into a meaningful college curriculum must be spelled out in greater detail. Again, without explicit attention to the academic major, these proposals are unlikely to produce the full range of outcomes their proponents hope to see.

Transition to a proficiencies approach will not be painless, whether it occurs in response to inside or outside pressures. What it will require is a dramatic rethinking of the purpose of the academic major. It will require identifying the proficiencies that departments seek to develop in their majors. It will require faculty members to rethink how they organize and teach their courses. It will require them to transfer greater responsibility for learning to their students.

The benefits will come from the greater attention given to what students are learning and satisfactions that flow to faculty members as they see their students respond to the enhanced learning opportunities open to them. Only with an integrated approach to undergraduate education, one that examines how learning at successive levels of education is linked from high school through college graduation, will our colleges and universities be able to graduate ever-larger numbers of liberally educated college graduates.

NOTES

1. Bok includes in his definition of general education what I would call both core intellectual skills and liberal education courses. The AAC&U divides the curriculum into five separate parts, one of which includes the academic major. Another is called "intellectual and practical skills," which is somewhat broader than my concept of core intellectual skills.
2. Though a general consensus prevails, various alternative approaches to the subject have been advocated, ranging from Nelson (2006) to Becker (2007).
3. This orientation toward preparation for graduate study ignores the fact that in any single year no more than two percent of baccalaureate degree recipients subsequently enter graduate economics programs (personal communication from John Siegfried).
4. The original five proficiencies set out in 1986 grew to six in 2001, subsequently increased to seven where it has remained. However, in this paper the seventh proficiency has been

reworded from "asking pertinent and penetrating questions" to "questing for knowledge and understanding."

5. Examples of the kinds of active learning activities that have worked well in my undergraduate classes are described in Hansen (1993a, 1993b, 1998a, 1998b, and 2001).

6. I base this assertion on my own experience. Originally, I cited the well-known "research finding" that people retain 20 percent of what they read, 30 percent of what they hear, 40 percent of what they see, 50 percent of what they say, and so on. When pressed by the editors of this volume for the source, which I had not supplied, I searched mightily but without success. Finally, Myles Boylan at the National Science Foundation referred me to an article that I commend to you: "The Ten Percent Solution: anatomy of an Education Myth" in Skeptic http://findarticles.com/p/articles/mi_kmske/is_4_10/ai_n29087271 (accessed 21 April 2009).

7. Such a requirement does not preclude students from enrolling as freshmen in introductory economics courses, which might mean their intellectual skills are not as well developed as they should be.

8. One commentator on this study asked whether the proficiencies might have been given some implicit rather than explicit emphasis. Based on my reading of the free response comments, that did not seem to be the case. As noted in the cited paper, students wanted much more in the way of applications to reinforce the formal material they were learning.

9. In the interest of transparency, I served on the AAC economics task force and pushed mildly for mention of the proficiencies approach in our report. I should also report that the 1985 AAC report refers to my description of the economics major, drawing on a draft of my 1986 paper.

PART 4

Structural problems and the interdisciplinary
nature of economics

13. The integrative nature of the economics major

Jessica Holmes

While I agree that an assessment of the role of the major in the liberal education is warranted, my initial reaction is that such analysis would reveal economics to be one of the more integrative disciplines – fulfilling the generalist need for both breadth and depth better than most other fields.

First, economics departments typically require fewer classes than many other disciplines (for example, economics students typically take eight to ten classes to fulfill the major while science and language students often have to complete 15 or more courses). Thus, economics majors have more flexibility than most to enroll in a variety of courses across the curriculum; they are given ample opportunity for both depth in their field and breadth across the curriculum.

Second, economics is one of the most common building blocks in the ever-increasing number of interdisciplinary programs that have emerged on college and university campuses. At my institution for example, students must take numerous economics courses to fulfill requirements for programs in international studies, international economics and politics, and environmental studies. The growth of these interdisciplinary programs suggests that the economics discipline does not operate in a silo, but rather extends beyond the boundaries of the major itself, exposing students across many disciplines to the ideas and tools of the economist. The growing abundance of interdisciplinary programs also suggests that "faculty homes" are less and less likely to be located within individual disciplines and students themselves are less and less likely to align themselves within specific departments.

Third, the economics departments are often at the forefront of an integrative movement to incorporate civic engagement and service-learning within and across the curriculum. The service-learning projects that have emerged from this movement are typically designed to empower students with both general knowledge and transferable skills, instill a strong sense of values, ethics, and civic engagement, and foster critical problem-solving, quantitative, research and communication skills – all stated goals of a liberal education. That said, I agree with many of the insights and recommendations outlined in the Teagle Report and add only a few more below.

If a liberal arts education is meant to teach students to integrate the insights of different disciplines and to think critically about broad issues, we must model this type of learning for them. One way to accomplish this is through interdisciplinary teaching; colleges/universities should offer more team-taught courses where general problems are approached by passionate specialists from a variety of disciplines (economists, historians, political scientists, sociologists, psychologists and so on.). As the Teagle Report acknowledges, faculty are often limited by the specialized nature of their own graduate training. They design courses around textbooks written by the top specialists in their field and rarely question the assumptions and limitations dictated by their own discipline's paradigm. As the Teagle Report also suggests, specialists often stray from the "big think" questions. Successful interdisciplinary teaching tackles the "big think" questions by focusing on the complex issues and problems that one discipline alone cannot solve; it fosters an interdisciplinary synthesis of ideas and methodology in ways that ensure that the sum is greater than the disciplinary parts.

For example, imagine an interdisciplinary course that teaches students about poverty and its underlying theory/implications from the perspective of historians, geographers, economists, sociologists, political scientists, psychologists, philosophers, human biologists, and scholars of philosophy, religion, and literature. Specialists from across the disciplines could contribute their expertise (and passion) to the discussion and in so doing, expose students to numerous and varied approaches to the problem of poverty/inequality. In my opinion, this course would be better served by five devoted specialists with depth of knowledge than one generalist with breadth of knowledge.

Of course, the success of any interdisciplinary course depends on the subject matter, the relationship between the faculty members, and the organizational structure of the course. In an ideal interdisciplinary course, the topic is invented by the specific faculty members teaching the course (that is, there is not likely to be an appropriate textbook already written), the material is presented in an integrative, not additive way (that is, the course is not simply a parade of disconnected lectures by faculty from different departments) and students are asked to rely on and sometimes reconcile the insights from several disciplines in thoughtful and creative assignments. Since interdisciplinary courses are likely to be quite time-intensive, faculty should be awarded extra teaching credits or financial bonuses for offering such courses.

If, as the Teagle discussion suggests, "economics neglects the development of certain skills of a liberal education that it could, and once did, include" (p. 15) then let's discuss ways to incorporate such skills into the curriculum. For example, the report discusses the poor training in both writing and communication that economists receive in graduate school. I agree and suggest that both undergraduate and graduate programs incorporate a course in oral and written communication into the economics curriculum. Or, even easier, tag existing field courses as writing/public-speaking-intensive and require that students take at least one or two such courses in fulfillment of the major and/or the PhD. It is not difficult to incorporate written assignments (for example, policy memos, op-eds, referee reports, and so on) and oral debates into almost any elective, and faculty should be encouraged to do so (perhaps by requiring that each department member teach at least one "tagged" course a year).

Departments should also develop a peer tutoring program that trains economics majors with strong communication skills to work directly with other majors who need improvement in oral and written communication; tutors assigned to specific courses would lighten the teaching burden of writing-intensive courses by, for example, working one-on-one with students on first drafts. Departments might also facilitate the organization of a student-run economics newsletter and/or student research conference.

Institutions and departments should encourage and reward faculty who integrate service-learning into their courses, particularly when the projects extend beyond the typical boundaries of the economics major and meet the objectives of a liberal education. Institutions without a civic engagement office should be encouraged to develop such a resource and faculty should be incentivized through course reductions or financial bonuses to develop service-learning assignments that allow students to apply concepts learned in the classroom to the communities in which they live. The optimal service-learning project not only provides our majors with the "real world applications" they desire, but if designed well, strengthens students' analytical, written, and oral communication skills. Ideally, an online public clearinghouse would develop where successful service-learning projects could be posted and reviewed; this would reduce some of the inherent risk associated with venturing away from the chalkboard and outside the classroom.

To encourage more breadth of study, colleges and universities should consider restricting the number of majors and minors a student can have. As a first step, eliminate double (and triple) majors and double (and triple) minors. This will encourage more exploration across the disciplines. Students with only one major and one minor could still signal to future employers their two specific areas of concentration. In addition, students could expand the section of their résumés that highlights "other relevant coursework" to convey information about transferable skills acquired in non-major or minor courses. To encourage more breadth, institutions should also consider introducing pass/fail options (if they don't already exist). This should encourage students to take intellectual risks and explore areas of the curriculum that might otherwise intimidate them. There are many ways to implement such pass/fail options. For example, students might be allowed to designate two or three (non-major) courses as pass/fail during their college career. To encourage students to remain actively engaged in the course material, institutions might set the passing threshold at C (rather than D–) or alternatively allow students to convert a passing grade back into their actual letter grade at the end of the semester.

Departments wishing to rely less on "formalism and technique" and more on "real-world problems and issues" should consider broadening their job candidate pool to include those who have both economics and public policy training. For example, consider hiring PhDs who have completed the core graduate economics sequence but whose degrees are from schools of public policy, forestry, public health, and so on. As demand for such "realists" increases, graduate programs will be forced to adapt their curricula to meet the needs of undergraduate departments.

14. The availability of interdisciplinary economics educators and the actions of deans: explaining the small contribution of economics to a liberal education

Arthur H. Goldsmith

In their monograph "The Teagle Report", Colander and McGoldrick claim that in its current state the economics department at virtually every liberal arts college is poorly suited to contributing meaningfully to the provision of a liberal education. In their view, the crux of the problem is that too few economics faculty are engaged in interdisciplinary teaching and research. They attribute the shortage of economics faculty with such skills and interests to graduate studies in economics being technical and discipline based, and that economics departments discount the value of interdisciplinary research when evaluating faculty. Thus, they assert that unless graduate education in economics embraces insights from other disciplines and economics faculty are evaluated in a more cross-disciplinary fashion, both of which they believe are unlikely, then the contribution of a major in economics to a liberal education will be modest.

I do not share this perspective, and believe that existing incentive structures in graduate economic education that reward high-quality work have already brought a sufficient supply of appropriately trained economics educators to the door of liberal arts colleges. The problem lies with senior administrators at liberal arts colleges who do not put in place policies that ensure their institutions will hire such faculty. Nor do they ensure that interdisciplinary scholarly output will be truly valued in the assessment process leading to tenure and promotion. In short, the problem is not a supply problem, but a demand problem. In this essay I will explain why the future of economics as a contributor to a liberal education can be very bright if senior administrators at liberal arts colleges act to establish an environment that values interdisciplinary-oriented economists once they arrive on campus and lead in a way that results in the hiring of such educators.

THE ECONOMICS MAJOR AND LIBERAL EDUCATION: IS ECONOMICS A PLAYER?

Colander and McGoldrick assert that "liberal education . . . empowers students with broad knowledge and transferable skills" and "instills in students a strong sense of values, ethics, and civic engagement" (p. 3). Moreover, a successful liberal education embeds in students "a passion for learning" (p. 4) that they carry throughout their life. Derek Bok worries that college majors are doing a poor job creating such a footprint and in providing students with broad skills, because they offer training that is too specialized. Colander and McGoldrick agree with this assessment of departments, including economics, and argue that interdisciplinary instruction and inquiry is need to provide the breadth and passion sought by proponents of a liberal education. However, they contend that such an approach to learning, even at liberal arts colleges, will be difficult to implement for four reasons.

First, faculties identify with their discipline and see interdisciplinary education as superficial, which limits their enthusiasm for engaging in such forms of instruction. Second, they believe that graduate schools do not produce faculty with either the interest or expertise to lead courses with an interdisciplinary orientation when exploring questions, because they have been trained to be researchers with a narrow focus – which maximizes their chances of winning grants and publishing papers. Third, departments hire faculty with narrow training, because they believe they will be successful scholars, who will bring prestige to both the department and the institution. Fourth, when departments hire faculty whose teaching and research are in line with the goals of a liberal education they will produce scholarly work that is not on the cutting edge of their discipline and they will explore broad questions that are difficult to answer. Consequently, such research will not be highly valued by their colleagues in the profession, and such faculty will find tenure difficult to obtain. Thus, self-interest will steer faculty away from acquiring the interdisciplinary skills as a scholar, which are fundamental to advancing the educational aims of a liberal arts college. In order to overcome the shortage of economics educators with interdisciplinary talents at liberal arts colleges, Colander and McGoldrick (p. 22) suggest that "schools might also consider creating a dedicated departmental home for those who teach liberal education courses" (for example, social studies) since they believe the only way to attract such faculty is to house them in a department that values cross-disciplinary discussion and inquiry.

The Market Works: A Bright Link Between Economics and the Liberal Arts

A striking development in economics in recent years is the increased flow of teachers/scholars leaving top-flight graduate programs who have conducted research grounded in conventional economics that incorporates ideas from a wide range of disciplines. This movement certainly coincides with the substantial increase in the share of graduate students in economics who are female and who have broadened the scope of questions being explored by economists. These newly minted professors are well positioned to teach in an interdisciplinary manner. Importantly, the existing incentive system, which rewards convincing research on questions of interests, is responsible for this sea change. Economists have increasingly come to recognize that theoretical work that fails to account for relevant ideas in other disciplines generates poor predictions and that empirical work that does not account for appropriate interdisciplinary insights suffers from omitted variable bias. Graduate students are aware of this, as are their advisors. Not surprisingly many graduate students who want to produce papers that are convincing and will be published in strong journals are accounting for ideas from a myriad of disciplines. Their advisors are increasingly embracing this approach because it enhances their reputation, and that of their graduate program, to produce new professors whose work is considered fresh, relevant, and convincing.

A perusal of top-flight social science journals respected by economists, including *The Journal of Human Resources*, *The Journal of Economic Behavior and Organization*, *The Journal of Policy Analysis and Management*, *Demography*, and *Social Science Quarterly* reveals that economic research informed by insights from psychology, sociology, history, and politics is published in each issue. Even the most highly respected economics journals are publishing interdisciplinary work by economists. For instance, the lead article in the September 2008 issue of *The Journal of Economic Literature* reports on what is known about the link between cognitive skills and economic development, which brings ideas together from psychology, neuroscience, economics, and public policy.

Graduate students in economics continue to receive a highly technical education during the formal course portion of their training. During the thesis stage the value of interdisciplinary thinking is taking hold. Young scholars are increasingly taking courses in departments outside of economics to enrich their understanding of the questions they are examining in their thesis. In addition, it is now commonplace for graduate students in economics to study, on their own, outside of the field of economics. They are doing this, in part, to obtain sufficient knowledge to develop a more appropriate formal theoretical model to evaluate their question of interest but also to identify what they must account for in their empirical work so that it does not suffer from omitted variable bias. This exploration prepares them to be strong liberal arts educators.

The range of interdisciplinary insights being embraced by economists is inspiring. Economic scholars are looking at matters such as the link between pre-natal nutrition and health status later in life, skin shade of workers and their treatment in the labor market, intra-family relations and wealth accumulation, birth position and school performance, and a range of other questions, all of which entail deep knowledge of ideas and evidence from other disciplines. Deans need to make clear to department heads that they will only allow job offers to be extended to candidates who have examined issues in their scholarly work from a host of perspectives and who have an engaging mind that values insight from other disciplines. However, even if economists with this mind set are hired at liberal arts colleges, efforts must also be undertaken to encourage them to follow through and actually teach in a fashion consistent with the mission of an institution committed to providing its students a liberal education.

The critical issue from the perspective of a liberal arts college is whether these scholars are willing to follow through and teach economics in a way that contributes to a traditional liberal education once they arrive on campus. Teaching in this fashion imposes two costs on the educators that are avoided by economists who instruct in the conventional, more narrow, fashion. First, there are the psychological costs associated with any uncertainty they may hold over whether they have a sufficient amount of relevant interdisciplinary knowledge. Second, there are virtually no economics textbooks around which to organize classes, because the currently available books are conventional. Therefore, the instructor must invest time and energy in developing appropriate readings. Faced with these disincentives, economic educators, even those who have the skill and background to teach in an interdisciplinary manner, must be convinced that the benefits of doing so outweigh the cost associated with this alternative form of economic pedagogy.

Some economists, especially those who have been recently minted, are acutely aware of the importance of incorporating insights from other disciplines – such as sociology, psychology, history, and political science – in providing a rich understanding of the questions they examine in their teaching. In class they are likely to explore a wide range of issues with their students that lead to insights about factors such as the influence of race, ethnicity, and gender on socioeconomic outcomes and on the connection between economic developments and poverty or the environment. These economic educators will be comfortable in a liberal arts college setting and will prudently gravitate to interdisciplinary instruction with economics playing a central role.

However, another group of economists are aware that insights from related disciplines might enrich their teaching, and their scholarly work, but perceive the costs in terms of preparation to be too high to engage this approach. A final group of economics professors is simply unaware of what other disciplines have to offer them as educators and scholars. One way to advance economics instruction that fits the liberal arts college setting is to inform, and convince, these latter two groups that the rewards to them and their students of interdisciplinary education exceed the costs – by substantially reducing the costs and by pointing out the merits of this approach.

The remainder of this essay makes the case that for most faculty the costs of engaging in economics instruction that draws on insights from disciplines outside of economics are smaller than perceived. In addition, I will identify the benefits of interdisciplinary economics instruction for those economists who currently teach in a conventional fashion – using formal economic models to help students learn to think like economists. Moreover, I will offer examples that suggest that economists who teach in this manner will promote in their students a passion for learning, will confront them with ethical dilemmas, and will provide them with transferable skills – the very traits that Bok, Colander, and McGoldrick believe are fundamental to a liberal education. I will argue that senior administrators are the fundamental roadblock to economics playing a more central role in providing students with a liberal education. Moreover, I offer concrete examples to support Colander and McGoldrick's contention that economics instruction that draws on ideas from other disciplines allows economics education to make a greater contribution, than standard forms of economics instruction, to the mission of a liberal arts college.

IDENTIFYING AND ASSESSING THE COSTS AND BENEFITS OF INTERDISCIPLINARY ECONOMICS BASED EDUCATION: MYTHS AND REALITY

The perceived costs of interdisciplinary instruction in economics-centered courses arise from additional preparation and the stresses associated with teaching in this fashion. The norm in economics is to teach non-principles economics using textbooks and to supplement the text with articles either from readers or from conventional economics outlets like the *Wall Street Journal*, the *Financial Times*, and the *Economist*. This is understandable because it provides familiar explanations for the questions at hand.

However, this practice is problematic for liberal education in two ways. First, these materials are rarely interdisciplinary. Second, these publications too often fail to highlight how economists with interdisciplinary knowledge go about the thinking or analysis that leads to the conclusions they draw. Thus, there are important shortcomings – from a liberal education perspective – embedded in the materials typically used to teach economics because it is the thought process that interdisciplinary-oriented economists use that is largely transferable and permanent and that provides students with another approach to examining the world.

Toss the Text

The first hurdle to overcome is the anxiety associated with giving up the crutch of the economics text. Fortunately, the profession has provided a ready substitute, and it is one that is well respected – the *Journal of Economic Perspectives*. In addition, a variety of other, equally well-respected outlets offer interdisciplinary examinations – which are readable for students with limited exposure to formal economics – such as *The Future of Children*, *Journal of Policy and Management*, *Demography*, and *Social Science Quarterly*.

I Only Know Economics: So, Be a Lifelong Learner

A second obstacle that diverts many economists from engaging in interdisciplinary instruction is the widely held notion that as economists we are ill-prepared to discuss issues with students from a host of perspectives – we simply are not experts in other disciplinary viewpoints. This fear is unwarranted. Students learn that a liberal education provides them the foundation to read and think critically and to apply these skills to whatever questions they confront. Certainly, as professors of economics we can embrace what we ask of our students – apply our ability to think and analyze to the accumulation of new ideas from disciplines outside of economics. We can understand and incorporate insights acquired in this manner into our instruction without becoming experts – after all, we teach students how to write analytical papers and we are not members of the English department.

I want to Teach the Economist Way of Thinking: Can I Do This in an Interdisciplinary Way that Provides Substantial Benefits Over Conventional Instruction?

A third concern to overcome, in order to encourage economics faculty to incorporate into their teaching ideas from other disciplines, is the belief that proceeding in an interdisciplinary fashion moves us away from teaching economics – especially the *economics way of thinking* (p. 19, Chapter 1, this volume). Actually, the opposite is true. Economists observe matters of interest to society and policy makers. Then, they *wonder and ponder* until they develop an *educated guess or hypothesis* to explain this intriguing outcome. Readings can be selected that expose students to educated guesses from a host of disciplines, including economics, and these ideas can be aired in class discussions.

Economists use *formal models* – visual representations of their educated guesses – to explore the implications of various developments. Students with a principles of economics background are familiar with the workhorse models of economics: cost–benefit analysis, production functions, and supply and demand. Conventional economic models are flexible and fluid enough to incorporate ideas from other disciplines. For instance, students might account for the psychological costs of joblessness – when formulating the marginal costs of being without work – in investigating the notion of an optimal level of unemployment. Thus, interdisciplinary instruction does not mean abandonment of economic-type modeling, but embellishment of this practice.

1. Improved theory instruction: a benefit of interdisciplinary teaching

Students become more proficient in the development and use of formal economic procedures to obtain insights when they figure out how to incorporate knowledge from other disciplines into conventional economic models, such as production functions or marginal cost and marginal benefit curves. Ideas from other disciplines will help them see that non-economic factors play a role in explaining outcomes of interest to economists. Moreover, insight from other disciplines may lead them to believe that, on theoretical grounds, the impact of economic factors on an outcome of concern may be contingent upon non-economic factors. Such an insight leads to a deeper understanding of the link between economic elements and outcomes that would be missed without taking an interdisciplinary perspective. Moreover, it reveals to students the connection between the issues they discuss in economics and the ideas they learn across campus in their other courses – and brings economics clearly into the liberal arts fold for students. Thus, teaching students to incorporate notions learned outside of economics into standard economic models provides a platform for highlighting the process of developing sound social science models and does not move economists away from modeling – a sacred feature of modern economics instruction. Therefore, there are real tangible benefits in terms of analytical skills that derive from taking an interdisciplinary perspective when developing and applying formal economic models.

Consider the following example of the benefits that flow from interdisciplinary inquiry in the arena of economic theory. In recent years, economists and other social scientists have been asking why is there a schooling achievement gap between children from families that are well off and those who are members of less privileged households. Standard economic thinking is that children from higher socioeconomic families receive better-quality education and have parents who are better equipped to help them learn. Thus, a policy recommendation often advanced is to encourage less-educated parents to spend more time assisting their children with their school work, suggesting that they are doing a poor job as parents with regards to the academic accomplishments of their children. But other factors associated with developmental psychology may also contribute to the educational achievement gap. For instance, today a quarter of high-income parents choose to delay, for a year, enrolling their children in kindergarten. They do this because they believe their children will be more mature physically and emotionally, allowing them to gain more from their education, and they can afford another year of preschool. Evidence reveals they are correct and the gains these children realize in primary school do not erode as they age. However, the schooling achievement gap between well-off and less privileged children is substantially smaller when children of the same age are compared. Thus, an interdisciplinary examination of the achievement gap in school outcomes suggest that the parents of poor children are not responsible for the gap that has been observed between less privileged and well-off children.

Exploring the educational achievement gap through an interdisciplinary lens provides richer insights into the source of the gap and promotes the development of broad critical analysis skills. Moreover, the classroom conversation on this topic is sure to lead to a conversation about the ethics or morality of more well-off children being able to more easily take advantage of the gains associated with delaying kindergarten enrollment. Hence, this is just one of countless examples of how economic education that embraces ideas from other disciplines will promote the very ideals that are central to a liberal education.

Students exposed to interdisciplinary economics instruction see clearly the usefulness of developing formal frameworks of analysis that are informed by insights from a host of disciplines and want to develop the capacity for analyzing using such a framework. Consequently, they become more engaged learners and the passion to explore and debate is fostered. In the process, ethical and moral features of the issues being investigated rise to the surface and warrant discussion. Thus, economic theory that embraces contributions from other disciplines and incorporates them in the traditional economic mode of analysis contributes to all of the goals laid out for a liberally educated person.

2.   Improved econometrics instruction: a benefit of interdisciplinary teaching

Economists are proud of their social science orientation and believe it essential to evaluate hypotheses to determine if they are consistent with data. Thus, instruction in how to go about proper evaluation of hypotheses is a central element of modern – scientific – economics. Economics majors are required to take a basic statistics course that introduces them to regression analysis and in many cases they are asked to take a course that specializes in regression analysis. In most cases, some familiarity with econometrics is sufficient for majors and non-majors to be able to read work from interdisciplinary journals that address questions of interest to economists. Fortunately, interdisciplinary theorizing leads to empirical work that is more convincing on many topics and provides students with opportunities to challenge and advance their understanding of how to properly test hypotheses.

The convention is to begin by specifying an empirical model in which some outcome of interest (Y) is explained by a key variable (K) – that economic thinking identifies as influencing the outcome of interest – and a host of control variables (X), along with stochastic elements captured by an error term (ε),

$$Y = \delta(K) + \beta(X) + \varepsilon \tag{14.1}$$

Variables – called Z – that are also expected to influence Y, based on insight from other disciplines can be accommodated either as elements of X or as factors that have been contained in ε and should be directly accounted for in the model specification so their impact on Y can be examined, leading to a reformulation of the model as,

$$Y = \delta(K) + \beta(X) + \psi(Z) + \varepsilon \tag{14.2}$$

Estimation of equation (14.2) allows a discussion of the relative importance of economic (δ) and non-economic (ψ) variables in explaining Y, and the pitfalls of estimating a model that omits Z, which may be correlated with X and/or K leading to estimates of δ (the key coefficient of interest) and β that are biased – which highlights the importance of taking account of ideas from other disciplines to engage in sound social science analysis. Reflecting on the soundness of empirical procedures leads to better instruction on conventional empirical tools of economic analysis – which is fostered by basing empirical models on interdisciplinary theorizing. Of course, better empirical work leads to more informed policy conclusions – the final element of "thinking like an economist" (pp. 16–20, Chapter 1, this volume).

Interdisciplinary thinking is also an ideal way to further educate students on another central tenant of economics – that the relation between variables is often nuanced or complex. There are two forms of complexity that economists hope students come to appreciate that are easily illuminated using interdisciplinary reflection. First, that one or more variables that explain an outcome of interest may be mediated by or contingent on one another. For instance, theory may point toward the impact of schooling (K) on wages (Y) depending on the emotional well-being of a person (Z). This can be captured by a model specified as,

$$Y = \delta(K) + \beta(X) + \psi(Z) + \lambda(K*Z) + \varepsilon \qquad (14.3)$$

If this model is estimated and λ is significantly different from 0, then the evidence is consistent with a mediating relation between K and Z.

Alternatively, theory from economics and another discipline may suggest that an outcome and one of its determinants might be jointly determined. For example, emotional health influences wages, and in turn wages impact emotional well-being. This characterization of relations can be tested by examining an empirical model such as,

$$Y = \delta(K) + \beta(X) + \psi(Z) + \varepsilon \qquad (14.4)$$

$$Z = \theta(M) + \nu(R) + \pi(Y) + \mu$$

where M is an element that influences Z, without explaining Y, and R is a set of controls. The point is that a student's understanding of hypothesis testing can be directly enriched by exploring interdisciplinary ideas to explain an outcome, because such an examination may lead to more complex notions of how a variable is determined and thus more complex empirical model specifications.

The tradition of evaluating hypotheses of interest can be maintained and advanced as part of an interdisciplinary exploration of issues of interest to economists – and the empirical background students need remains a course in statistics that culminates with a discussion of regression analysis. As students discuss evidence on the relation between economic and non-economic factors in explaining outcomes of interest they learn to think critically and broadly, which contributes to their liberal education.

CONCLUSION

The purpose of the discussion, by Colander and McGoldrick in Chapter 1, is to identify and discuss ways to better integrate the teaching practices of economists with the ideals of a liberal education. They believe that economics as it is currently taught is contributing little to the mission of liberal arts colleges and that there is little reason to believe that this situation will improve unless concrete actions are taken to develop a cadre of economists with the ability and interest to teach economics in an interdisciplinary fashion. While I agree that economics education that incorporates ideas from other disciplines is critical for economics to contribute more fully to the liberal education of students, I do not share their perspective that the problem is one of limited supply. Rather I believe the problem is one of limited demand. Not only is the supply of newly minted economists with interdisciplinary teaching and research interests sufficient to meet the needs of liberal arts colleges, but if given the right signs of support from administrators they will actually join liberal arts colleges and teach in an interdisciplinary manner. Moreover, those same signs of commitment to economic education and scholarship that draw on ideas from other disciplines will also encourage some existing faculty, who currently are not interdisciplinary in their teaching, to become more so.

The solution to the problem identified by Colander and McGoldrick is straightforward. First, deans at liberal arts colleges, and other senior administrators, must establish a policy of only extending job offers to economist-scholar-educators who conduct research that accounts for insights from other disciplines and who indicate they intend to teach in such a fashion. Second, these very same administrators must inform both the head of the economics department and the members of committees that evaluate economists for tenure and promotion that interdisciplinary teaching and research is to be valued as much, if not more, than more narrow economic teaching and scholarship. These policies will establish a viable demand for interdisciplinary-oriented economists at liberal arts colleges. Next, these two policies must be communicated to administrators of graduate programs in economics and to their graduate students. This development will promote the supply of new scholar-educators in the field of economics who will have the teaching orientation desired by liberal arts colleges that adhere to the Bok perspective on what a liberal education provides. Moreover, by establishing a clear commitment to economics being taught in an interdisciplinary manner, existing economics faculty will become more interdisciplinary in their teaching and research.

Recent developments in graduate economics education have produced an outpouring of new PhD holders in economics that have ideal preparation to teach economics in an interdisciplinary way. Thus, as a discipline, economics is poised to make a greater contribution to liberal education than in past decades. The challenge is to enlighten senior administrators at liberal arts colleges to this development and to motivate them to establish policies that bring these economics educators to their campus and to value their interdisciplinary teaching and scholarship when they arrive. If economics fails to be a major contributor to a liberal education on the campus of liberal arts colleges the culprit won't be a lack of appropriately trained economists but a lack of will on the part of college administrators.

15. The economics major at a crossroads

David Kennett

Colander and McGoldrick's "Teagle Report" has forced us all to think hard about, among other things, liberal education and how traditional disciplines can contribute to that objective. Before I venture to offer my own feelings about the analysis and recommendations laid out in the main report, it might be useful for readers to learn something of my own education because our backgrounds help form our preconceptions about the shape of liberal education and therefore the appropriate policy recommendations.

I grew up in the United Kingdom in a system where disciplinary concentration started at an even earlier age than in the United States. I had a very broad education, and I would say a very liberal one up to the age of 16, when I took national examinations in nine subjects. However, I was then required to focus on a much narrower curriculum and forced to choose between an arts and a science concentration. I selected science with some misgivings. My best subjects were probably history and literature but I chose, with half an eye on a career objective (Prime Minister Harold Wilson was then waxing about the "white heat of the technological revolution") to focus in the sciences for the next two years taking mathematics, physics, chemistry in addition to a course in general studies. The latter covered a wide range of topics, among them literature, drama, philosophy, history and civics, but was broad and not deep. It was not taught by staff trained in general education but by a rotating faculty of disciplinary specialists.

During the next two years I had a hard job imagining myself in a science career and my performance was much better in general studies. I decided at the age of 17 to take a degree course in economics. I knew little of what it meant and I was, in retrospect, lucky. The mathematics and some of the science were useful in the economics program and so too were the extensive history and geography that I had taken earlier in my career. I chose the University of Sussex, a newly established university, at that time well-funded with a self-described mission to "redraw the map of education." The most obvious feature of this iconoclasm was the abandonment of traditional departments, with both instruction and research to be located within "schools of study." I was in the School of Social Studies but economics students and faculty were scattered across European Studies, English and American Studies, African and Asian Studies, and Educational Studies.

Even with the hindsight of 40 years, I continue to think that my education at Sussex was extremely good but it did have costs. Less of my time was spent in purely economics courses with fellow economics students and much more was spent with psychologists, philosophers, sociologists, and even literature specialists than would have been the case in the average UK economics program. Courses were designed for a much broader clientele than economists alone. For example, the material that would in most universities be taught as introductory micro- and macroeconomics was embedded in a broader course entitled the "The Economic and Social Framework." The basic statistics course was common to all social scientists and was taught by a mathematician from the School of Mathematical and Physical Sciences. It was less directed to regression models than was the case in economics departments even then. I spent more time on interdisciplinary material than economics students in other universities and, importantly, I learned to speak the language of other disciplines.

This formal structural interdisciplinarity, and its informal counterparts, had a strong appeal and for me lasting effects, many positive. Some, however, in the immediate aftermath seemed negative. For one thing it meant that I was a less "well-trained economist" than the output of most other UK undergraduate programs. I had spent only about 60 percent of my university career (a total of three years) on economics course work while the average at most British undergraduate institutions at that time was nearer 90 percent. My mathematical economics and econometrics were not "up to snuff." Despite high grades and good recommendations, I was denied access to the LSE one-year MSc and admitted only to the two-year program; this was probably a correct decision because the greater breadth of my Sussex education necessarily neglected the depth that would have made a UK graduate school an easier transition, but I declined the offer. In this sense I was an early harbinger of the problems that my own students today have in gaining admission to top graduate schools in the United States.

As a side note, but one relevant to our discussion here, the Sussex attempt to "redraw the map of education" was largely unsuccessful. Traditional academic departments showed considerable resilience. Initially, disciplinary colleagues would meet under the aegis of "subject groups" that grew progressively stronger. Research funding and graduate programs required strong disciplinary concentration in most subjects, not just in economics, and the grand interdisciplinary experiment slowly expired as departments rose from their coffins.

When I did enroll in the Columbia PhD program in 1972, despite my rough handling by the LSE, I had few problems. In those days most of my classmates were recent economics graduates of the US liberal arts education system and the depth of my training was certainly comparable to theirs. Clearly this is not a situation that would pertain today when it's very hard for even the best liberal arts economics graduates to gain entry. The majority of graduate school recruits today tend to be neither economics majors nor American.

I was also struck by the "econocentric" and technical nature of the course work in graduate school. While some of my professors doubtless took a liberal and comprehensive view of the world, it was clear that Columbia's immediate mission was to raise the research output of the faculty and this involved recruiting a younger faculty more focused on theory and technique than on context and policy relevance. I tended to select away from this. The greatest influence on me was probably Bill Vickrey, a brilliant theorist but also a man you could run into in any one of Columbia's many seminars on history, sociology, urban studies, political economy, and philosophy. He was deeply concerned about the policy relevance of his work and his heavily normative commitment appealed to me.

After three years of funding my support ran out and I needed a job in easy reach of Columbia. Initially I went as a part-time instructor to Queens College in the New York City system. If Gerald Ford had not told the city to "drop dead" that year I would probably have stayed at Queens but the city's fiscal crisis propelled me to find other work and I took a one-year job at Vassar. I had only a fuzzy idea of what "liberal arts" in the full-blown US sense of the word was and it is with some surprise that it's provided a happy home for me for 32 years. However, my own under-graduate experience was as close to US liberal arts as could be found in the UK and my own indecision between science, social science, and arts had given me a background that prepared me well for my Vassar experience. I have subsequently come to think that, when done well, the US liberal arts education is simply the best available to unlock student potential and that we should fight hard to defend its basic precepts against the internal and external pressures that it faces.

This brings me to confront more directly the issues raised in the report. One of the most important is the origin of the liberal element in a liberal arts education. Must it be found in every course, or should it be an essential part of every program of major study or can it be achieved by the balance of courses that a student takes during a four-year college life? What are the responsibilities within our own discipline? Must the department assume the responsibility and indeed say *if an economics student is going to get a liberal education, it's up to the economics curriculum to provide it?*

One line of argument is to say that since economic courses represent roughly a third to at most one-half of the class work that a student can take, the "liberal" part of a "liberal education" can be comfortably provided by the work outside of the major. This conveniently relieves the department of the responsibility for a student's general education. However, if all departments are concentrated on their own disciplinary foci and core research, a student is unlikely to come away with an interdisciplinary and integrated view of the world but rather a series of snapshots of the disciplinarily-oriented view from various, and perhaps competing, ivory towers. This approach asks the student to perform a vital task that many faculty members find both difficult and unwelcome, that of putting together an integrating view of the world that encompasses many disciplines.

This is, I believe, why David and KimMarie write that "if one wants to achieve a liberal education, one needs some body of the professorate who have a substantial commitment to that liberal education, not to a specific discipline or major" (p. 11). Only if the faculty of a liberal arts college has within it teachers who are themselves knowledgeable in, and committed to, a liberal vision can the students' liberal education be achieved. Whether the role of these individuals is to maintain the liberal content of their own disciplinary major or to teach integrative courses and enhance the advising function may be open. Certainly with respect to economics I would favor more numerous offerings in the history of economic thought, economic history, and comparative economics that have the scope for deeper student reading – particularly the reading of the economic "classics." That would certainly give economics a more liberal content than the anti-historical, technical, and in many ways pre-professional discipline that we are becoming. However, I still cling to the belief that much of the liberality must come from understanding other disciplines and integrating their perspectives into a broader view of the world.

This raises the question of where the people committed to liberality are to come from, what their specific role should be in the college and how they are to be given appropriate incentives, evaluated, and retained. When we at Vassar are recruiting economics faculty, we tend to look for candidates who have a liberal arts undergraduate background because such scholars are more likely to understand our mission. Frankly, this is harder all the time because, as we have discussed elsewhere, not many liberal arts students actually want to do an economics PhD and those that do, have a hard time getting into major graduate schools. Moreover, those that do have the appropriate set of skills to gain admission to our leading graduate schools are not generally those who have availed themselves fully of the liberal ideal while in college but rather have focused on a limited, not general, curriculum – learning at least as much mathematics as economics, and not spreading themselves across the range of disciplines. I find the statistic in the report that those students entering into economics PhD programs have a mean 772 Quantitative GRE score, and a mean 562 verbal score to be quite chilling. One wonders how with such limited communication skills any future economist could sit down and write any kind of "essay in persuasion."

While most would admit that this assessment is substantially correct, the next step in the authors' argument is one that causes some to baulk:

> This leads us to the proposition that if one wants the goals of a liberal education to be the focus of undergraduate education, one needs a set of professors whose research goals and whose teaching interests are in line with the broader questions that liberal arts programs focus on, and less on the specialized research that characterizes most disciplinary research. (p. 13)

This is an important question, whether it's necessary that a liberal arts teacher's research interests be liberally oriented. It might ideally be the case, but I am not convinced. I know many excellent teachers (in many disciplines) with broad teaching interests but whose research foci would be described by the broader mass of both students and faculty as specialist. I have team-taught with a literature professor whose work was on a German poet unknown to me before and unheard of since and a biologist concerned with quite mysterious micro-organisms. I learned from both of them, factually and methodologically, as did our students – independent of the nature of their research, which was, however, a vital part of their own professional lives. In my experience those who can teach with a high content of generalism and integrative skill are not necessarily those whose research is as liberally oriented as the course content. Such a discussion, however, raises the whole topic of research, its link to teaching and the growth of the "research college," issues, which, though important, I cannot fully address here.

Of more importance still is how these generalists get trained. The authors have the idea that we should "[i]ncrease the number of professors whose training is designed to promote good teaching of undergraduates, not to promote research" (p. 21). Should these people continue to be the output of research-oriented graduate programs who select undergraduate teaching while in graduate school, or should they be the product of specialist programs in undergraduate teaching?

If the former, how do we increase the size of the cohort and the talent embodied at the stage of entry to graduate school? At present, graduate school is neither attractive nor accessible to would-be teachers. It is a cruel fact that most (if not all) placement officers at the major PhD-granting institutions regard liberal arts colleges as the place to put students who have not the research promise to survive elsewhere. Some dissertation advisers tend to shy away from students who express a desire for a teaching career as they are unlikely to have the output that will give them reflected credit in years to come. The system of graduate student support is biased to support, in the first rank, those spotted early as having research potential. The second rank tended to be those who can do the bulk of teaching of economics to undergraduates in a research institution, while (during my time at Columbia at least) the teaching of general education in Columbia College was left to those who had not attracted much interest from the members of the economics department at all. These graduate students were often left in an educational limbo, as their needs and teaching demands took them farther away from the department and stretched out their time to completion, which (sadly) contrived to make them relatively unattractive even to the liberal arts colleges that might have benefited from their skills.

Even if our economics graduate schools did begin to look with greater favor on the education of those committed to teaching at the college level, it's not clear that they possess the necessary skills to develop teaching facility in others. Perhaps things have changed (I suspect not) but my graduate school teachers were not very impressive in the classroom. I cannot think of a class that truly inspired me by its methods, and many were just disappointing. Some teachers tended to show more concern for their students and class presentation, but such behavior was viewed with apparent condescension by the research heavy brigade. While my experience is dated, it's hard to see how subsequent generations of graduate school professors, recruited for research technique not communication, might fare any better.

That said, a possibility is the creation within existing graduate schools of tracks devoted to the production of teachers. My fear is that both the students and the teachers in such a subdivision would be viewed, at best, patronizingly by the research-oriented faculty and students, just as those economists who were sucked into the vortex of teaching "general education" were back in the 1970s. Similarly, in those institutions whose PhD output mainly goes into teaching there is often a wish to "improve" the program by increasing the research output of both faculty and graduate students. Moreover, it's not clear to me that those "taught to teach" are necessarily the better teachers. I have been involved in several efforts at improving teaching at my own institution and while some skills that raise student approval are easily conveyed (organization, timeliness, availability) excellence in teaching comes in many forms, and is hard to instill.

To give some balance, in recent evaluation/certification missions I have encountered wonderfully energetic teachers, essentially ABDs (all but the dissertation), who have no real thirst (or time) for completing their PhD or pursuing an active research agenda. Under present arrangements they will be taken advantage of by their current institutions and probably pushed out after six years of service. If there were a well-respected certification for undergraduate teaching separate from a research-oriented PhD training, they would have been ideal candidates. Certainly their students were more than happy with their performances and their departments would be the weaker for their absence. In a similar vein, many major universities now make "clinical" appointments taking advantage of the teaching skills of PhD economists who have no zest either for continued research or for departmental administration. Even if we finesse the problem of the relationship between teaching and research, and avoid the question of why research might promote the teaching skills of some professors but not others, the issue of class and status remains, and it may be key, especially in the close residential world of the "elite liberal arts college." As a result I remain skeptical that establishment of specialist teaching programs at the graduate school level is a means to solving the "general education" issue at the collegiate level.

Where then might we look for help in saving liberal education? There is some potential in improving the quality of student advising. Leaving a freshman to choose his or her own courses is not a reliable route to a balanced general education. Nor, in my view, would a return to more specific requirements be very helpful. Advising must be a vital part of "leading out" (the real meaning of education) and must be preceded by a deeper investigation of student interest and aptitude, and more monitoring of those aspects as a student progresses, than is commonly allowed. If advising were closer and more informed, I for one would be more comfortable that the mission of general education might be achieved by crafting a balance of classes and disciplines within a four-year curriculum. But who might do such advising? A disciplinary-focused faculty member is not ideal but a concerned and involved "tutor," to use an old term, would be. Some thought about how to realistically improve advising as a continuous process would be time well spent.

A further possibility lies in the increase of multidisciplinary programs, a development that can help solve the problem for specific students but does not resolve the issue for the economics major. I believe that the growth of such programs has contributed a lot in my own college to the promotion of more balanced liberal education. For most of the last 20 years I have been a director of such a multidisciplinary program, Vassar's Program in International Studies. Within that program I think we have achieved most of the objectives of general education. An agreed set of guidelines espoused by a multidisciplinary steering committee sets out the essential objectives and requirements – balance, quantitative aspects, languages, a thesis, peer presentation and so on – and these are applied in a continuing advisement process that allows change as students' interests mature and alter. The drawback in today's bleak financial environment is cost. Essential components are team-teaching, personal advisement, and small-size seminars – elements that might be too expensive even at the prices we are charging. However, the results are good. I recently did an e-mail survey of all of the graduates of the program over its 20-year history to gauge ex post satisfaction. I got a more than 50 percent response to a single e-mailing and all but one of the respondents was positive about the experience, and would repeat it. That one felt that although she knew "a little about a lot" she lacked the satisfaction of knowledge in depth – a trade-off liberal arts must always face.

In conclusion, I would like to address the specific issues of the economics program because I believe we are at a very crucial crossroads where economics as a liberal discipline is under attack from not one but two directions. We have discussed extensively one nexus: that graduate schools are demanding from entrants the skills for a narrower, more technical, and more theoretical version of economics than has been commonly taught in liberal arts schools. This feeds back into those schools as they respond to those stimuli and because the incoming faculty at liberal arts schools have been trained to produce a more technical student.

The second assault is student and employer driven. Most students of economics from liberal arts schools do not go on to graduate school in economics but the majority find employment in business and consultancy with the preferred destination, at least before the meltdown of recent weeks, being the New York City financial sector. Industry leaders pay tribute to the advantages of liberal arts education and its role in producing the leaders of tomorrow, and look, they say, for the "best brain" and a "world view." However, the internships are more often awarded by individuals on a lower rung of the management ladder on the basis of course work in finance and facility with spreadsheets. Students know this and line up for any course with finance in the title and pressure departments to offer more. Having seen the "survey monkey" results prepared for these discussions I followed up with students at my own college about what they saw as the deficiencies of our program. A strong complaint was inadequate preparation in finance, and this came most vocally from overseas students, certainly among our brightest, who had come to the US for the chance of a good education with substantial financial aid, but who did not really subscribe to the ideal of liberal arts and were more focused on pre-professional training. Holding the line that divides economics from business preparation will be increasingly difficult and, somewhat ironically, much harder if the current finance-led collapse leads to a tight job market.

Would these students be better served by a major that contained elements of economics but not the detail and depth since their interest is only tangentially linked to the major as currently taught? The big question here is how such an admittedly "pre-professional major" could exist in the liberal arts environment. Isn't overt pre-professionalism anathematic to the liberal arts ideal? Economics is not the only major to face these problems; for example, successful programs in film, media studies, and drama rely a lot on practical work and pre-professional internships, and I suspect that the role of such off-campus applied study will grow. It will be difficult but essential either to accommodate this movement within the liberal arts curriculum or to resist its inroads. That will be one of the challenges of the twenty-first century.

16. Crafting the economics major as an exercise in property rights

Neil T. Skaggs

Since other commentators have taken the license to apply economic reasoning to the problem at hand, I will do likewise. One might look at the problem of crafting an economics major as an exercise in property rights. In universities, including my own, and probably in most liberal arts colleges, departmental faculty members have wide latitude in defining the major. Those acquiring a major have limited control over its content. One could make a strong argument that professors within a discipline are best qualified to determine the content of the major, but such an argument overlooks the problem of incentives. I would guess that at least a substantial minority – perhaps a substantial majority – of academic economists would argue that students should engage in more directed writing assignments than they do. Yet these same economists are frequently loath to require substantial writing assignments because of the time consumed in grading them. Time spent grading is time not spent on research. The incentive structure leads all of us – including myself, though I require some writing even in my large principles sections – to tailor assignments so as to minimize grading time. (Like many professors, I am hesitant to have my assistants grade essays, even when I'm quite happy to have them grade problem sets.) Faculty incentives cannot help but affect the nature of the major.

The incentive problem strikes again when we look at the research programs pursued by the vast majority of academic economists. It is quite possible that liberal arts colleges have different standards for ranking journals and rewarding research performance than do universities. Since I've spent my entire career in a state university, I will speak of what I know. My department uses widely recognized ranking schemes to systematically discriminate against journals that fail to follow the leaders. Economists largely agree on the top tier of journals, and, if my department is any indication, are pretty well agreed on the second tier (top field journals and strong general journals). But there the agreement ends, at least on my part, for journals that don't follow the standard neo-classical approach tend to be downgraded, primarily because their citation counts are relatively low. Many journals have low citation counts simply because no one has bothered to count them. For example, *History of Political Economy* is the only history of economic thought journal to be included in standard citation counts. That means that all the citations to *HOPE* that appear in the *Journal of the History of Economic Thought*, the *European Journal of the History of Economic Thought*, and two or three other journals never show up in the citation rates – and the empiricists in my department assign *HOPE* to purgatory and the remainder of the HET journals to hell proper.

Now I'm a wizened veteran, a full professor who can afford to react to such nonsense with scorn and continue doing what I do. It may cost me a few dollars in salary increases, but it is preferable to re-crafting my research career at this late date. But such an incentive structure virtually guarantees that few younger faculty members will be so foolish as to work in such an undervalued area. The obvious result of such incentives is a narrowing of the types of courses that are taught.

But perhaps such a claim cannot be substantiated. Lots of economists teach courses outside their specialty areas, and they are perfectly capable of following a textbook and acquainting students with the material. Many, no doubt, do a commendable job of it. But a lingering suspicion remains: are students taught to think broadly about issues and problems, or are they taught to think deeply but narrowly? My department currently consists of 16 economists, a large majority of whom could be categorized as micro-econometricians. Most of them are excellent neo-classical economists, who can apply the standard maximization approach to a substantial range of problems. Most of their work is quite sensible. Hardly any of it addresses the broader reaches of economics. One or two pay a little attention to the Coase Theorem (I/O, Law and Econ, Environmental); hardly anyone pays substantial attention to the broader implications of transaction costs. Even our "Managerial Economics" course is taught in neo-classical terms. What might students learn from an extensive encounter with Coase or Kirzner in such a class?

If most (and perhaps I'm being overly pessimistic) departments are targeted so narrowly because it is clearly in the faculty members' interests to focus narrowly, then change will have to come from the outside. If economists don't voluntarily avail themselves of the breadth of approaches available *within* the discipline, they can hardly be expected to integrate their knowledge with *other* disciplines. If the highest goal of education is a liberal education, then the incentive structure must change.

I'll end with a final word regarding the desires of our students. I'm sure that many students in top liberal arts colleges love to read, enjoy being challenged by new ideas, and are capable of making well-reasoned arguments in well-written prose. The vast majority of students at State U. read little, even when the readings are "required," are dumbfounded (or incensed) by truly new ideas, and can't write a lick. As articles in both the popular and education literatures (for example, *The Chronicle of Higher Education*) have started to note, the current generation of students differs from its predecessors. This generation entered school during the heady years in the early 1990s when the latest craze in education schools was the notion that no child could fail. Their attitudes and academic work ethics differ greatly from earlier generations'. Such students will not demand a liberal education; they will be forced to obtain one, if they are to obtain it at all. Assigning property rights to the students would be disastrous. But there is hope: as the world outside of the North American-Western European sphere impinges more and more upon us, the range of topics that can be addressed fruitfully with the variety of economic approaches now available to economists might lead to greater breadth in both topics and approaches. So long as economists don't get so caught up in theory that we fail to apply our theoretical and empirical tools to the understanding of real-world behavior, the very course of events may multiply our approaches and pull us into more interdisciplinary investigations. Our students will benefit if this mildly rosy future comes to be.

17. Preserving liberal arts education: a futile endeavor

Brendan O'Flaherty

The difficulties that US liberal arts colleges are facing may be a little deeper than Dave and KimMarie make them out to be in Chapter 1, and the challenges may be correspondingly more interesting. Colleges (not necessarily disciplines) may have to change a lot more than they think they should, and this change will be for the better.

Two trends are driving a lot of what is happening in the economics profession, and both of them are working against the traditional US major: globalization and technological change. These are trends that economists talk about affecting other people all the time; but they also affect us.

First, globalization. Economics graduate education is now an international enterprise. Students in the top universities come from all over the world, and so do the faculty. Students of any one nationality, including the US, are now a minority (and a large proportion of US students are immigrants or children of immigrants). This has created a wonderfully diverse society. It's nice to step out into the hallway and see, for instance, a Bulgarian, Chinese, Israeli-Arab trio, all friends, joking with each other.

The problem for traditional liberal arts education in the US is not that international students aren't good teachers; the problem is that they have different options. Occasionally, US students win our teaching prizes, but usually it's the international students – probably more often than their representation among teaching students. And many international students think about big questions. What sets them apart from Americans is that they have better employment opportunities outside the US.

Many international students adopt the following job market strategy: try the US market, see if you get a great offer, and if you don't, go home. Even among students who primarily want to teach, going home has significant advantages over staying in the US: you can teach in your native language, you can be with your parents as they age, in some cases you can be a big fish in a small pond, and you don't have to rely on strangers in a country that is extremely unfriendly to immigrants to grant you tenure. Different countries have different teaching traditions, and you may think you can teach better in the tradition in which you were brought up. For a student who wants to have an impact on the world – a future Ernesto Zedillo, Andres Velasco, or Domingo Cavallo – the advantages of going home are quite clear. Staying in the US is ok, but only in a high profile position – not teaching principles.

Until US liberal arts colleges can offer an alternative at least this attractive to international PhDs, they will not see most of the best teachers who come out of graduate school. (Of course, world welfare is probably maximized by putting the best teachers in Brazil and China, and so it may not be socially optimal for US colleges to attract these teachers.)

The second trend is the improvement in computing and information technology. The basic idea is simple comparative advantage. In a year, Socrates could have two insights into the meaning of life or (maybe) calculate one simple OLS regression. In a year I can have (maybe) one insight into the meaning of life or run hundreds of regressions. Who should think about the meaning of life and who should run regressions? Who should be taught how to think about the meaning of life and who should be taught how to run regressions?

At Columbia a few years ago the Statistics Department started a master's program in financial engineering. It is thriving. Some professors think of this success as evidence of the collapse of Western civilization (they see the fact that economics has more majors than history and English combined as further evidence). I think of this success as evidence that the demand for sophisticated reasoning is highly price elastic. MA graduates of this program can probably perform in a week the kind of analyses that a half-century ago only Nobel Prize winners could have performed in a year. Why shouldn't a lot more people learn how to do this?

Closer to home for most of us, this technological change shows up in the willingness of Wall Street and consulting firms to offer high salaries and attractive locations to job market candidates (probably not this year, but generally pretty often). Having a lot of money (I'm told) contributes greatly to one's quality of life, and many people find the excitement and practicality of these jobs exhilarating. We teach our undergraduates that wages approximate in some way the marginal social contribution that a worker makes, and so it is hard for the profession to disparage these jobs credibly (especially when we might have to ask their holders for alumni contributions).

Thus, PhD programs now are not primarily training students to teach in US universities and colleges. Foreign universities and businesses of all kinds hire large proportions of graduates, and so do a lot of governmental and quasi-governmental organizations. After the first or second academic job, even more economists move in this direction. Most of these employers are not hiring people to ask (and not answer) big questions.

Splitting up graduate students by eventual employer is not a viable option. Students want the security that comes from diversification, and they don't understand their options until they examine them. More than once I've seen graduates have competing offers in hand before deciding whether to work for an investment bank or an overseas university. More than once I've seen graduates and colleagues move from academics to Wall Street. US liberal arts education is going to be a minority career choice for economics PhDs. The tail is not going to wag the dog.

What does this mean for undergraduate liberal arts education? The obvious implications are negative. Liberal arts colleges are not going to change graduate economics education by asking for a change. Moreover, they are unlikely to change the nature of specialization in the profession because even among their own professors, the next job is almost as important as the current job. One quick implication is that it may be more productive to establish interdisciplinary majors and let the students do the integrating (since they have an incentive to get an integrated education) than to ask faculty to integrate it for them. Having the world make sense to you is the sort of personal responsibility that can be no more successfully delegated to a well-meaning stranger than brushing your teeth.

More positively, I would decouple undergraduate education from any particular place or group of professors. Groups of professors want to be with each other, not any particular group of students. Students would be organized into groups by administrators, who would then send them together around the world to take various classes from various groups of professors. This is essentially "junior year abroad" without any other years around. Students would hang out with students and learn from each other; professors would hang out with professors and learn from each other. Some groups of students would stay pretty close to home, but they would visit different groups of professors in the same metropolitan area. If this sounds like what life is like in academia now, with students making their way all over the map and faculty drawn from every continent and every walk of life (adjuncts), and administrators rather than professors directing student life, then you should realize that what I am recommending is nothing radical, just to go with the flow.

What economists can tell other academics is that the structure of an industry depends on the technology of the industry and on relative prices, and that when technology and relative prices change, the industry changes. The structure of education depends on a contrast between economies of agglomeration (more students in a classroom, more brilliant colleagues to bounce ideas off), and the costs of homogeneity (students want teaching that matches their skill level and interests, faculty want people they can talk to). This is the classic product differentiation problem. When you expand the market – through globalization, more students in general, or easier communication – the industry changes in the direction of greater variety and greater specialization. I don't know the dimensions on which adjustment will come. But preserving late twentieth-century US liberal arts education is a futile endeavor.

PART 5

Views from the administration

18. Good researchers make good teachers

Catharine Hill

The authors of "The economics major as part of a liberal education" (Chapter 1, this volume) discuss the goals of a liberal arts education and the role of the major in meeting these goals. They then go on to talk specifically about the economics major, arguing that both the major generally and the economics major specifically do not serve well the goals of a liberal education. They propose a variety of both radical and more incremental changes to address their concerns.

My concerns with much of the paper have to do with whether one sees the glass as half full or half empty, and more importantly, whether the glass is being filled up or slowly emptied. The authors assume the glass is definitely being emptied, and this informs many of their arguments and proposals. Economists know all about the importance of assumptions. They make it possible to devise elegant models to address particular issues. In some cases, it does not matter whether the assumptions are "true" – they may still be useful. But, in other cases, some assumptions will make it impossible for the model to address particular issues. For example, a model that assumes full employment won't be particularly useful during economic downturns. Too many assumptions are made in this paper that then drive the conclusions.

THE MAJOR GENERALLY

The authors assume that there is too much emphasis on the major, with too much "narrow preparation in a single area" (p. 3). It is not at all clear to me that this is in fact the case or a problem. The authors call for balance between depth and breadth in the major and between the major and the rest of the curriculum. My own experience suggests that there isn't clear evidence that we've gone too far in one direction consistently across the curriculum. Some majors probably lack depth, while others may have gone too far. Seeking balance makes sense, both within majors and across the curriculum, but we need to be as aware of majors that have lost depth, for a variety of reasons.

I agree that education succeeds when students leave college with a passion for learning, having come to understand its value and how to continue to learn after college. I am less certain about the authors' recipe for instilling passion. And, the notion that the major should play a catalyst role in generating passion is fine, but this shouldn't be independent of the specific content of the major. There is a worry that teachers with specific research issues, "disciplinary specialists," can't teach broadly. I doubt that this is true. As an economist who started my career as a development economist but then moved on to work in higher education, I still strongly believe that I could teach almost any course in the economics curriculum at the undergraduate level. I could certainly teach any of the required courses, despite specific research interests. Importantly, being actively engaged in research supports a certain amount of intellectual discipline that is important to teaching. My own experience is that successful researchers make some of the very best teachers. They understand how to make an argument, how to think through a problem, how to understand what we know and what we don't know. This discipline in going about addressing an issue is what we are trying to instill in our students. If we don't practice it ourselves, it may be more difficult to teach to others.

The argument about general and specific skills is misleading. General skills, such as critical thinking, quantitative and communication skills, can truly be honed within the major. These need not only come from the general education part of the curriculum. In fact, in many cases, the depth of a major can significantly aid in learning these skills. Mastering these skills in fact may truly need the tools and the discipline of the major. One needs to be critical of what a major field or discipline can and cannot contribute to a particular issue, but one cannot do this without understanding the discipline first in order to make these judgments.

The discussion of "big think" and "little think" questions is related to this discussion of the major. First, I can't help but comment on the value-laden use of big and little. Little microchips, tumors, and floods are better than big ones, while some other things are better bigger. According to the authors, big think questions are likely ones that can't be answered, that involve breadth and not depth, and that "question the foundation of the disciplinary analysis and that transcend disciplines" (p. 5). Depth and little think questions involve smaller questions that possibly can be answered. Where to start! Both are incredibly important, but I would argue that depth is necessary for breadth to have much value. Depth involves intellectual discipline and careful reasoning. Big questions are addressed, defined, approached in large part by lots of careful, smaller questions and answers. To sit around and talk about "big" questions with no tools could be a waste of time. We will get as far as we can on big questions by breaking them down into pieces, some of which we can answer and some of which we cannot. Being able to clearly think this through will have come from understanding the importance of depth.

The authors also assume that there is a link between discussing the "big think" questions and creating a passion for learning on the part of students. Discussing questions to which there are no answers might in fact generate a certain disdain on the part of some students. To have learned how to go about discussing these, with background (depth) in one or more disciplines might in fact generate more intellectual engagement and enthusiasm. Some of our students might in fact be incredibly excited by the idea of making progress on knowledge, in fact answering some new questions on the margins of what is known, and not from spinning their wheels on unanswerable questions.

GRADUATE EDUCATION

The authors move to a discussion of graduate education, suggesting that it has caused the reduction in breadth in undergraduate liberal arts education. Also, by focusing on educating researchers and not teachers, it undermines a liberal education because researchers are not passionate teachers. This seems a string of untested assumptions. Why can't a graduate student who is incredibly excited about pushing out the frontiers of knowledge also be, or be just as likely to be, passionate about his or her field as the graduate student who hasn't had success at research? Should we have a teaching caste and a research caste? Can someone who has little interest in or ability to do research be a passionate teacher? Probably. Are they likely to be the most effective teachers? This is assumed, but it isn't clear to me that this would be the case.

It is implied that the passionate researcher can't teach intermediate or introductory courses with passion. "When the passion and excitement isn't there, the course does not provide the catalyst to further learning that is the key to a liberal education" (p. 8). Is there actually any evidence for this? I worry about this statement on two different levels. I don't know what "passion" in the classroom means. Having evaluated people's teaching for almost 20 years now either as a senior member of a department or at the college-wide level, effective teaching takes many forms. Some of it is quiet and thoughtful, some of it is flashy and exciting, some of it is challengingly rigorous and difficult. There are many ways to instill interest and curiosity about a particular subject matter, and I'm not sure that the professor wearing his or her passion or excitement for the field on his or her sleeve is either necessary or sufficient. It is assumed that our research-trained professors will more naturally display passion in their upper-level courses, which are narrowly focused on their research interests. Again, is this really true? Faculty with strong research interests may be particularly interested in asking questions and thinking through how to address them, and this can happen on many levels and in many contexts. Thinking critically, communicating orally and in writing, and understanding the limitations of any discipline and/or approach can happen at any level of the curriculum. We do hope that a student's ability to do this will grow over the four years, in part from working with a more sophisticated set of tools after exposure to the depth of a particular discipline.

It is suggested that faculty trained to be researchers and the strength of disciplines at undergraduate institutions lead to incentives to provide the best training for the discipline, but at the expense of a liberal education. It is not clear that commitment to a discipline means that faculty cannot both teach broadly and be committed to such teaching. And, clearly the institutional leadership can insure that such a commitment is part of success at liberal arts institutions. "People are best at training students to do what they themselves do" (p. 9). This suggests that current training in graduate school leads faculty to be best at training future researchers and not liberally educated graduates. But, research and teaching are not mutually exclusive or even necessarily substitutes. In fact, teaching students to think critically and analyze a problem, something researchers do, is core to liberal arts education.

In the end, I don't believe that a strong commitment to a liberal education is in conflict with a commitment to a specific discipline or major. In fact, a commitment to understanding a specific discipline or major is necessary to an effective liberal education. And, such a commitment need not come at the expense of having a faculty who can teach broadly. Institutions that are committed to this have a variety of means of creating incentives to this effect. There is no reason that good researchers can't be good teachers, whether they address big or little think questions. On the other hand, having a faculty that did not include many deeply involved in research in their disciplines seems like a sure way to put the quality of a liberal arts education at risk.

THE ECONOMICS MAJOR

When turning to the economics major more specifically, rather than the major in general, the goal of thinking like an economist and thinking like a liberally educated person are set against each other. But understanding one discipline well, along with its limitations, is an important component of a liberal education, and there is no reason a major, and in particular an economics major, can't meet multiple objectives. It is true that the nature of economics has changed, as the language used has become more mathematical both at the graduate and undergraduate level. This has been valuable in many ways, allowing for more careful modeling of certain concepts and ideas. Some concepts in economics are so much more easily explained with mathematics or statistics than with words or graphs. And, over time, some issues that economists would have previously considered part of the discipline have moved to other fields, and this may in fact have happened as a result of the increased use of mathematics. But this happens in many fields, with the issues of central or primary interest changing over time. When there are important issues that one discipline chooses not to address, experience suggests that some other area will pick them up. Important issues will find a home someplace in the curriculum at liberal arts institutions, and it isn't so important exactly where.

The authors' discussion of the freshman seminar and the role of the economics major is a bit misleading. The verbal GRE scores of students in economics graduate school is clearly something affected by the increasing international nature of graduate training, particularly in economics, in the United States. In addition, not all disciplines should contribute equally to all goals of a liberal arts education. Quantitative reasoning is an equally important skill, and is more apt to be effectively taught in some disciplines than in others. Effective writing is important in all disciplines, but it is important to note that the nature of effective writing will differ by discipline. But the logic of a closely reasoned and careful argument will cross disciplines. Many courses offered in the economics major can be quite effective in teaching careful argument, written and oral.

PROPOSALS

The proposals to change the research focus of graduate education and the disciplinary emphasis of undergraduate education are recognized as radical by the authors and unlikely to be implemented. Turning to the more incremental changes discussed, many of the proposals would be appropriate for a glass half full or half empty. Increased emphasis on working with graduate students on teaching seems a reasonable direction. I wouldn't want to go so far as to give up hiring graduates with strong training in research skills, but recognizing that many graduate students will also spend some of their career teaching suggests that some education in this area would be appropriate. I do think that learning to teach may be something that is better learned on the job, and that given the various approaches to teaching at different institutions, it may be more productive to offer training at the institution of employment, rather than in graduate school. Would you work on large lecture formats, or small class seminars and tutorials? If teaching matters to an institution, offering assistance to new faculty and weighting success in the classroom throughout the promotion and tenure process could send appropriate signals about the values of the institution.

The proposals to certify teachers and to create pre-professional programs in business and public policy seem less appealing. What exactly would be certified? While there are some basic skills that most good teachers possess, there are a variety of ways of being a highly effective teacher and it isn't clear how they could effectively be certified. If one is worried about the economics major being too focused on graduate school, the proposal to design pre-professional programs in business and public policy at the undergraduate level are really looking for a way to include in the curriculum some areas that previously might have been addressed in the economics major and may now be receiving less emphasis. But, this could be done without moving a liberal arts curriculum too closely to a pre-professional curriculum that has risks of its own. The authors link these issues, in that "[g]raduate content is determined by its relevance for research, not its relevance for teaching" (p. 29), suggesting that economics graduate students aren't learning material appropriate for an undergraduate curriculum. While graduate school may not emphasize some issues that could be very useful to have as part of an undergraduate curriculum, such as a variety of public policy issues, many economists leave graduate school with the tools to address such policy issues, and can and do teach these effectively. I suspect that if the authors are right and economists stop teaching policy issues, institutions will evolve and important policy issues will be addressed elsewhere in the curriculum. And the suggestion to hire faculty trained in graduate schools with a public policy focus seems reasonably to follow.

Examining the principles course also seems a reasonable recommendation. By now, you can probably guess that I wouldn't design it to focus on "big think" questions. This seems a wonderful way to suggest to students that they can just analyze any issue without learning much first. I'd much rather have students learn the basics, in historical context, understanding the limitations of what they learn and where else the discipline has moved over time. Discussing what should be taught in principles does seem important, recognizing that some of our students will stop without taking any more courses in economics. But, jumping into "big think" questions seems a way of encouraging some students to "talk like an economist" without really knowing much economics.

CONCLUSION

"We believe it is better to have the 'wrong' content taught passionately than the 'right' content taught perfunctorily" (p. 37). Surely, we can do better. We can design an interesting and challenging curriculum and have it taught effectively, which leads to students being excited both about the material and the learning process. I'm not convinced that passion for learning necessarily comes from passionate teachers or discussing "big think" questions. It comes from an appreciation for the value of what is learned, and an understanding of how it can be used to further one's knowledge of the world around us.

19. Overstating the challenges, underestimating the solutions

George Daly

From my perspective – that of an economist/administrator – Colander and McGoldrick's Teagle Report has two principal themes. The first is that there are important flaws in the training provided for economics (and other) majors at many US universities. The second is that the best way to correct this problem is through the recognition and discussion of these problems among faculty members through what the authors term a "bottom up" process. I believe their paper raises important issues and does so in interesting ways. My chief criticism is that, having identified a problem, it tends to misjudge both its seriousness and the ease and appropriate methods of correcting it.

THE PROBLEM

The authors see the training of economics undergraduate majors in US universities as unduly narrow and technical. This is due to an agency problem in which the faculty pursues objectives that are inappropriate to the great majority of the students they teach. Specifically, faculty members want to teach cutting-edge research topics consistent with what they view as the tastes of their professional peers. Reflecting this, the economics curriculum fails to achieve the broad, liberal learning goals the authors see as the major purpose of undergraduate education. Instead, economics majors are often taught a curriculum designed as if most students were desirous of going on to graduate school in economics when, in fact, the vast majority of these students will pursue other career paths for which broad liberal arts training would better prepare them.

While I believe that such an observation has real descriptive validity, it can be overstated. Are, in fact, economics departments turning out majors ill-equipped to deal with the world most of them will enter? I have occasion to chat with a number of Georgetown undergraduates. Most of these students will pursue post-graduate training although very few will select a graduate program in economics. I am struck by how focused they are on their professional futures and how carefully they structure their educational programs in line with this focus. I believe they can identify a "research-oriented" bias in economics or any other major and that they adapt accordingly, whether through taking courses in other social science departments, interdisciplinary courses, or even extracurricular activities. The authors seem sometimes to portray the problem as if the *only* adjustment mechanisms were within the economics curriculum when, in reality, the primary adjustments may well originate elsewhere.

SOLUTIONS

The second half of the paper discusses methods of correcting the imbalance on which they focus. Given the authors' view that the preferences of faculty are the major source of the problem, it seems rather ironic to me that they repeatedly emphasize that all such changes should originate from the voluntary actions of individual departments and faculty members. Thus, in their conclusion they repeat a theme found throughout the paper: "We strongly believe that positive change in any discipline does not come from the top down; it comes from the bottom up, and major change builds on the initiatives of individual schools" (p. 37).

I rather doubt that many economics faculty members in departments that focus primarily on technical skills are under the (mis)impression that the vast majority of their students plan to pursue a PhD in economics or dislike real-world examples and discussion. Rather, I suspect that these economists, like most faculty members, teach what they do because of some combination of belief in the value of their discipline and the rational self-interest they believe to be central to human behavior including, presumably, their own. If this is the case, it seems to me unlikely that these economists can or will be persuaded of the error of their ways simply by the provision of a perspective that differs from their own (and their perceived self-interest), especially given the daunting and glacial politics of curricular change in most universities. In this regard, it is worth recalling that the "Great Books" curriculum instituted by Robert Maynard Hutchins at Chicago was an example of "top down" change.

A related set of reforms proposed by the authors focuses on changing the graduate training provided academic economists to reflect the broadening they believe desirable. While I believe the broadening of undergraduate training in economics is desirable, I am doubtful that changing the nature of graduate training in economics or credentialing requirements is likely to prove easy or an efficient way of achieving it. While it is also desirable for economists to become better versed on issues of public policy or "big think" issues, I am not sure that graduate school is the best place to receive such training. The authors also urge changing the departmental/disciplinary structure of the university, another reform that is difficult for me to envision occurring, especially in the "bottom up" manner they endorse.

My final quibble with the paper is that it tends to implicitly assume that highly specialized and technical academic research makes little, if any, contribution to the undergraduate teaching function because it is neither accessible to nor desired by most undergraduate students. Indeed, a major contribution of the authors is to illuminate the manner in which this distraction may operate: through different curricula, taught in different ways, and for different ends than that which they believe maximizes social welfare.

I feel that publishing research in leading journals, quite apart from its substantive value as "knowledge," signals a key quality of mind and expression of its authors: the ability to participate in a sophisticated dialog among leading thinkers and thus the capability to digest and creatively react to the content of this dialog. This quality, in turn, is a good proxy for long-term teaching viability. Ironically, this perspective suggests that even if, as some critics claim, academic research is worthless drivel, it is nonetheless valuable to the academic enterprise.

SUMMARY

Colander and McGoldrick have done an admirable job of outlining the nature of an important challenge to undergraduate education in the US. Their solutions are in my view more problematic. My hunch is that many of the problems they outline are currently mitigated to some extent, albeit largely outside individual majors. Likewise, I suspect that the reforms they propose are less likely to spring from a "bottom up" dialogue among economists than from "top down" methods in the form of changed reward structures implemented by various chairpersons, deans, and provosts who are motivated by the need to sell an increasingly expensive product in an increasingly competitive marketplace to increasingly demanding clients informed by everything from classroom visits to magazine ratings to RateMyProfessor.com.

20.   How the shifting landscape affects our students

David W. Breneman

David Colander and KimMarie McGoldrick have written a thoughtful and provocative piece on the relationship of the undergraduate major in economics and the goals of liberal education. The question they raise is whether this increasingly popular major, as currently taught, is contributing positively to the goals and objectives of those colleges and universities that embrace the liberal arts tradition and its corresponding philosophy of education. Sadly, the authors conclude that in far too many ways and on far too many campuses, the economics major is not a positive contributor to the breadth and vision espoused by this educational model.

The authors, however, are modest in their hopes for their report, sponsored by the Teagle Foundation as part of a broader project encouraging re-examination of the undergraduate curriculum. They note that the AEA's Committee on Economic Education, when asked to undertake this task, was reluctant to commission a committee report, in part because the economics major appears to be thriving – as measured by enrollments – and thus is not considered ripe for reform. Instead, we have a co-authored essay, designed to spark discussion that might lead to modest but imaginable improvements. In short, the Colander-McGoldrick report is not a bold educational manifesto, but rather a thoughtful analysis of the forces shaping undergraduate education in economics, together with some ideas and suggestions for change. It is a document that one hopes faculty members, department chairs, deans, provosts, and presidents will read with profit, leading, where conditions are right, to educational improvements.

THE ARGUMENT

The basic premise for the report is drawn from the recent work of the Association of American College and Universities that focuses on strengthening liberal education. In a recent publication, *College Learning for the New Global Century*,[1] AAC&U put forth a view of liberal education for the twenty-first century that Colander and McGoldrick adopt as the basis for their work. Two hallmarks are that a liberal education should provide more breadth and less depth, and a perspective that sees liberal education as a way of learning as opposed to learning specific content. Colander and McGoldrick argue that to succeed in the above, a liberal education must instill in students a passion for learning, and that in turn requires faculty who share that passion. The dilemma for the undergraduate major is now established: faculty in the major field are prepared in graduate school for research careers, and thus seek depth as opposed to breadth in their teaching, emphasizing specific content as opposed to a way of learning. Indeed, much of the report focuses on the graduate preparation of faculty and the incentive structure within colleges and universities that influences faculty activity. The story they tell is not a new one, and has led to numerous criticisms of graduate education as focused exclusively on research training, thus failing to prepare people for teaching positions. Faculty with this orientation have no incentive – and often no ability – to teach other than as they have been taught, to focus on small, solvable research questions rather than on the big, unanswerable questions that undergraduates should pursue. This issue is not unique to economics, but as the most technical of the social sciences, is more pronounced in this field than would be the case in history, sociology, anthropology, or political science. In that respect, economics shades closer to the hard sciences than toward the humanities.

A related issue, which Colander and McGoldrick do not explore in detail, is the orphaned state of general education, the first two years of the college curriculum. An institution filled with faculty trained in the disciplines has a difficult time finding faculty who are willing and able to teach engaging lower-division courses that cross disciplinary boundaries, provide breadth of knowledge rather than depth, and that explore what Colander and McGoldrick call the big "unanswerable questions." Most institutions simply do not have such faculty, and thus general education often deteriorates into a series of introductory courses in specific disciplines, designed more for potential majors than for students seeking a broad understanding of the field. In order to prepare students who are liberally educated, one must have a faculty similarly educated, but the process of natural selection that operates in our colleges and universities tends to eliminate such people. Rewards and promotion go to specialists, and liberal education of the young suffers accordingly.

PERSONAL OBSERVATIONS

Several of us who have served as college or university administrators were asked by the authors to comment on their report from that vantage point. In my case, the most relevant part of my experience was the six years I served in the 1980s as president of Kalamazoo College, a private liberal arts college in Michigan. When we hired new faculty, generally at the beginning stage of careers with new PhDs, I made it a point to conduct the final interview before offers were made. My standard question was why the candidate was applying for a position at Kalamazoo College rather than at a university. In some cases, the story would emerge that an undergraduate college was a second choice, that indeed the candidate was primarily interested in research, secondarily in teaching, but that the labor market had not been kind to his or her aspirations. This type of response, hardly likely to bring forth an offer, was usually carefully couched in qualifications and nuance, but underneath the evasive language, the truth would come out. In other cases, a common story was that the candidate had attended either a liberal arts college or an honors college at a state university as an undergraduate, and although he or she had enjoyed the move to graduate school and had experienced success and pleasure at conducting research, still looked back at the undergraduate experience as uniquely valuable and as the type of environment in which to shape a meaningful career. Needless to say, when I found excellent candidates who presented that story, they were almost always the ones I hired. I should note that it is most fortunate that liberal arts colleges are an exceptionally productive source of students who go on to earn the PhD.

I do not want to come across as believing in a simple-minded research versus teaching view of the world, for there are many excellent teachers in research universities and excellent scholars in liberal arts colleges. But the emphasis on how one spends one's time is different in the two settings, and those who have attended both a liberal arts college as undergraduates and a research university for graduate school, know and understand that difference. At Kalamazoo, we always tried to protect the untenured faculty from engaging too deeply in the life of the college at the expense of beginning a research agenda and completing a book or articles drawn from the dissertation. I counseled young faculty that I could not guarantee tenure at Kalamazoo, and thus they must in their own best interest maintain sufficient research activity to be viable candidates for positions elsewhere. But we also made clear that we valued quality teaching highly, and encouraged them to take their teaching very seriously, working on areas of deficiency, and broadening the scope of their areas of teaching competency. Only with faculty motivated in this fashion did I believe that

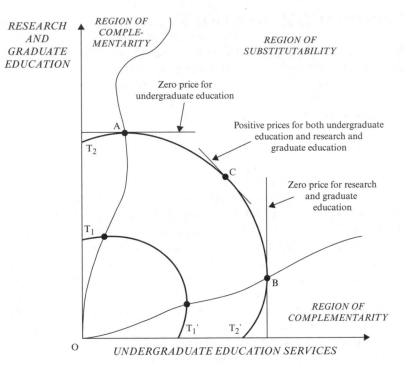

Source: Nerlove, M. (1972). On tuition and the costs of higher education: Prolegomena to a conceptual framework. *Journal of Political Economy*, **80** (3), S205.

Figure 20.1   Combinations of undergraduate education and of research and graduate education showing the regions of complementarity and the region of substitutability

we were being true to the educational promises that we made to students and their families.

My view of the relationship of teaching and research is that presented years ago by Marc Nerlove (1972) in a figure from his paper in the *Journal of Political Economy*, reproduced as Figure 20.1. His argument is that, on a production frontier for an institution producing both undergraduate education and graduate education and research, there are combinations where the activities are complementary and combinations where they are substitutes. My sense is that a good liberal arts college provides incentives to faculty to ensure that the college is operating in the region of complementarity on the right side of the figure, and not in the region of substitutability where research and teaching collide for faculty time. One should also note that the logic of the figure suggests that virtually all universities are operating in the region of substitutability. If that is accurate, the dilemma for producing the highest-quality undergraduate education in a research university is clear.

This discussion prompts another thought from my experience. To the best of my knowledge, the notion of a research liberal arts college was just starting to be floated in the 1980s, and it has now apparently achieved some sort of meaning or reality, as Colander and McGoldrick refer to it several times. When those early discussions were under way, I remember feeling deeply ambivalent about what was intended. A colleague president at the time explained that the most wealthy and most selective liberal arts colleges (Kalamazoo was neither) wanted to compete with the leading research universities for faculty, and that as a result they had to offer similar salaries and working conditions to be successful. As a consequence, teaching loads were being reduced to university levels, and evaluation methods were shifting away from whatever balance between teaching and research had obtained to an increased emphasis on research. While I understood the motivation, that shift seems to set up the core issue that prompted Colander and McGoldrick to write their paper. If faculty at Amherst, Williams, and Oberlin are being held to promotion and tenure standards that are similar to those obtaining at Harvard, Princeton, and Chicago, then how do the colleges attract and retain the type of faculty interested or motivated to teach in the way that the report advocates?

In the 1990s, universities came under considerable pressure to do a better job at undergraduate teaching, and responses have included creation of teaching/learning centers, faculty mentoring programs, and efforts to provide pedagogical instruction to graduate teaching assistants. Nonetheless, a growing chorus of sophisticated external (and internal) critics of higher education has lost sufficient trust in faculty performance that a major move is under way to establish independent measures of student learning. The National Center for Public Policy and Higher Education with which I am associated has produced five biennial reports on state-level performance of higher education during this decade, and we have consistently given the states failing grades for not developing measures of student learning.[2] The Spellings Commission report, *A Test of Leadership: Charting the Future of U.S. Higher Education*, released in 2006, included among its findings that:

> At a time when we need to be increasing the quality of learning outcomes and the economic value of a college education, there are disturbing signs that suggest we are moving in the opposite direction. As a result, the continued ability of American postsecondary institutions to produce informed and skilled citizens who are able to lead and compete in the 21st century global marketplace may soon be in question.[3]

In an opinion piece published in *The Chronicle of Higher Education*, I challenged the leaders of elite colleges and universities not to ignore the findings and arguments of the Spellings Commission, as I feared too many of them were doing. My concern was that if leaders of higher education ignored the criticisms of thoughtful business and political leaders, the result may be actions taken out of anger, such as taxing endowments or attempts to impose tuition caps, that could be severely damaging.[4]

In yet another sign of external concern, regional and specialized accrediting associations are all adding major components to their evaluation tool kits, focused on whether institutions have meaningful ways to assess student learning. Faculty are struggling, and in many cases opposing, these unaccustomed pressures and questions about the quality of their services, but higher education functions in a trust market, and once trust is lost, stringent measures are required to re-establish it. Surely the Teagle Foundation effort is a response, in part, to the criticisms leveled at higher education, and one of the more helpful and positive efforts to bring about improvement in teaching and learning.

COMMENTS ON CHANGES TO CONSIDER

One strand of thinking in the report is an effort to modify traditional doctoral programs so that they include some forms of preparation that are more attuned to the needs of undergraduate students, particularly the vast majority who major in economics with no intention of going on to graduate school in that field. I am reminded of the significant effort made by the Carnegie Corporation of New York in the 1970s to promote a new degree, the Doctor of Arts, which would be a primary teaching degree rather than a research degree. Despite spending millions of dollars to fund universities to create such a degree, the venture was a failure. Regardless of all that was said about the logic of such a degree, it was always viewed by potential graduate students and faculty as a second-class degree, and what rational student would opt for a degree so stigmatized? Similarly, some years ago the University of California tried to create a degree called the Candidate in Philosophy, or CPhil, which if memory serves would be awarded to ABDs to signify the achievement of "all but the dissertation," in the hope that community colleges and other teaching institutions would give its holders credence. Again, this effort to supplement or displace the PhD from its central role in faculty certification failed miserably.

Thus, I am not optimistic that the path to change lies through the graduate schools. A more promising set of ideas lie in the proposals for post-graduate experiences, created in some cases by consortia of liberal

arts colleges that would seek to provide professional development opportunities to broaden the educational vistas of traditionally prepared PhDs.
Ideas such as this one, while not new, are worth considering, as the incentives of the employers (the colleges) can be used to influence the incentives
of their own faculty. Rather than simply preaching about change, such
programs would give concrete shape and substance to the type of teaching
being sought.

Another proposal envisions creating an alternative ranking system to
those such as the US New & World Report, which places heavy emphasis
on research measures in the disciplines. Presumably some way of giving
greater weight to books and essays in general publications would provide
an incentive to faculty to broaden the vision of what counts in the reward
system. Beyond the implausibility that any such ranking would be technically or economically feasible, I would simply note that nothing prevents
individual colleges now from being explicit in promotion and tenure
guidelines regarding what counts. One need not have an external rating
system to implement a system of meaningful price signals that faculty
would understand.

Distinct tracks within the economics major might be a promising way
to broaden the type of teaching provided under that label to undergraduates. Surely all faculty members in economics departments know that
the vast majority of the majors are not going on to doctoral programs in
economics, and thus might benefit from a more liberal-arts-oriented form
of education. A broad undergraduate major in economics should include
more focus on institutions, industrial organization, economic history, and
the history of economic thought than the theoretical approaches provide.
An undergraduate so prepared would be in a position to discuss and
understand the significance of recent moves by the Treasury and Federal
Reserve Board to recapitalize the banking system, knowing in what ways
these moves represent departures from past responsibilities. A focus on
the history of economic thought would move a student close to the history
of philosophy, linking the economic concept of utility, for example, to the
broad tradition of utilitarian thought in political philosophy. Economic
history provides a student with an understanding of the forces and impediments to economic growth, which is highly important for understanding
the evolving nature of a global economy. I have no difficulty imagining
an economics major of enormous interest and relevance, firmly in the
liberal arts tradition, but not necessarily focused on preparing students for
graduate school. It seems to me that nothing stands in the way of such a
curriculum other than the lack of interest of disciplinary faculty.

Many of today's students are committed to volunteer work in the
community, which can engage them in a series of questions regarding

affordable housing, child care, health care, pre-school education, environmental issues, waste disposal, transportation, energy use – the list goes on and on. An understanding of economics is vital to the assessment of policy proposals designed to remedy such concerns, and thus an economics major that involved a strong public policy component would likely have enormous attraction for activist-oriented students. In the new Batten School of Leadership and Public Policy at the University of Virginia we are developing such an undergraduate major, and although few liberal arts colleges have policy schools, such schools are normally staffed by faculty trained in social science fields that are present on liberal arts campuses. Thus, I see no inherent obstacle preventing an enterprising college from mobilizing faculty resources around a public policy major, or certificate program, within the existing curriculum. Skillful packaging of areas of faculty interest could carry such a program a long way toward realization.

The report concludes with several useful thoughts and suggestions for improving the pedagogy of instruction, not a strong point with most economics faculty members. Adoption of any of these practices will depend upon incentives that would motivate individual change. As students bear an ever-larger share of the cost of higher education, they are understandably becoming more demanding in what they expect for their parents' money. Pressure from students may force economists (and other faculty as well) to devote more time and attention to how well they do in the classroom, and how effectively they are able to enhance student learning. Economists, if any group, should understand this effect of market behavior.

CONCLUSION

I have been involved in higher education for more years than I like to acknowledge, as a student, faculty member, and administrator. The issues that Colander and McGoldrick have chosen to tackle are among the most difficult and intractable components of what we do as academics. How we actually perform the day-to-day work of teaching is intensely personal and generally left to the discretion of each faculty member. Colander and McGoldrick are too experienced to advocate wholesale, revolutionary change, but I am glad they have taken on the task of nudging all of us to think more carefully about how well we are serving the undergraduate students of today. In the not-too-distant past, when tuitions were low, and students were not incurring significant debt for their college degrees, it was perhaps understandable that faculty prerogatives and values held sway over the curriculum, but in today's world of high-priced education, we owe our students better than that. Colander and McGoldrick are gently calling us to recognize our moral and civic obligations to provide the best education possible to the young, who are paying substantial sums for it. I commend their thoughtful work, and hope it gains a responsive audience.

NOTES

1. AAC&U (2007).
2. National Center on Public Policy and Higher Education (2000).
3. Commission Appointed by Secretary of Education Margaret Spellings (2006, p. 13).
4. David W. Breneman (2008).

21.   The role of incentives (and culture) in rebalancing the economics major

Bradley W. Bateman

In many ways, I find David and KimMarie's essay in Chapter 1 to be both insightful and helpful. For instance, I think they are smart to begin their examination of how we might better integrate the economics major into a liberal education by suggesting that this is actually a problem that faces all disciplines. In doing so they have correctly identified a problem that exists for every discipline on every liberal arts campus I have visited in the last dozen years; from anthropology to zoology, there is no discipline that currently trains its graduate students to come to a school like Denison or Grinnell and to thrive as a liberal educator. I also think that David and KimMarie are wise to include a discussion of incentives in their report. In my comments, however, I would like to frame the need for those incentives a bit differently by rebalancing the relative demands of liberal education against the demands of the discipline of economics.

Before going any further, I should note that from 1987 until 2007, I was a faculty member in the Department of Economics at Grinnell College. In July 2007, I became the provost at Denison University, where I also have the privilege of an appointment as a professor of economics, but where I have not taught a class. In writing this response to David and KimMarie's report, they agreed that I would work from the original framework of the comments I drafted in May 2007, when I was still a faculty member at Grinnell and several of us met at Middlebury to discuss an earlier draft of their report. Nothing that I have learned at Denison has changed what I believe about the role of the economics major in a liberal education, but in this essay I discuss how I came to my beliefs in the context of my work at Grinnell. Where appropriate, I have added comments about my observations as an administrator at Denison.

During my last several years at Grinnell, I spoke each August to the new faculty as a part of their orientation, and I said each year to this group that every discipline I know of discourages its young from entering undergraduate teaching and from working at liberal arts colleges. When I would say this, the heads of all the new faculty members would bob up and down as they reflected on their own training and the admonitions they received not to ruin their careers by doing the work they had been hired to do at Grinnell. I have now had the same experience at Denison in speaking to the new faculty; they likewise confirm that they were discouraged from seeking the work they are about to begin and certainly were not prepared for doing it while they were in graduate school.

The technical requirements of contemporary literary theory make demands on young graduates in English that are not so different in kind from those made upon young economists. And the structure of rewards within English is virtually the same; they are stacked toward achievement in the discipline and away from "general education" and liberal education. It is nearly as hard to find a new English PhD who wants to teach freshman writing as it is to find a new economics PhD who wants to do it. I think that newly minted graduates in English may be more receptive to a job at a liberal arts college than their graduate professors are to them taking these jobs because their job market is much weaker on the demand side; but you can be sure that the mavens running the graduate programs in English have just as low a regard for a job at a liberal arts college as do the mavens running graduate programs in economics. Thus, the problem that David and KimMarie describe of poor preparation to teach at liberal arts colleges is definitely real, and it occurs across all the disciplines in the arts and sciences, not just in economics.

But despite the poor preparation of most graduate students to teach undergraduates and their virtual complete ignorance of the traditions of liberal education (unless they happen to be a graduate of a liberal arts college), I am not sure that the situation for liberal education is dire. There are many ways to jigger the incentives to help build a professorate of liberal educators and there is lots of "cultural" work that can be done to help you get what you want. If I find a fault in David and KimMarie's report, it is that they focus too much on the incentives and not enough on the "cultural work." In this sense, they are well-trained economists in the neo-classical tradition; they focus on marginal changes and not on the broader questions of how society (in this case the small liberal arts college) is structured. In writing this way, they certainly have a much better chance of being read sympathetically by other economists. However, I am not sure that they have given enough thought to the reality of the fact that a small liberal arts college is not a research university and that even at very good liberal arts colleges (where many of the faculty publish peer-reviewed scholarship) the terms of employment are simply different than they are at a research university and the demands on the faculty must, accordingly, be different. In short, I think that David and KimMarie coddle their colleagues a little and (until the very end of the report) fail to take seriously enough the reality that no matter what kind of research trajectory one is on at a liberal arts college, one has responsibilities to engage broad questions, help develop students' critical thinking skills, and work with them to become better writers. These three broad categories of work that I have described are the responsibility of every liberal educator in every discipline, including economists. If economists do not want to do that work, they need to look for employment at a different kind of institution. It is perfectly fine to teach at a research university, a technical college, or a business school; but if you want to be employed at a liberal arts college, then you need to do the work of a liberal educator.

But, of course, it is impossible to ensure that the work at hand gets done without a good incentive structure, and David and KimMarie point out correctly that one way that the incentives can be structured is in the hiring, tenure, and promotion policies of a college. This involves a complicated mix of "cultural work" and incentives. For instance, to be hired, you can require that people be interviewed by people in other disciplines and these people from outside the discipline can report on the candidate's suitability to teach in a liberal arts college. This helps a college to avoid the most egregious mistakes (and also builds cross-disciplinary dialogue about what it means to be teaching at a liberal arts college). There are also good small liberal arts colleges where the department does not prepare the tenure dossier. This is done at some schools by the individual, sometimes with a letter from the department, sometimes without. Such a structure means that one's letters of support and evaluation can come from people who are not in your own discipline. Such a structure guarantees that the department's needs are not weighted more heavily than the college's in the decisions that people make about their courses and research. (Neither Denison nor Grinnell do this, but I have been on campuses where it is the practice and I can attest that it creates economists who are very different than the ones described by David and KimMarie.)

At Grinnell, we were able to weed out most of our job applicants simply by placing a requirement in the advertisement that they include a statement about their teaching philosophy. Some did not even bother to include the statement we requested. The majority of those who did include it did not say anything that was compelling. But while this practice indicates that there are lots of job candidates that would never make it through the initial screening at Grinnell, there were still always people in the applicant pool who were interested in the positions and who showed promise.

Still, I share David and KimMarie's concern that many (most) graduate programs do not produce people who are prepared to be good undergraduate teachers. Frankly, I think that most of the people who run graduate programs are very parochial in their approach to the training of economists; they only seem to want to prepare people who are just like themselves, rather than the people that the market is looking for. Sometimes I suspect that most of those who teach in graduate programs are so enamored of the power of stories about division of labor and specialization, that they lose sight of the fact that most of their graduates, who will enter very specialized niches in a highly segmented market for PhD economists, will not do what they themselves do for a living. Many graduate professors in economics do not seem to understand that their students are in training to do something that is not being a professor at a research university.

After all, PhD economists do not all do the same thing; and the training that would prepare one to work at Stanford and Harvard may not be the training that would be best to prepare you for a career at Hope College or Earlham College. Yet, the economists at Hope and Earlham are also PhD economists and their work (and the preparation to do it) deserves serious attention. If any graduate program would specialize in the production of graduates in economic history and the history of economic thought, and they also provided some serious training in the teaching of writing, their graduates would be gobbled up in the liberal arts college market. Work in either of these fields gives one a wide understanding of the discipline (or of history) that provides a good basis for the kind of experience that one is likely to have teaching in a liberal arts college where a broad vision of human knowledge is indispensable. However, we could even forget the strictures I have placed here on the graduate student's field choices; if any graduate program worked seriously to prepare people to teach writing and critical thinking, their graduates would also be gobbled up by the many liberal arts colleges in the market every year. (Are there more new jobs each year at the top 20 graduate programs, or at the small liberal arts colleges?) How many graduate programs talk seriously to their students about any career other than one at another graduate program? How many graduate programs offer thoughtful and intentional preparation for the work that their graduates who will come to Denison or Grinnell will do? It's not many.

Because the people in most disciplines are not well prepared to teach at a place like Denison or Grinnell, we have to do a lot of "cultural work" to help them make the transition to the world where they are now working. In economists' lingo, we have to clean up the mess created by the market failure in the market for liberal arts college professors. Since the failures occur on the supply side, we have to clean them up on the demand side. At Grinnell, they run an orientation program every year for new faculty in which we have workshops on what a good undergraduate syllabus looks like, and they have them meet with students who talk about what they experience in the classroom and what differentiates a good from a bad classroom experience. They also run a series of springtime workshops every year for all the faculty to help prepare them to teach the freshman writing course. EVERY faculty member, in every discipline, must teach the freshman tutorial (not every year) and so they provide preparation for all of them. They also run summer workshops in teaching writing and in teaching oral communication skills. These many workshops are the places where they teach people to be liberal educators. Attendance is strong, participation is robust, and the participants are from all the disciplines.

A crucial piece of ensuring a student's liberal education also comes through advising. At Grinnell, they do not have any distribution requirements, believing instead that the acquisition of a liberal education should come through a process of dialogue between the adviser and the student about the meanings and purposes of liberal education. Their students should study chemistry not because it is a box they can tick off on the natural science requirement, but because they understand, for instance, that they will never be able to participate seriously in the democratic solutions to environmental problems if they cannot adjudicate between good science and bad. To cut to the quick, they have incentive structures in place that encourage this advising work, and we also do the "cultural work" necessary to support it with a pair of faculty workshops they run annually: one on advising and mentoring and one on articulating the meaning(s) of liberal education.

How much of this kind of cultural work takes place on other campuses, I cannot be sure. But I have visited many campuses in this decade to help spread some of these best practices and I believe that most economists at liberal arts colleges come to understand fairly quickly that they are working in a different environment than the one in which they attended graduate school. David and KimMarie do not really focus in their report on the kind of cultural work I have described, preferring instead to situate the economists at liberal arts colleges as if they have property rights to function in the limited way they were trained in graduate school rather than as liberal educators, and that they can only be moved away from that position reluctantly and with great effort. I have no doubt that there is resistance by some economists to engaging in the full work of being a liberal educator, but my own experience at two very good liberal arts colleges (and as a visitor at several others) is that the kind of intellectual arrogance and refusal to fully engage liberal education that David and KimMarie describe is not the case everywhere, not even at all top liberal arts colleges with "publishing faculty."

I also would like to challenge David and KimMarie's description of disciplinary work as involving "little-think questions." Much of the work done by economists involves very "big-think questions." The whole basis

for applied microeconomic analysis, for instance, depends on a sophisticated philosophical argument about the nature and primacy of individual
choice in describing desirable policies. In fact, such analysis is completely
and utterly utilitarian and it has no claim on our attention except that the
superstructure of that philosophical argument has been carefully worked
out through several generations of philosopher-economists. If one chooses
not to ignore that philosophical content, one can easily question the
assumptions of neo-classical economics and its descriptive and normative
content; the possibility of those questions derives, for instance, from the
fact that it involves a "big-think question" to undertake a benefit–cost
analysis of a dam project in a developing nation and report out the results
of that analysis in isolation from other ethical considerations. All economists should be well-versed in the philosophical basis for applied microeconomic analysis and all economists should share those underpinnings
with their students. If they don't, they are not doing their job. To be sure, it
takes a lot of course work and a lot of practice to be able to do applied microeconomic analysis well; it could take months (or years) of work to learn the
techniques and to be able to use them well. One could (and many do) spend
considerable resources on gaining this technical proficiency without ever
having to deal explicitly with the philosophical questions that underpin the
work. But the fact remains that their work makes no claim on our serious
attention without its philosophical underpinnings. And that philosophical underpinning provides an easy means for any economist working as a
liberal educator to engage her students in "big-think questions."

Likewise, applied macroeconomic analysis involves many "big-think
questions." This essay was being revised during the first two weeks of
October 2008, when the credit markets around the world were on the brink
of freezing up as confidence collapsed in virtually all financial institutions.
One can surely spend years mastering the technical tools for analyzing
financial markets and not have to face the "big-think questions" implicit
in one's work. But the fact remains that there are "big-think questions"
that underpin the work we do in monetary economics and those are always
available for discussion and use in an undergraduate economics class. As
this essay is being written, most citizens of the world consider it to be a
"big-think question" what the nature and limits of responsible regulation
are in financial markets.

As against David and KimMarie's position, I would say that the
methodologies in virtually all disciplines, from English and economics to
biology, reduce frontier research to very small questions. But that doesn't
mean that the "big-think questions" have disappeared or cannot be taught
as a part of an undergraduate economics class. It is the methodologies
that limit an individual's research project and reduce it to answering only

small questions; the disciplines still strive to provide guidance in exploring "big-think questions".

So just what would a good economics department in a liberal arts college offer in the curriculum? What would be available in the set of courses that majors have access to that would also be of value to non-majors who are seeking a liberal education? A good one-semester introductory class should be available for all undergraduates. We should offer classes in international trade and environmental economics that can be taken by people who have taken the one-semester course in introductory economics. We should have a good history of economic thought course available that philosophy majors, English majors, and biology majors can take as cognates to the work they do in more depth in those majors. The courses offered in an economics major are valuable parts of a liberal education, but I think we can make this contribution largely through the courses we already teach and that fit well into a good major. A good economics major will perforce make a strong contribution to liberal education.

Ultimately, I think that what KimMarie and David have identified in their paper is largely a problem of poor economic education at the graduate level. It is a very personal observation and somewhat anecdotal, but I have visited many campuses and talked with many economics students and economics professors, and I believe that many economists at research universities are not doing the work that Lee Hansen and others suggest is necessary for a really robust and worthwhile undergraduate education in economics. How many teach writing courses, real writing courses in which we work with drafting, editing, and revising a piece of student work? How many economists teaching at research universities work with their undergraduate students on developing the skills of preparing a briefing on some economic policy issue, or on finding original source material to support an argument? I suspect that the number is not what it should be and I think that many of our tribe hide behind arguments about specialization and division of labor to avoid the fact that these skills need to be developed in all good undergraduate economics courses and integrated into our teaching. But if poorly educated graduate students are not told the truth about what will be expected of them when they seek employment as liberal educators and are not given opportunities as graduate students to develop the skills they will need to do that work, then it will remain necessary for small liberal arts colleges to continue to do triage to repair the market failure that exists on the supply side of the market for undergraduate economic educators. But the truth is, the need to do this for economists is not so different than it is for graduates in any other graduate discipline.

PART 6

Views from the students

22. What economics majors think of the economics major

Steven Jones, Eric Hoest, Richie Fuld, Mahesh Dahal, and David Colander[1]

Students have a unique perspective on the economics major, and in some ways are in the best position to judge it. This chapter tries to tap into their collective mind set. It reports the results of two surveys of economics majors at various undergraduate institutions across the country. One survey was a randomized survey of economics majors at all types of undergraduate institutions.[2] The second survey was a more directed survey of economics majors at 11 top research liberal arts colleges.[3] Combined, the surveys give a good sense of what students think of the economics major.[4]

This report builds on earlier work, which looked at the economics major from a number of perspectives.[5] Some earlier works include Brasfield et al. (1996), which showed that colleges with business programs reported less of a decline in economics majors in the 1990s than other colleges. Salemi and Eubanks (1996) developed the discouraged-business-major hypothesis, which demonstrated that many students at colleges with restricted-entry business programs took economics as a second choice, a point that is reinforced by results from our surveys. However, none of these studies have specifically tried to address the particular questions that are the focus of this report, although they have looked at relevant issues. Additionally, studies that contain information from other majors can provide an important context for many of the findings in this report.

The organization of this chapter is as follows: for each aspect of the economics major, we first discuss the overall results from the survey; then we contrast responses of sub-groups of the survey where they seemed sufficiently different to warrant discussion, or did not differ where we expected them to differ. These sub-groups include state colleges, liberal arts colleges, colleges with or without business programs, colleges with restricted-entry or unrestricted-entry business programs, and men and women. Finally, we consider the responses from the research liberal arts college survey to questions that are not present in the larger survey.

HOW IS THE ECONOMICS MAJOR PERFORMING OVERALL?

To find out how the economics major is succeeding, we asked students how satisfied they were with the major. Overall, the economics major is succeeding reasonably well, as can be seen in Figure 22.1. In response to the question, "How satisfied are you with the economics major?," overall 78 percent of students responded that they were highly satisfied or satisfied with the major. Figure 22.1 also shows satisfaction levels broken down into state colleges, randomly selected liberal arts colleges, and research liberal arts colleges. As can be seen, students at randomly selected liberal arts colleges were significantly more satisfied than students at both state and research liberal arts colleges.[6]

We suspected that a key reason for the differences in satisfaction levels across these groupings of colleges was the presence or lack of business programs of differing degrees of selectivity.[7] In Figure 22.2, we compare satisfaction levels at colleges with different types of business programs, and without any business programs, in order to identify the effect of business programs. A much higher percentage of students were very satisfied with the economics major at colleges with unrestricted-entry business programs as compared with colleges with a restricted-entry business program. This

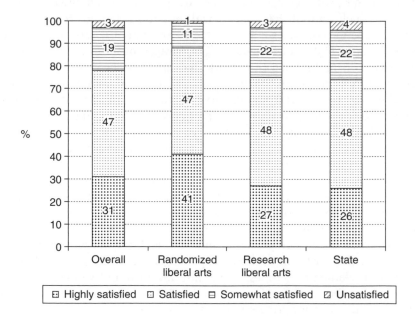

Figure 22.1   Student satisfaction with the major

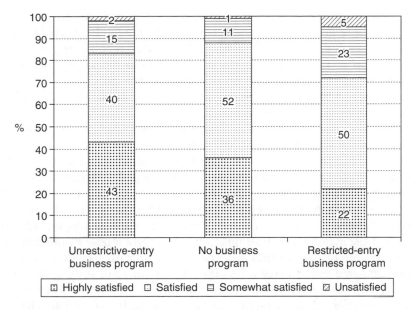

Figure 22.2   Student satisfaction with the major (business school comparisons)

is logical because many students at colleges with a restricted-entry business program may have taken the economics major as an alternative to
the business program they could not get into, and therefore would not be
as satisfied because it is not the track they would have chosen ideally. As
the business program increases in selectivity, more students will become
economics majors who actually do not want to be economics majors. At
colleges with unrestricted-entry business programs, students who want to
study business, but choose to take economics because it is the closest to
business, shouldn't be present, and thus these colleges have the highest
percentage of highly satisfied students.

It should be noted that the percentage of very satisfied students at colleges with unrestricted-entry business programs was also higher than the
percentage for all students, and more specifically for colleges with no
business programs and research liberal arts colleges. These data suggest
that the presence of an unrestricted-entry business program has a positive
impact on the satisfaction levels of economics majors. When such programs exist, the economics major is not forced to balance both the goals
of students who would rather be in business programs with the goals of
students who prefer to study economics as opposed to business; therefore
the economics major can more easily suit all of its students' demands. We

also suspect that the presence of business majors accounts for some of the difference in satisfaction levels between the randomly selected liberal arts colleges and research liberal arts colleges, since no business programs are present at the research liberal arts colleges in the survey but some randomly selected liberal colleges do have business programs. However, satisfaction levels at research liberal arts colleges are still lower than other colleges without business programs.[8]

An additional measure of the success of the major can be obtained by looking at student satisfaction levels by class. An increase in student satisfaction levels as students progress from freshman to senior year may indicate that the economics major is exceeding the expectations they had for the major when they began it. Constant satisfaction levels may indicate that students are achieving exactly what they expected from the major. However, the results actually point to the third possibility, indicating that the major is not meeting students' expectations. The differences, however, are relatively small. One percent of sophomores were unsatisfied compared with 3 percent for juniors and 4 percent for seniors. This increase in dissatisfaction levels may be due to students' expectations being too high. Also, sophomores usually have the option to change majors and/or they have only just declared their major. Hence, it would be expected that declared sophomore economics majors would have higher satisfaction levels because, otherwise, they would not have declared their major yet.

THE RELEVANCE OF THE MAJOR TO FUTURE CAREERS

Another question on the survey asked students how relevant they felt the skills and information they learned in the economics major were to their likely career. As can be seen in Figure 22.3, 28 percent of students feel the skills and information in the economics major are highly relevant to their careers and the majority of students feel the skills and information they learn in the economics major are somewhat relevant to their careers. Additionally, 19 percent of students responded that the job-training aspect of the economics major was very important, and 55 percent of students said that the job-training aspect of the economics major was somewhat important.

As can be seen in Figure 22.3, fewer students at research liberal arts colleges feel that the skills and information they learn in the economics major are relevant to their career. Nineteen percent of students at research liberal arts colleges reported that the skills they learned in the economics major were not very relevant, or almost irrelevant, to their likely careers

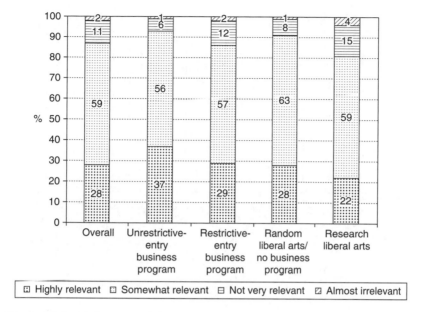

Figure 22.3   Relevance of the economics major

compared with 9 percent at randomly selected liberal arts colleges without business programs.[9] The reasons for this discrepancy are unclear, but may simply be due to higher technical demands and expectations of students at research liberal arts colleges.

Figure 22.3 also shows that fewer students at colleges with restricted-entry business programs view the skills and information they learn in the economics major as relevant to their career. Fourteen percent of economics majors responded that the skills and information learned in the economics major are not very relevant or almost irrelevant to their likely careers as compared with 7 percent at colleges with unrestricted-entry business programs. This percentage was 9 percent at colleges without business programs.[10] The likely reason for this difference is the presence of students at colleges with restricted-entry business programs who would rather be in the business program and therefore do not find the economics major to be very relevant, at least compared with the business program.

HOW HARD IS THE ECONOMICS MAJOR?

Another question asked of students was "What is your perception of the difficulty of the following majors?"[11] The economics major was considered

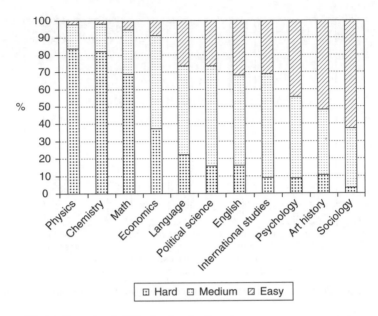

Figure 22.4   Perceived difficulty level of majors

hard by over one-third of students, 37 percent, and medium by the majority of students, 54 percent. Only 9 percent of students considered the major
easy. Figure 22.4 contrasts these views with economics majors' views of
the other majors. The social sciences and the humanities were considered
significantly easier, and the natural sciences and math were considered significantly harder. This suggests to us that the economics major has found
a balance in terms of analytic difficulty and general understanding, as
compared with the natural sciences and mathematics on the one side and
sociology, art history, and psychology on the other.

Students generally considered the majors more difficult at liberal arts
colleges than at state colleges. The difference is most pronounced in economics, considered hard by 25 percent of state college students compared
with 40 percent of students at liberal arts colleges. At research liberal arts
colleges, the major was considered even harder; 44 percent of students
considered the economics major hard.

Part of this discrepancy may be attributed to business programs, especially restricted-entry business programs, which are only present at state
colleges in this survey. At colleges with restricted-entry business programs,
only 23 percent of students rated the economics major hard, whereas at
colleges with unrestricted-entry business programs, 37 percent of students rated the economics major hard. The percentages for colleges with

unrestricted-entry business programs are almost completely equal to that of students overall. The reduction in perception of difficulty found at colleges with restricted-entry business programs may be due to the existence of a business program that is considered more difficult because it is harder to get into, or the economics major may actually be easier at these colleges because it has to develop a program for students who did not get into the business program, but who wanted to, and for students who prefer to study economics for its own sake.

WHAT DO STUDENTS SEE THEMSELVES AS LEARNING IN THE MAJOR?

One of the questions gave students a list of the five skills and knowledge categories from Figure 22.5 and asked them to state whether or not they had learned each of them in the economics major.[12] As can be seen in the figure, the highest percentage of students felt that they have learned the economic way of thinking, while economic literature appears to receive the least focus in the major.

Figure 22.6 compares responses across different types of colleges. As you can see, students report lower levels of learning in these categories

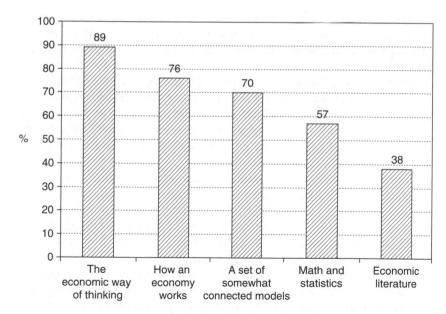

Figure 22.5   What have students learned in the economics major?

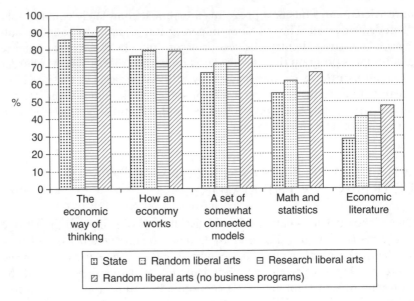

Figure 22.6   What have students learned in the economics major? (School comparisons)

at state colleges than at liberal arts colleges. Economic literature is the most lacking at state colleges, 28 percent, compared with 41 percent at randomly selected liberal arts colleges and 43 percent at research liberal arts colleges.

Figure 22.6 also shows that students at randomly selected liberal arts colleges from the larger survey felt that the major was more successful than did students at research liberal arts colleges at teaching these specific economic skills except for economic literature. Interestingly, if liberal arts colleges with business programs are factored out, the randomly selected liberal arts colleges in the larger survey score higher than research liberal arts colleges in all categories including economic literature. Figure 22.6 illustrates these discrepancies.

When asked what changes they would make to the economics major if they could, 63 percent of students responded that they want more discussion of real-world issues; 53 percent of students wanted more discussion of business-relevant issues.[13] A higher percentage of students who picked more discussion of business-relevant issues also picked more discussion of real-world issues, 67 percent, and vice versa, 57 percent. Although the increase is relatively small, it demonstrates that some students may view business-related courses as dealing with the real world.

WHY DO STUDENTS BECOME ECONOMICS MAJORS?[14]

The majority of students, 52 percent, became economics majors because they did well in early courses and found it interesting. The least selected reason was that the economics major was the closest to a business major; 25 percent of students stated this reason. The overall responses are presented in Figure 22.7.[15]

In general, students at both state colleges and liberal arts colleges chose to become economics majors for the same reasons. However, there is one glaring exception. Forty-seven percent of students at liberal arts colleges chose the economics major because it offers the best job opportunities, while only 18 percent of state college students chose the economics major for the same reason. This is most likely due to the fact that state colleges offer business programs that are viewed as better for getting a job than economics. In fact, all the state colleges in this survey have a business program. Liberal arts colleges, on the other hand, often have no other track that students feel logically connects to business.

Figure 22.7 also shows that students' reasons for becoming economics majors are different at research liberal arts colleges than at the randomly selected liberal arts colleges in the large survey. Students at research liberal arts colleges chose the economics major most often because it provides the best job opportunities, and relative to students at liberal arts colleges in the larger survey, more students chose the economics major because it was closest to a business major. In this instance, the discrepancy between

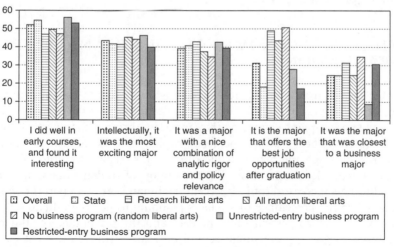

Figure 22.7   Reasons for choosing an economics major

research liberal arts colleges and randomly selected liberal arts colleges can be partially attributed to the presence of business programs at some of the randomly selected liberal arts colleges.

As can be seen in Figure 22.7, only 9 percent of students at colleges with unrestricted-entry business programs chose the economics major because of its closeness to business compared with 31 percent at colleges with restricted-entry business programs. Students at colleges with unrestricted-entry business programs would not be expected to take economics if they wanted to study business because they could simply attend the business school. At colleges with restricted-entry business programs, students may not be able to get into the business program, and hence economics can become a backup major.

It should be noted that when comparing unrestricted-entry business program colleges to restricted-entry business program colleges, all of the percentages for reasons for becoming an economics major decline, except for the business major reason, which increases. This decline reinforces the conjecture that students are taking economics as a backup to the business programs they could not get into rather than because of other reasons. In fact, several students even stated under "other" reasons that they majored in economics because they did not get into the business program.

Additionally, colleges without any business program had a relatively high percentage of students who took economics because of its closeness to business, 35 percent, and the highest percentage of respondents became economics majors because it offers the best job opportunities, 51 percent.[16] The other three reasons were less common among students at colleges without business programs.

WHAT ARE ECONOMICS MAJORS' PLANS AFTER GRADUATION?

In the larger survey, the highest percentage of students plan to work in business after graduation. What is more interesting than the overall results is how student plans change as they progress through the major. Figure 22.8 illustrates how students increasingly plan to work in business as they progress through the major, while other plans, especially graduate and professional schools, diminish. The percentage of students planning to go into business increases from 21 percent freshman year to 43 percent senior year, while the percentage of students planning to go to graduate school decreases from 26 percent to 11 percent and the percentage of students planning to go to professional school decreases from 26 percent to 14 percent.[17] In fact only about 4 percent of economics majors actually go

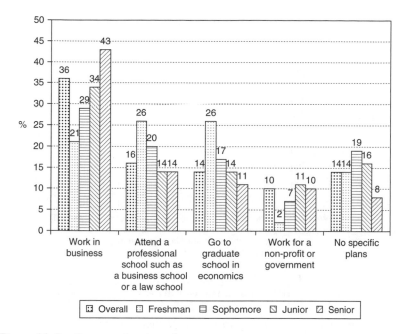

Figure 22.8   Post-graduation plans

on to graduate school, so even in their senior year more than two times as many students are considering graduate schools than actually go.[18]

Comparing different types of colleges shows that state college economics majors have a lower percentage of students who plan to go into business, 31 percent, compared with 41 percent for randomly selected liberal arts colleges. Research liberal arts colleges have an even higher percentage, 55 percent. For all other post-graduation plans, the order is reversed as can be seen in Figure 22.9. Because all of the state colleges have a business program, it is to be expected that many students who want to go into business will be directed towards the business programs, leaving a higher percentage of students focused on other plans such as graduate school. However, the percentage of students planning to go into business at state colleges is still high, showing that business programs do not attract all business-oriented students from the economics major. Also, if the business programs are restricted-entry at state colleges and limit enrollment, some students interested in business may still have taken economics because they could not get into the business program.

Interestingly, the presence of business programs does not appear to have a demonstrable influence on post-graduation plans for students at randomly selected liberal arts colleges, since little change occurred when

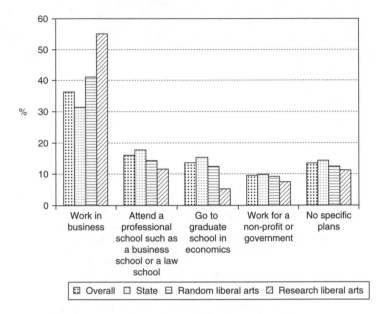

Figure 22.9   Post-graduation plans (school comparisons)

liberal arts colleges with business programs were removed.[19] Compared with randomly selected liberal arts college students, research liberal arts economics majors have a greater focus on business and a lesser focus on graduate studies and all other post-graduation plans whether or not colleges with business programs are eliminated from the randomly selected liberal arts colleges. The difference therefore must have something to do with the nature of research liberal arts colleges and the randomly selected liberal arts colleges rather than the effect of business programs. The results are shown in Figure 22.9.

HOW IS THE MAJOR CONTRIBUTING TO THE GOALS OF A LIBERAL EDUCATION?

In his book, *Our Underachieving Colleges* (2006), Derek Bok discusses eight goals that students should be achieving in their four years at college. Figure 22.10 shows how well students felt the economics major is achieving those goals.[20] As you can see, the economics major is most successful at achieving the goals of critical thinking and living in a more global society, and least successful at achieving the goals of moral reasoning and living with diversity.

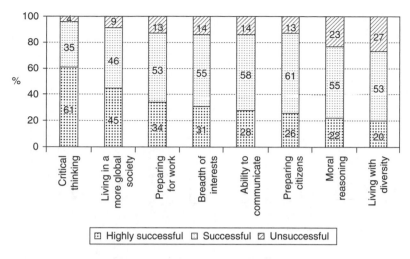

□ Highly successful □ Successful ▨ Unsuccessful

Figure 22.10   Derek Bok's eight goals

We also asked students whether they felt the economics major's focus on these goals should be changed.[21] Figure 22.11 illustrates that students did not view moral reasoning and living with diversity as important since they had the two lowest percentages of students who wanted to increase the focus on these two goals and the two highest percentages of students who wanted to decrease the focus. According to students, preparing for work and the ability to communicate require the greatest increase in focus.

By compiling the information from Figures 22.10 and 22.11, we can see that critical thinking and living in a more global society are in students' opinions the most successful and possibly important goals. Although these two goals were considered the most successful, a relatively large number of students still want to increase focus on both goals. Also, students feel that the economics major is struggling to achieve the ability to communicate goal, and that this goal needs to receive a much stronger focus.

The economics major is generally considered less successful by students at achieving the eight basic goals of an undergraduate education at state colleges than it is at randomly selected liberal arts colleges.[22] Living with diversity, which was the least important goal, is the only exception. Twenty-two percent of students considered it unsuccessful at state colleges, compared with 28 percent at randomly selected liberal arts colleges. Students at state colleges also want to increase the focus on all eight goals more than students at randomly selected liberal arts colleges. When compared with responses of students at colleges with an unrestricted-entry business program, a larger percentage of students at colleges with a

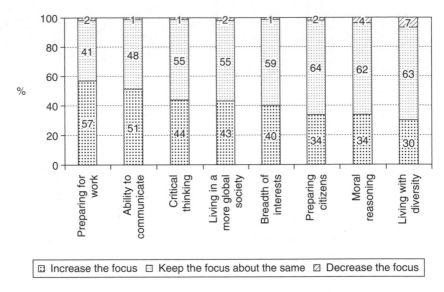

Figure 22.11   Changing focus on Derek Bok's eight goals

restricted-entry business program report the economics major to be unsuccessful at achieving all eight goals.[23]

GENDER DIFFERENCES

Figure 22.12 shows the overall ratio of men to women respondents as well as a breakdown of the data by college type and types of business program. As you can see, state colleges have a higher percentage of men than randomly selected liberal arts colleges, but research liberal arts colleges actually have the highest percentage of men when all-women's colleges are removed. Colleges with business programs have a higher percentage of men, and of those colleges, colleges with restricted-entry business programs have an even higher percentage of men.

Relative to men, women feel that they have learned less economic literature and more math and statistics. Thirty-one percent of women report learning economic literature and 61 percent report learning math and statistics while the numbers are 37 percent and 56 percent for men respectively.[24] The fact that a larger ratio of the women are at liberal arts colleges may help to explain the difference for math and statistics, but this possibility fails to address the discrepancy in economic literature learning, which has a higher percentage at liberal arts colleges.

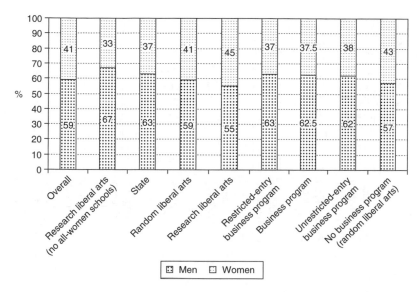

Figure 22.12   Gender ratios by institutional category

Additionally, we found that while men and women were in general agreement on what goals the economics major is achieving, they disagree on what goals the major should achieve. While preparing for work and ability to communicate are considered important to both sexes, men tend to favor a stronger focus on critical thinking while women favor a stronger focus on living in a global society, breadth of interests, and living with diversity. Figure 22.13 shows the data for men and women.

HOW IS THE ECONOMICS MAJOR PERFORMING AT RESEARCH LIBERAL ARTS COLLEGES? QUESTIONS FROM THE SMALLER SURVEY

The survey of research liberal arts colleges contained some questions not present in the larger survey. The additional questions provide deeper insight into the economics major's situation at research liberal arts colleges.

One of those questions was how successful economics majors felt that their liberal arts education (rather than just their economics major education) was at achieving Derek Bok's eight goals. A comparison of student responses to this question and the question regarding the economics major's success in achieving these goals shows where the economics major contribute to a liberal arts education. The economics major makes its

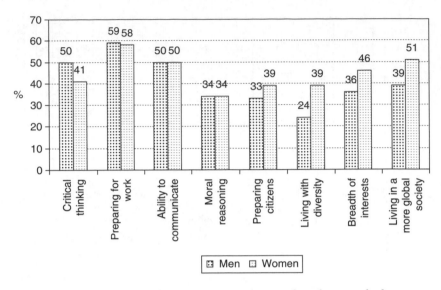

Figure 22.13   Gender differences in perceptions of goals in need of an increase in focus

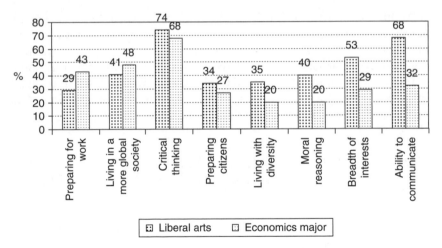

Figure 22.14   Major's success in achieving liberal arts goals (% who view as highly successful)

strongest contribution to the goals of preparing for work and living in a global society. It makes the weakest contribution to the goals of moral reasoning, ability to communicate, and breadth of interests. The results are shown in Figure 22.14.

Because research liberal arts colleges do not offer a business program, a number of their majors see the economics major as the closest to a business major, and take it as an ersatz major, not as a true choice. To discern the size of this group, we asked a couple of questions.

The first question explored how students who were interested in business ended up at these colleges that have no business major.[25] Fifty percent of research liberal arts students responded that before they chose to attend a college, they did not think about whether or not the college offered business-related courses, and 34 percent of students responded that a college's offerings or lack of offerings of business-related courses were not a significant factor in their choice of college. These numbers indicate that most students picked their college based on other criteria than the match of the courses it offered to their interests.

Only 37 percent of students indicated that they chose their particular college because it was a liberal arts college and they were not especially interested in business-related courses. These students are most likely to be those who became economics majors because of an interest in economics rather than business. The 27 percent of students who responded that if they had thought about it they would have preferred a college that offered more business-related courses, are the ones who are most likely to be taking economics as an ersatz business major. An additional explanation for how students interested in business ended up at these research liberal arts colleges is simply that their interests changed while in college.

Another question asked students if they would have been interested in a business-friendly math or science major if it existed.[26] Thirty-eight percent of students who considered being a natural science major stated that they would be interested in such a major, and 32 percent of students stated that they might be interested.[27] Only 30 percent of students who considered natural sciences responded that they would not consider such a major.

Another question directed at the same issue asked students if they would be interested in a "leadership" major designed to give students a broad liberal background in a variety of fields.[28] Thirty-one percent of students said they would be interested in such a "leadership" major, while 41 percent of students said they would not be interested.

The last question on the smaller survey asked students if they would still be economics majors if they found out that employers preferred the aforementioned leadership major. Twenty-five percent of students responded that they would not remain economics majors. This percentage captures the students who are most likely taking economics as an ersatz business major. Thirty-three percent of respondents stated that they would remain economics majors even if they found out that employers preferred leadership majors. This percentage probably represents majors who have a genuine interest in economics.

Combined, the preceding responses show that at research liberal arts colleges between a quarter and a third of students are taking economics as an ersatz business major, whereas about a third of economics majors are strongly interested in economics for its own sake. Additionally, students in the middle group probably lean towards business since 65 percent of students responded that they want an increase in the number of business-oriented courses.[29] This number shows that even students who do not want an entire business major still want more preparation for the world of business.

CONCLUDING REMARKS

There are a number of general conclusions that can be drawn from these surveys. The first is a positive one: overall, the economics major is succeeding. Most students are generally satisfied with the major. They perceive the major to be relatively challenging, and they see the economics major as generally relevant to their future careers. For the most part, economics majors see the economics major as making contributions to the broader liberal education agenda, primarily in the areas of critical thinking, living in a more global society and preparing for work.

The economics major does, however, face challenges and questions about its contribution to a broader liberal education. Its contribution to knowledge of its own literature is smaller than one might expect from a major, and its contribution to achieving a proficiency in communication skills is small. Programs may want to reflect on that result and modify the major to provide better training in that area.

How well the major is satisfying students depends on the nature of the college. Economics majors at liberal arts colleges perceive the economics major to be more satisfying and challenging than do economics majors at state colleges; they report learning more than do students at state colleges. Additionally, economics majors at randomly selected liberal arts colleges report being more satisfied with the major than do economics majors at research liberal arts colleges. Research liberal arts college economics majors find the major more challenging, but not in a way that they feel contributes to their learning, since they report learning less than do students at randomly selected liberal arts colleges. These differences may reflect the tension between the more technical research interests of the faculty, which are best suited to preparing students for further study in economics, and the broader business and real-world relevant interests of over half their majors.

Students in programs that had an alternative business-oriented option that students could choose were more satisfied with the economics major. At these colleges students felt the major was more relevant and challenging, and that they were learning more. The problem that research liberal arts colleges face in meeting the desires of two different groups of students is even more pronounced for state colleges with a restricted-entry business program. Satisfaction levels at these colleges were lower than at all other colleges, and students felt that they were learning less than students at the other colleges.

These programs without a viable business-oriented alternative for students may want to consider institutional changes, such as creating multiple tracks within the major, or having other majors besides economics become more business-friendly. Such changes might create a better match between what that portion of the students are looking for in a major, and what they are getting.

NOTES

1. Steven Jones compiled and drafted the report as part of his CAJ Research Assistant position at Middlebury College. Eric Hoest and Richie Fuld together with David Colander created and administered the two surveys as a project for Professor Colander's senior seminar. Together with Mahesh Dahal, they began analysis of the survey responses. David Colander oversaw the administration of the surveys and guided the writing and editing of the report.
2. Every eighth four-year undergraduate instructional program generated by Carnegie Classifications was selected (82 colleges in total), and e-mails were sent to economics department chairs requesting that they forward the electronic survey on to their majors. For those colleges that did not respond, a second and third e-mail was sent, but economics majors from some colleges nonetheless did not participate. From those institutions that did forward the electronic survey to their majors, a total of 1072 students from 38 institutions participated; 515 of those students attend state colleges, and 555 students attend liberal arts colleges; two students did not indicate their college.
3. In this report, these colleges are referred to as "research liberal arts" colleges because their faculty are heavily evaluated on the basis of research and are given lower teaching loads to accommodate their doing research. Additionally, these colleges are all listed amongst the top 20 liberal arts colleges. The participating colleges were Bates, Colby, Colgate, Grinnell, Hamilton, Middlebury, Mt. Holyoke, Vassar, Wellesley, Wesleyan, and Williams. This second survey included the questions in the randomly selected survey, but also a number of other questions; 666 students participated in this survey.
4. We combine the results of the two surveys unless otherwise noted. We do not combine the two surveys when research liberal arts colleges provide a large enough discrepancy that they would substantially change the results.
5. Relevant sources include Siegfried et al. (1991b), Brasfield et al. (1996), Conrad (1996), Salemi and Eubanks (1996), Willis and Pieper (1996), and Allgood et al. (2004).
6. The randomly selected liberal arts colleges include some colleges that can be considered research liberal arts colleges, namely Pomona, Carleton, and Barnard. However, the differences between student responses from the second survey of research liberal arts colleges and the randomly selected liberal arts colleges in the larger survey shows that

the presence of these three colleges does not significantly dilute the data for randomly selected liberal arts colleges. These three colleges are not removed from the data for randomly selected liberal arts colleges because the data for this sub-group are intended to represent the full range of liberal arts colleges.

7. Restricted-entry business programs are only present at state colleges, and this may provide a bias for some results because it will be difficult to tell if the difference occurs due to differences between state and liberal arts colleges or between restricted-entry and unrestricted-entry business programs. Similarly, some randomly selected liberal arts colleges have unrestricted-entry business programs while no business programs are present at research liberal arts colleges. In total, 732 students attend colleges with business programs. Of those students, 359 students attend colleges with unrestricted-entry business programs and 373 students attend colleges with restricted-entry business programs.

8. Figures 22.1 and 22.2 show all data referred to in this paragraph.

9. Liberal arts colleges with business programs are not included because they distort the comparison of research liberal arts colleges and randomly selected liberal arts colleges. Differences arising from the presence of business programs are discussed, where notable, in separate sections from comparisons of liberal arts colleges. Both comparisons use Figure 22.3 to avoid using unnecessary space.

10. This is the same data as liberal arts colleges without business programs because no state colleges in the survey lacked a business program. Research liberal arts colleges were not included in this statistic because, as the preceding paragraph demonstrated, other factors besides the presence or lack of business programs are affecting student responses from research liberal arts colleges.

11. These are the perceptions of economics majors. A survey of all students may yield different results, but we cannot be sure how the results would differ. On one hand, students may view their own major as easier because it is their strength. On the other hand, students may view their own major as more difficult due to a sense of pride they have for their own major.

12. The specific question was "Which of the following describe what you have learned in your economics major?" Students could choose multiple responses.

13. The specific question was "If you could change the economics major, which changes would you make in it?" Students could choose multiple responses.

14. The question on the survey was, "Which of the following describes your reason for choosing to become an economics major?" Respondents could select more than one response.

15. Research liberal arts colleges are not represented in the overall statistics here.

16. Research liberal arts colleges are not included in these data.

17. Only 42 freshmen participated in the survey. Most students do not have to declare a major freshman year, which explains the low number of freshman respondents.

18. An estimated 2 percent of economics majors enter PhD programs after graduation, and an additional 2 percent attend master's programs.

19. Since all state colleges in the survey have some sort of business program, it is impossible to perform a similar comparison for state colleges.

20. The survey question simply stated "How successful do you believe the economics major at your college is in achieving the following goals?" Students could rate the achievement of each goal as highly successful, successful, or unsuccessful.

21. The survey question was "Which of the following skills would you suggest that the economics major increase or decrease focus on?" Students were expected to indicate increase the focus, decrease the focus, or keep the focus about the same for all eight skills.

22. Data from research liberal arts colleges are not mentioned due to a difference in surveys, which is discussed in the last section.

23. Only state colleges are used here because the differences between state colleges and liberal arts colleges would provide an additional bias.

24. The percentages are from the larger survey because the smaller survey contained all-women's colleges, which would bias results.
25. The specific question was "Which of the following describes your reasoning in choosing to come to your school?" Students could choose multiple responses.
26. The survey question was "If other majors, such as math, chemistry, or biology had business-friendly majors that would prepare you for business and other types at real-world jobs rather than majors designed to prepare students to go to graduate school in the science would you have been interested in such a major?" Students could select "yes," "no," or "maybe" as their response.
27. Students who considered a major in the natural sciences are used rather than all students because students who did not consider a major in the natural sciences would most likely not be interested in any sort of science major, and therefore their inclusion would only bias the results.
28. The specific question was "If your school had had a 'leadership' major that was composed of sequences of courses in science, economics, math, social science, and history that were centered around giving you a broad liberal arts background in a variety of fields, would you have been interested in such a major?" Students could once again select "yes," "no," or "maybe."
29. The survey question asked students, "Should the economics major increase or decrease the number of business-oriented courses in its curriculum?" Students could choose "increase," "decrease," or "keep focus about the same."

PART 7

Conclusion

23. Really thinking like an economist
John J. Siegfried

In the most quoted passage from the 1991 study of the economics major that I coordinated (Siegfried et al., 1991b) we asserted that the overarching goal of economics education should be to "enable students to develop a capacity to think like an economist" (p. 21). Unfortunately, as Colander and McGoldrick suggest, the language we used in our report was not as sharp as it might have been. Our statement was rather easily shortened to "teach students how to think like an economist," from which it was but a small step to "teach students to think like an economist." Our committee did not believe that all students should think like economists everywhere and all of the time. Indeed, we explicitly articulated among ourselves that we hoped students would understand how to think like an economist, and then use that method of analysis when, and only when, they thought it appropriate. To emphasize the point, we should have said that the goal is to enable students to understand how to think like an economist when such thinking is appropriate, rather than to teach them *to* (always) think like an economist, as our statement has subsequently been interpreted. Students should be shown the opportunities and disadvantages of various methods of analysis, but then left to themselves to decide when it is appropriate to "think like an economist." To think like an economist means to know when to use economic thinking, and when not to do so.

The distinction is important because it gets at many of the issues that are discussed in this volume: how much of a liberal education should be provided within the economics major, and how much should be provided by other courses within a student's broader education. The major is only one part of a liberal education and what the economics major should try to do depends on what is done elsewhere. In this final word, which the editors have given me, I will highlight some of these issues that came out in the discussion, and give my sense of where we are in the economics major.

HOW INTENSE SHOULD THE MAJOR BE? THE BREADTH/DEPTH ISSUE

A theme that the 1991 report and the discussion in this volume keeps coming back to is depth versus breadth. How do individual disciplines, like economics, fit into a "liberal education?" The report authors cite Derek Bok's call for more breadth in majors as a means toward achieving a more liberal education. For some majors that is probably necessary, but it is not clear that the call for more breadth is as relevant for economics. While many would argue that we don't need more depth in terms of technical tools, the economics major offers a widely accepted structure that likely enhances depth of understanding. In the jargon of the discipline, economics has a comparative advantage in teaching depth. An economics major is not just a random collection of courses; rather, the major at almost all four-year colleges and universities follows a structure of first introductory economics, then intermediate theory and an introduction to economic statistics, and finally applied field courses. As students move from introductory to intermediate theory courses, and on to applied fields, and (for some) eventually graduate study, similar questions are addressed at ever-increasing depth (generality), employing forms of analysis that gradually release restrictive assumptions used to make the questions tractable at each level. This depth of understanding provided by the structure of the economics discipline is one of its major strengths, and has led one of this volume's authors to call economics the "just right" liberal arts major (Colander, 2009). In many ways, the economics major has addressed the difficult trade-off between breadth and depth to consider when choosing college courses to maximize a goal – say, a "liberal arts education" – in the presence of a total course (time) constraint, and has arrived at a reasonable, if not optimal, result.

Does that compromise leave out some needed elements of a liberal education? Absolutely. But the economics major is not and should not try to do everything. Departments, especially those at research universities with large undergraduate enrollments, tend to focus primarily on their own major programs. This focus is not necessarily inconsistent with a broad liberal education. Context is important. Which implies more breadth: a curriculum consisting of 20 two-semester (that is, year-long) courses, each being the introductory sequence in a different discipline, or a curriculum consisting of ten one-semester introductory courses in various disciplines, followed by ten one-semester courses in each of three disciplines, that is, a triple-major? Would your answer differ if the triple-major were in economics, history, and political science, rather than in economics, English, and chemistry? The answer to this question is not obvious to me, especially if a modicum of intensity of learning is necessary to understand the fundamental concepts in a discipline. Bach and Saunders (1965) found, for example, that college graduates seem to retain a non-trivial amount of what they may have learned in college economics courses *only if* they have taken at least five courses in the subject.

If effective learning occurs only after a certain threshold of study is reached in a discipline, and that threshold lies beyond just the introductory courses, there may be room in a curriculum for exposure to only a limited number of disciplines. And, while a triple-major of ten courses in each of three disciplines may exaggerate the persistence required to reach the threshold, it, nevertheless, highlights the relevant considerations. Breadth and depth are subtle and complex; neither is a single dimension concept.

THE CONTEXT AND CONTENT OF ECONOMICS IN A LIBERAL ARTS EDUCATION

Beyond the question of how intense a curriculum is needed to attain the minimum threshold required to generate long-run benefits from study, is the more fundamental concern about the content of the economics curriculum and the role of that content in a liberal education. In an important recent treatise by the author of another chapter in this book, Stephen Marglin (2008) argues that economists have become advocates for a particular kind of thinking that he calls "algorithmic." Algorithmic knowledge is knowledge based on logical deduction. It is analytic, geared to falsification, impersonal and impartial. It can be decomposed and reconstructed. It is reproducible. It is understandable across cultures. In contrast, what Marglin calls experiential knowledge is understanding based on intuition, experience, and authority. It concerns human relationships, and is partly based on learning from literature and reading history.

Experiential knowledge sounds a lot like "moral reasoning," a subject not unrelated to economics. In the late eighteenth century, Bishop James Madison, president of the College of William and Mary, included political economy in his lectures on moral philosophy, using *The Wealth of Nations* as a text. According to Lawrence Leamer, "Bishop Madison was probably the first teacher anywhere to seek to make economics an element in a truly general education appropriate to a free society" (Leamer, 1950, p. 20).

Marglin concedes algorithmic knowledge serves a useful purpose. It is just that modern economics unduly places it on a pedestal, elevating its prestige so much that experiential knowledge is thereby marginalized. He pleads for more balance between algorithmic and experiential knowledge as the basis for understanding society. He is particularly concerned that the "textbook economics" taught to undergraduates consists of sterile modeling, with little thought devoted to whether the assumptions used in the models accurately characterize human nature. Of a reasonable three-step process of inquiry: (1) describe the world and the incentives induced by its institutions, (2) model the incentives and deduce their implications, and (3) compare the results of the model with actual experience, Marglin thinks that much of modern economics is obsessed with only the middle of the process.

He has a point: modern textbook economics is enamored with logical deduction, to the exclusion of learning *about* the economy, or dealing with ambiguous "big think" questions. Be that as it is, one might counter that economics classrooms *should* emphasize algorithmic knowledge because it is in such short supply relative to experiential knowledge in other learning environments. Algorithmic knowledge is usually learned through schooling, which occupies only a small fraction of anyone's life. Algorithmic knowledge, it could be argued, therefore is at a severe disadvantage when compared with experiential knowledge. Moreover, economics garners but a miniscule share of the time allocated to formal education. If most other knowledge learned in school is experiential, and virtually all knowledge acquired outside of formal schooling is experiential, a course or even an entire major emphasizing algorithmic knowledge may be just what the well-balanced (otherwise algorithmic deprived) liberally educated college graduate needs. In short, economics may fill a yawning gap in a liberal education, namely precise scrutiny of the internal logic of arguments.

Much of the controversy in this volume revolves around differences about how much of these two types of learning students should be provided within the economics major. Marglin, and a number of the other discussants find that today, economics majors are exposed to too much algorithmic and too little experiential knowledge, caused perhaps by a misguided zeal for the kind of certainty produced by logical deduction.

I am less concerned about an overexposure to algorithmic knowledge than is Marglin, in part because I have conducted exit interviews of undergraduate economics majors at many colleges and universities. Even at leading research universities and highly selective liberal arts colleges, economics graduates exhibit a startling dearth of algorithmic knowledge. It is a knowledge that is only slowly learned through constant repetition, and thus needs to be given considerable attention. The need for algorithmic knowledge is made even greater by the fact that much of the knowledge students get in other non-science and mathematics courses is experiential knowledge. The "correct" balance depends on what other courses the students take. Does it have to be balanced within subjects rather than just balanced across them? If it is the former, the humanities and other social sciences (philosophy excepted) face a daunting challenge to add a sufficient amount of algorithmic knowledge to their curricula to attain a scintilla of within-subject balance. If it is the latter, asking each discipline whether it conveys the appropriate balance between algorithmic and experiential knowledge seems to be an irrelevant question. It is, instead, the total package that matters.

A persuasive case for a concentrated dose of algorithmic knowledge in economics classrooms can spring from its scarcity elsewhere. Perhaps if all college students were required to take a course in informal logic as part of their general education requirements, economists could back off their obsession with algorithmic knowledge, but such a requirement is rare and, indeed, the role of general education requirements seems to be waning in favor of free (and potentially algorithmic-knowledge-free) choice. In the absence of assurance that logical deduction will be emphasized elsewhere in the curriculum, maybe the best use of economics courses is to fill that gap aggressively.

PASSION VERSUS CONTENT

In their report, Colander and McGoldrick rightly stay away from prescribing any particular curriculum, basing their argument on the contention that content is less important than the passion of teachers. I strongly agree with this proposition. The trade-off in economics largely favors freedom of content – let them teach whatever they wish – in order to maximize passion because the essence of what is taught in most applied field courses is the same, regardless of the specific questions and institutional context of the subject matter covered in the course. Economists teach the basic principles of economics – opportunity cost, marginal analysis, the role of prices as signals, incentives, specialization, unintended consequences – regardless of the name of the course to which they are assigned. The ideas are the same whether the applied field course focuses on factor markets or product markets.

There are some exceptions worthy of attention. The content of core courses that are used as prerequisites for other courses must be transparent and fairly stable so that those counting on student understanding of prerequisites can organize their courses to take advantage of the sequential nature of the curriculum and move on to deeper analysis. Moreover, if a course is truly idiosyncratic, students should be aware of that fact. I believe that the most effective way to stimulate a passion for learning is through honors courses, programs, and theses (Siegfried, 2001) and senior seminars that require students to synthesize various skills and knowledge they have accumulated prior to taking the seminar. Honors work, in particular, is also good preparation for subsequent graduate study, and provides relevant evidence of a graduate's capacity for post-graduate work.

SPECIALIST TEACHERS

Despite their call for maintaining property rights over content with the professors of record, one doesn't need to read deeply between the lines of the report to see where Colander and McGoldrick's hearts lie in terms of content. They would prefer to see more professors whose passion lies in providing students with a broader understanding, especially those teaching at the principles level. (The content of introductory economics is a different issue than the appropriate curriculum for majors discussed above, because 95 percent of principles students do not continue on to become economics majors; Hansen et al., 2002.)

In the case of introductory courses, Colander and McGoldrick argue that much more teaching specialization is needed. They propose that more specialist teachers be hired by (especially) research universities and research colleges. I suspect they are right, and, in fact, there is now evidence that such a movement is already underway. While some specialist teaching faculty are tenured or tenure-track (for example, the University of Kentucky has two), most hold full-time non-tenured or tenure-track appointments with titles such as instructor or senior lecturer. The percentage of economics faculty teaching at a sample of 59 PhD-granting universities who are classified as full-time non-tenured or tenure-track has grown from 3.9 percent to 7.9 percent over the decade from 1999 to 2009. A similar comparison for a sample of 86 colleges that offer no post-baccalaureate degrees in economics shows a rise from 6.5 to 11.9 percent in full-time non-tenured or tenure-track faculty over the decade (Scott and Siegfried, 2009, Table 5, p. 644). It is unlikely that many of these non-tenured faculty are research professors. While not all of those in these positions are specialist teachers, specialist teachers are likely to dominate this category of faculty.

THE ROLE OF JOB SKILLS

Colander and McGoldrick argue that graduate education today is designed to produce research scholars rather than undergraduate teachers. Successful research emanates from ambition, specialization, persistence, and focus, traits that do not serve "liberal education" as well. Pressure to emphasize narrow research questions and specialized skills comes not only from research faculty teaching undergraduates at universities that also award PhDs, but also from employers, who may produce rhetoric about seeking especially well-rounded employees to be future executive prospects, but also want them tooled up to the frontier in state-of-the-art vocational skills.

Colander and McGoldrick contend that economists are deficient in teaching communication skills. As a result, economics graduates do not excel in communication, and the ones that go on to teach in PhD programs most likely perpetuate the deficiency. Colander and McGoldrick's intuition is supported by data. Graduates fault their PhD training quite seriously on this front. Three hundred and eight-five economists who earned their PhD in 2001–02 rated communication as the most important among eight skills for their job performance (the other skills, in order of rated importance, were application, critical judgment, analytics, creativity, computation, instruction, and mathematics). However, when asked about the relative importance of the same eight skills in achieving success in their PhD programs, they rated communication below analytics, critical judgment, mathematics, computation and creativity (Stock and Hansen, 2004, Table 2, p. 268). So, how do we break the cycle of bad communicators serving as role models for a future generation of poorly communicating economists? It is not difficult to diagnose the problem; a means to treat it remains elusive, however.

The situation grows worse as younger economics faculty progressively increase the emphasis on technical skills, and the relevance of economics increasingly diminishes for the vast majority of undergraduates who are looking for a humanistic/quantitative liberal arts foundation. The emphasis on algorithmic knowledge is exacerbated by the growing proportion of international PhD students, changing from roughly 25 percent of those awarded PhDs in economics in the US in the 1960s to almost 75 percent today (see Scott and Siegfried, 2008, Table A, p. 633). As relatively more economics PhD students come from different cultures, there is naturally an increasing emphasis on content that is less dependent on culture, namely algorithmic knowledge. With algorithmic knowledge as the medium of exchange, people can communicate easier across cultures. To the extent that institutions and historical context remain important, many of those with different cultural backgrounds struggle. As their numbers rise, many of the new assistant professors of economics who studied in the US on temporary visas slowly redefine the discipline into one that is of less interest to most US undergraduates, even though it could be of considerable value to them.

IMPROVING LIBERAL ARTS TEACHING

An agreement among elite liberal arts colleges to give interview preference, and nothing more, to job candidates who have had at least one course in economic history and/or the history of economic thought might signal the importance of these subjects. To be successful, the movement would have to start with those highly selective liberal arts colleges that offer the most attractive appointments to PhD graduates, and it would have to be agreed upon by a large fraction of them in order to be effective, because their faculties are small and their hiring infrequent. The idea is not to require an economic history or history of economic thought background in order to secure an interview, but rather just to give interview *priority* to those having taken such courses.

The important question is whether PhD programs would try to accommodate such a change in criteria for securing interviews in the job market. The PhD students who are likely to care the most are those who themselves were undergraduate students at liberal arts colleges, because many of them aspire to return to the tranquility of Mr. Chips professing to motivated and curious undergraduates. There is evidence that economics graduate students who earned bachelor's degrees at one of the 60 leading liberal arts colleges are relatively more successful than others enrolled in PhD programs, so it might be difficult for PhD programs to ignore these students (Stock et al., 2009). On the other hand, liberal arts college graduates constitute only about ten percent of students in PhD programs, and revealing an interest in subsequently working at a liberal arts college is thought by many of them to be career stifling (Colander, 2007, p. 22). Most faculty at the leading PhD programs want to train graduates who make significant long-lasting contributions to economic research. Indicating an interest in teaching can limit choices available to students in PhD programs. While it is peculiar that a goal pertinent to relatively few PhD students (perhaps in ten years making the "shortlist" of candidates for the American Economic Association's John Bates Clark Medal) dominates the structure of graduate programs, as a discipline we behave similarly at the undergraduate level, where we myopically structure curricula to prepare bachelor's graduates to enter PhD programs, even though only about 2 percent of undergraduate majors ever do so.

I like the Colander-McGoldrick idea of a post-doctoral program to prepare PhD economists to be better liberal arts and/or liberal arts college teachers. The challenge is not overwhelming. This seems like an attractive project for a foundation, supplemented by modest financial support from a (hopefully large) coalition of liberal arts colleges and those research universities that promise a strong liberal arts education to their undergraduates.

It could be organized as a six-week "summer institute," with a three-week break in the middle (to accommodate intensive reading and the families of participants), followed by a post-doctoral "internship" taking the form of a visiting professorship at a liberal arts college. The second summer the participants might reassemble for a third and final three-week session. Suppose 30 selective liberal arts colleges were to agree to provide a one-semester teaching internship in alternate years (every fourth semester). Each would compensate the intern, but the net cost would be modest, as the intern would be expected to teach two big-think-related elective courses during the internship semester. In effect, the internship would take the form of a visiting professorship. In the other semester, participants would be expected to read ten of the "Great Books." In addition, the group might meet for a few days in January after the Allied Social Science Associations (ASSA) meetings to add continuity to the program. Thirty economists could move through the program every two years. The idea is not that all of these people would take jobs at liberal arts colleges. Indeed, many of them are likely to be faculty at major research institutions and continue to work there, but with a substantially different menu of teaching responsibilities after the training.

A PRE-PROFESSIONAL DEGREE

I am pessimistic about the idea of a separate pre-professional undergraduate economics major with less technical emphasis, primarily because it is risky to students. What is the degree worth if a student does poorly and does not get admitted to the professional (for example, law, business) school of his or her choice? I think this is one reason why there are no real "pre-med" degrees, regardless of what students announce to their family and friends, or how intercollegiate athletes are described by television announcers during pre-game introductions.

CONCLUSION

In conclusion, let me return to the issue of thinking like an economist. As I said at the beginning, as we meant to interpret it in our 1991 report, understanding how to think like an economist involves much more than applying economic reasoning to every issue. It involves not only applying economic reasoning, but also knowing when to apply it. Colander and McGoldrick call this thinking like a liberally educated person, but the difference seems largely semantic.

In the 1991 report, my committee gave the economics major a B–. Colander and McGoldrick also gave it a B–. These B–s need be kept in perspective; they are B–s awarded by hard graders who avoid grade inflation. In terms of fitting in to a liberal arts curriculum, economics does a much better job than most majors, and it is discussions such as those in this book that help maintain that pace.

Finally, I note that examinations often serve to establish goals. For example, the Advanced Placement examination in economics was devised in large part in order to influence the content of high school economics courses. To advance the cause of promoting attention to what is thought to be a more liberal education than that which currently occurs in undergraduate classrooms, perhaps someone or some group could develop a list of 20 *carefully crafted* "big think" questions, in response to which every liberally educated undergraduate economics major (and perhaps the faculty, too!) should be able to write a thoughtful, well-constructed hour-long essay. What would those questions be, and how many of our students (and faculty) would feel comfortable tackling five (of their choice) among the 20 as a senior comprehensive examination? It is an agenda that could make a difference.

References

Adkins, R. and Newsome, M. (2006). Designing the economics curriculum. *Journal of Economics and Finance Education*, **5** (2), 7–16.

Adler, M. What is liberal education?, http://www.ditext.com/adler/wle.html (accessed 20 April 2009).

Adler, M. (1951). Labor, leisure, and liberal education. *The Journal of General Education*, **VI** (October), 35–45, http://www.sourcetext.com/grammarian/adler2.html (accessed 20 April 2009).

Allgood, S., Bosshardt, W., van der Klaauw, H.W. and Watts, M. (2004). What students remember and say about college economics years later. *American Economic Review (Papers and Proceedings)*, **94** (2), 259–65.

American Association of University Professors (AAUP). (1915). *General declaration of principles*. Columbia University.

American Association of University Professors (AAUP). (1967). *Joint statement on rights and freedoms of students*. Washington, DC: AAC&U.

Angelo, T.A. and Cross, K.P. (1993). *Classroom assessment techniques: A handbook for college teachers*. San Francisco: Jossey-Bass.

Association of American Colleges (AAC). (1985). *Integrity in the college curriculum: A report to the academic community. Project on redefining the meaning and purpose of baccalaureate degrees*. Washington, DC: AAC.

Association of American Colleges (AAC). (1990a). *The challenges of connecting learning: Liberal learning and the arts and science major*. Vol. 1. Washington, DC: AAC.

Association of American Colleges (AAC). (1990b). *Reports from the fields: Learning: Liberal learning and the arts and science major*. Vol. 2. Washington, DC: AAC.

Association of American Colleges and Universities (AAC&U). (2006). *Academic freedom and educational responsibility*. Washington, DC: AAC&U.

Association of American Colleges & Universities (AAC&U). (2007). *College learning for the new global century: A report from the national leadership council for liberal learning and America's promise*. Washington, DC: AAC&U.

Association to Advance Collegiate Schools of Business (AACSB). (2008). *Eligibility procedures and accreditation standards for business accreditation*. Tampa, http:www.aacsb.edu (accessed 21 April 2009).

Bach, G.L. and Saunders, P. (1965). Economic education: Aspirations and achievements. *American Economic Review*, **55** (3), 329–56.

Bartlett, R.L. and Feiner, S.F. (1992). Balancing the economics curriculum: Content, method, and pedagogy. *American Economic Review*, **82** (2), 559–64.

Becker, W.E. (1997). Teaching economics to undergraduates. *Journal of Economic Literature*, **35** (3), 1347–73.

Becker, W.E. (2007). Quit lying and address the controversies: There are no dogmata, laws, rules, or standards in the science of economics. *American Economist*, **51** (1), 3–14.

Becker, W.E. and Watts, M. (2001). Teaching economics at the start of the 21st century: Still chalk and talk. *American Economic Review*, **91** (2), 446–51.

Becker, W.E. and Watts, M. (2008). A little more than chalk and talk: Results from a third national survey of teaching methods in undergraduate economics courses. *Journal of Economic Education*, **39** (3), 273–86.

Beyer, C.H., Gillmore, G.M. and Fisher, A.T. (2007). *Inside the undergraduate experience: The University of Washington study of undergraduate learning*. Bolton: Anker Publishing Company, Inc.

Biggs, J. (1999). *Teaching for quality learning at university*. Buckingham, UK and Philadelphia: SHRE and Open University Press.

Blaug, M. (2001). Is competition such a good thing? Static efficiency versus dynamic efficiency. *Review of Industrial Organization*, **19** (1), 37–48.

Bloom, B.S. (ed.) (1956). *Taxonomy of educational objectives: The classification of educational goals, handbook I: Cognitive domain*. New York: David McKay Company, Inc.

Boettke, P.J. (2002). Information and knowledge: Austrian economics in search of its uniqueness. *Review of Austrian Economics*, **15** (4), 263–74.

Bok, D. (2006). *Our underachieving colleges: A candid look at how much students learn and why they should be learning more*. Princeton: Princeton University Press.

Borg, J.R. and Borg, M.O. (2001). Teaching critical thinking in interdisciplinary economics courses. *College Teaching*, **49** (1), 20–29.

Bransford, J., Brown, A.L. and Cocking, R.R. (2000). *How people learn: Brain, mind, experience, and school*. Washington, DC: National Academy Press.

Brasfield, D., Harrison, D., McCoy, J. and Milkman, M. (1996). Why have some schools not experienced a decrease in the percentage of students majoring in economics? *Journal of Economic Education*, **27** (4), 362–70.

Breneman, D.W. (2008, 15 February). Elite colleges must stop spurning critiques of higher education. *Chronicle of Higher Education*, A40.

Carlson, J.L., Cohn, R.L. and Ramsey, D.D. (2002). Implementing Hansen proficiencies. *Journal of Economic Education*, **33** (2), 180–91.

Colander, D. (2001). *The lost art of economics: Essays on economics and the economics profession.* Cheltenham, UK and Northampton, MA: Edward Elgar.

Colander, D. (2007). *The making of an economist, redux.* Princeton and Oxford: Princeton University Press.

Colander, David. (2009). Economics is the "just right" liberal arts major. *Chronicle of Higher Education*, **55** (26), A72.

Colander, D. and Holmes, J. (2006). Capstone course in economics: To what, and for whom? In D. Colander, *The stories economists tell: Essays on the art of teaching economics.* New York: McGraw Hill Irwin, pp. 71–8.

Commission Appointed by Secretary of Education Margaret Spellings. (2006). *A test of leadership.* Washington: US Department of Education.

Conrad, C.A. (1996). Where have all the majors gone? Comment. *Journal of Economic Education*, **27** (4), 376–8.

Earl, P.E. (2000). Indeterminacy in the economics classroom. In P.E. Earl and S.F. Frowen (eds), *Economics as an art of thought: Essays in memory of G.L.S. Shackle,* London: Routledge, pp. 25–50.

Ehrlich, T. and Colby, A. (2004). Political bias in undergraduate education. *Liberal Education*, **90** (3), 36–9.

Ellerman, D. (2005). *Helping people help themselves: From the World Bank to an alternative philosophy of development assistance.* Ann Arbor: University of Michigan Press.

Entwistle, N.J. (1981). *Styles of learning and teaching.* Chichester: Wiley.

Feiner, S.F. (2003). On the history of teaching heterodox economics. Paper presented at History of Heterodox Economics in the 20th Century conference, University of Missouri at Kansas City.

Feiner, S.F. and Roberts, B.B. (1995). Using alternative paradigms to teach about race and gender: A critical thinking approach to introductory economics. *American Economic Review*, **85** (2), 367–71.

Fels, R. (1974). Developing independent problem-solving ability in elementary economics. *American Economic Review*, **64** (2), 403–7.

Ferber, M.A. (1999). Guidelines for pre-college economics education: A critique. *Feminist Economics*, **5** (3), 135–42.

Finkel, D.L. (2000). *Teaching with your mouth shut.* Portsmouth, NH: Boynton/Cook.

Fleischacker, S.F. (1999). *A third concept of liberty.* Princeton: Princeton University Press.

Foley, D. (2006). *Adam's fallacy: A guide to economic theology.* Cambridge, MA: Harvard University Press.

Fullbrook, E. (ed.) (2003). *The crisis in economics: The post-autistic economics movement*. London: Routledge.

Frank, R.H. (2000). Why is cost–benefit analysis so controversial? *Journal of Legal Studies*, **XXIX** (2), 913–30.

Frank, R.H. and Bernanke, B.S. (2009). *Principles of micro-economics*. Massachusetts: McGraw-Hill/Irwin.

Grant, R.R. (2005). A small college adventure with accreditation and assessment. *Perspectives on Economic Education Research*, 1 (1), 60–75.

Griswold, C.L., Jr. (1999). *Adam Smith and the virtues of enlightenment*. Cambridge: Cambridge University Press.

Groenewegen, J. (ed.) (2007). *Teaching pluralism in economics*. Cheltenham, UK and Northampton, MA, USA: Edward Elgar.

Halloun, I. and Hestenes, D. (1985). The initial knowledge state of college physics students. *American Journal of Physics*, **53** (11), 1043.

Hansen, W.L. (1986). What knowledge is most worth knowing – for economics majors? *American Economic Review*, **76** (2), 149–52.

Hansen, W.L. (1991). The education and training of economics doctorates: major findings of the executive secretary of the American Economic Association's Commission on Graduate Education in Economics. *American Economic Review*, **29** (3), 1054–87.

Hansen, W.L. (1993a). Teaching a writing-intensive course in economics. *Journal of Economic Education*, **24** (3), 213–18.

Hansen, W.L. (1993b). Bringing total quality improvement into the college classroom. *Higher Education*, **25** (3), 259–79.

Hansen, W.L. (1998a). Improving classroom discussion in economics courses. With Michael K. Salemi, in Phillip Saunders and William B. Walstad (eds), *Teaching undergraduate economics: A handbook for instructors*. New York: McGraw-Hill Inc., pp. 207–26.

Hansen, W.L. (1998b). Integrating the practice of writing into economics instruction. In William E. Becker and Michael Watts (eds), *Teaching economics to undergraduates: Alternatives to chalk and talk*. Cheltenham, UK and Lyme, NH, USA: Edward Elgar, 79–118.

Hansen, W.L. (2001). Expected proficiencies for undergraduate economics majors. *Journal of Economic Education*, **32** (3), 231–42.

Hansen, W.L. (2006a). Proficiency-based economics course examinations. Paper presented at the Midwest Economics Association meetings.

Hansen, W.L. (2006b). Assessing the learning of economics majors based on an expected proficiencies approach. Department of Economics, UW-Madison. Unpublished.

Hansen, W.L., Salemi, M.K. and Siegfried, J.J. (2002). Use it or lose it: Teaching literacy in the principles of economics course. *American*

Economic Review, Papers and Proceedings of the American Economic Association, **92** (2), 463–72.

Harpham, E.J. (2000). The problem of liberty in the thought of Adam Smith. *Journal of the History of Economic Thought*, **22** (2), 217–37.

Hausman, D.M. and McPherson, M.S. (2006). *Economic analysis, moral philosophy, and public policy*. Cambridge, UK: Cambridge University.

Hayek, F.A. (1948 [1945]), The use of knowledge in society. In *Individualism and economic order*, Chicago: University of Chicago Press, pp. 77–91.

Huber. M.T. and Hutchings, P. (2007). Building the teaching commons. The Carnegie Foundation for the Advancement of Teaching. Available at http://www.carnegiefoundation.org/perspectives/sub.asp?key=245& subkey=800 (accessed 17 April 2009).

Johnston, C.G., James, R.H., Lye, J.N. and McDonald, I.M. (2000). An evaluation of collaborative problem solving for learning economics. *Journal of Economic Education*, **31** (1), 13–29.

Katz, A. and Becker, W.E. (1999). Technology and the teaching of economics to undergraduates. *Journal of Economic Education*, **30** (3), 194–9.

Keynes, J.M. (1936). *The general theory of employment, interest, and money*. New York: Harcourt, Brace, and World.

Keynes, J.N. (1891, republished 1955). *The scope and method of political economy*, 4th edition, New York: Kelley and Millman, Inc.

Knoedler, J. and Underwood, D. (2003). Teaching the principles of economics: A proposal for a multiparadigmatic approach. *Journal of Economic Issues*, **37** (3), 697–725.

Kronman, A. (2007). *Education's end: Why our colleges and universities have given up on the meaning of life*. Princeton: Yale University Press.

Krueger, A. et al. (1991). Report of the commission on graduate education in economics. *Journal of Economic Literature*, **29** (3), 1035–53.

Kuhn, T. (1962). *The structure of scientific revolutions*. Chicago, IL: University of Chicago Press.

Lavoie, D. (1995). The "objectivity" of scholarship and the ideal of the university. *Advances in Austrian Economics*, **2B**, 371–403.

Leamer, L.E. (1950). A brief history of economics in general education. In H. Taylor (ed.), *The teaching of undergraduate education*, supplement to the *American Economic Review*, **40** (December), 18–33.

Leftwich, R.H. and Sharp, A.M. (1974). Syllabus for an "issues approach" to teaching economic principles. *Journal of Economic Education*, Special Issue No. 1, 3–32.

Lucas, R.E. (1988). On the mechanics of economic development. *Journal of Monetary Economics*, **22** (1988), 3–42.

Lucas, R.E. Jr. (2000). Some macroeconomics for the 21st century. *Journal of Economic Perspectives*, **14** (1), 159–68.

Maier, M.H. and Simkins, S. (2008). Learning from physics education research: Lessons for economics education. Social Science Research Network working paper archive, http://papers.ssrn.com/sol3/papers.cfm?abstract_id=1151430 (accessed 20 April 2009).

Maier, M.H., McGoldrick, K. and Simkins, S. (2009). Implementing cooperative learning in introductory economics courses. In Barbara Millis (ed.), *Cooperative learning across the disciplines*. Vermont: Stylus Press/National Teaching and Learning Forum.

Mankiw, N.G. (2004). *Principles of economics*, 3rd edition. London: Thomson Learning.

Marglin, Stephen. (2008). *The Dismal Science: How Thinking Like an Economist Undermines Community*. Cambridge, MA.: Harvard University Press, pp. 359 + xvi.

McGoldrick, K. (2008). Doing economics: Enhancing skills through a process-oriented senior research course. *Journal of Economic Education*. **39** (4), 342–56.

McGoldrick, K., Hoyt, G.M. and Colander, D. (forthcoming). The professional development of graduate students in economics: students' perspectives. *Journal of Economic Education*.

Mill, J.S. ([1859] 1956) *On liberty*. Edited with introduction by C.V. Shields. Indianapolis: Bobbs-Merrill.

Moomaw, R.L. and Olson, K.W. (2007). *Economics and contemporary issues*. (7th edition). Mason: Thompson Southwestern Higher Education.

Moseley, F., Gunn, C., and Georges, C. (1991). Emphasizing controversy in the economics curriculum. *Journal of Economic Education*, **22** (7), 235–40.

Myers, S.C., Nelson, M.A., and Stratton, R.W. (2008). Weathering the perfect storm or thriving in a new environment: Assessing a proficiency-based economics major. Department of Economics, University of Akron. Presented at Annual Meeting of American Economic Association. Available at http://GoZips.UAkron.edu/~myers (accessed 21 April 2009).

National Center on Public Policy and Higher Education. (2000). *Measuring up 2000* (and subsequent reports in 2002, 2004, 2006, and 2008), www.highereducation.org (accessed 21 April 2009).

National Leadership Council. Report that spells out the vision behind the Teagle initiative on liberal education, http://www.aacu.org/advocacy/leap/documents/GlobalCentury_final.pdf (accessed 21 April 2009).

Nelson, C.E. (1989). Skewered on the unicorn's horn: The illusion of tragic tradeoff between content and critical thinking in the teaching of science. In L.W. Crow (ed.), *Enhancing critical thinking in the sciences*, Washington: Society of College Science Teachers, pp. 17–27.

Nelson, C.E. (1997). Tools for tampering with teaching's taboos. In W.E. Campbell and K.A. Smith (eds). *New paradigms for college teaching*, Edina: Interaction Books, pp. 51–77.

Nelson, J.A. (2006). *Economics for humans*. Chicago: University of Chicago Press.

Nerlove, M. (1972). On tuition and the costs of higher education: Prolegomena to a conceptual framework. *Journal of Political Economy*, **80** (3), S205.

Newcomb, S. (1886). Can economists agree upon the basis of their teachings? *Science*, **8** (179), 25–6.

Nussbaum, M.C. (1997). *Cultivating humanity: A classical defense of reform in liberal education*. Cambridge, MA: Harvard University Press.

Nussbaum, M.C. (2000). The costs of tragedy: Some moral limits of cost–benefit analysis. *Journal of Legal Studies*, **29** (2), 1005–36.

Paul, R. and Elder, L. (2001). *Critical thinking: Tools for taking charge of your learning and your life*. Upper Saddle River, NJ: Prentice Hall.

Perry, Jr., W.G. (1970). *Forms of intellectual and ethical development in the college years: A scheme*. New York: Holt, Rinehart and Winston.

Prosser, M. and Trigwell, K. (1999). *Understanding learning and teaching, on deep and surface learning*. Buckingham, UK and Philadelphia: Society for Research into Higher Education and Open University Press.

Ramsden, P. (1992). *Learning to teach in higher education*. New York: Routledge.

Rawls, J. (1971). *A theory of justice*. Cambridge, MA: Harvard University Press.

Richardson, J. (2004). Concept inventories: Tools for uncovering STEM students' misconceptions. *Assessment and Education Research*.

Salemi, M.K. and Eubanks, C. (1996). Accounting for the rise and fall in the number of economics majors with the discouraged-business-major hypothesis. *Journal of Economic Education*, **27**(4), 350–61.

Salemi, M.K. and Siegfried, J.J. (1999). The state of economic education. *American Economic Review*, **89** (2), 355–61.

Schaur, G., Watts, M., and Becker, W.E. (2008). Assessment practices and trends in undergraduate economics courses. *American Economic Review*, **98** (2), 552–6.

Scott, Charles E. and Siegfried, John J. (2008). American Economic Association universal academic questionnaire summary statistics. *American Economic Review*, **98** (2), 630–33.

Scott, Charles E. and Siegfried, John J. (2009). American Economic

Association universal academic questionnaire summary statistics. *American Economic Review*, **99** (2), 641–5.

Sen, A.K. (1999). *Development as freedom*. New York: Anchor Books.

Shackelford, J. (1992). Feminist pedagogy: A means for bringing critical thinking and creativity to the classroom. *American Economic Review*, **82** (2), 570–76.

Shackle, G.L.S. (1953). *What makes an economist?* Liverpool: Liverpool University Press.

Sharp, A.M., Register, C.A. and Grimes, P.W. (2008). *Economics of social issues*. (18th edition). Burr Ridge: McGraw-Hill Irwin.

Siegfried, J.J. (2001). Principles for a successful undergraduate economics honors program. *Journal of Economic Education*, **32** (2), 169–77.

Siegfried, J. and Stock, W. (2007). The undergraduate origins of Ph.D. economists. *Journal of Economic Education*, **38** (4), 474.

Siegfried, J.J., Bartlett, R.L., Hansen, W.L., Kelley, A.C., McCloskey, D.N. and Tietenberg, T.H. (1991a). The economics major: Can and should we do better than B minus? *American Economic Review*, **81** (2), 20–25.

Siegfried, J.J., Bartlett, R.L., Hansen, W.L., Kelley, A.C., McCloskey, D.N. and Tietenberg, T.H. (1991b). The status and prospects of the economics major. *Journal of Economic Education*, 197–224.

Simkins, S.P. and Maier, M.H. (2004). Using just-in-time teaching techniques in the principles of economics course. *Social Science Computer Review*, **22** (4), 444–56.

Simkins, S.P. and Maier, M.H. (2009). *Just in time teaching: Across the disciplines and across the academy*. Vermont: Stylus Press/National Teaching and Learning Forum.

Smith, A. ([1759] 1976). *The theory of moral sentiments*. D.D. Raphael and A.L. Macfie (eds). Oxford: Oxford University Press.

Stock, W.A. and Hansen, W.L. (2004). Ph.D. program learning and job demands: How close is the match? *American Economic Review Papers and Proceedings*, **94** (2), 266–71.

Stock, Wendy A., Finegan, T. Aldrich and Siegfried, John J. (2009). Completing an economics PhD in five years. *American Economic Review*, **99** (2), 624–2.

Strike, K.A. (1982). *Liberty and learning*. New York: St. Martin's Press.

Task Force on Teaching and Career Development (2007). A compact to enhance teaching and learning at Harvard, http://www.Auburn.edu/academic/other/biggie/resources/TeachingAndLearningAtHarvard.pdf (accessed 21 April 2009).

Thoma, G.A. (1993). The Perry framework and tactics for teaching critical thinking in economics. *Journal of Economic Education*, **24** (2), 128–36.

Underwood, D.A. (2004). Principles of macroeconomics: Toward a multi-paradigmatic approach. *Journal of Economic Issues*, **38** (2), 571–81.

Walstad, W. and Allgood, S. (1999). What do college seniors know about economics? *American Economic Review*, **89** (2), 350–54.

Walstad, W.B. and Becker, W.E. (2003). The instructional use and teaching preparation of graduate students in U.S. Ph.D.-granting economics departments. *American Economic Review Papers and Proceedings*, **93** (2), 449–54.

Watts, M. and Becker, W.E. (2008). A little more than chalk and talk: Results from a third national survey of teaching methods in undergraduate economics courses. *Journal of Economic Education*, **39** (3), 273–86.

Welsh, A.L. (1974). Foreword. *Journal of Economic Education*, Special Issue No. 1, 1.

Wight, J.B. (2009). Teaching economics. In Jan Peil and Irene van Staveren (eds), *Handbook of Economics and Ethics*. Cheltenham, UK and Northampton, MA, USA: Edward Elgar.

Wight, J.B. and Morton, J.S. (2007). *Teaching the ethical foundations of economics*. New York: The National Council on Economic Education.

Willis, R.A. and Pieper, P.J. (1996). The economics major: A cross-sectional view. *Journal of Economic Education*, **27** (4), 337–49.

Wyrick, T.L. (1994). *The economist's handbook: A research and writing guide*. Minneapolis/St Paul: West Publishing.

Index

academic majors, generally
    expected proficiencies approach to
        108–13, 118–24
    increasing importance of 8–9
    in liberal education, role of 4–6, 8,
        76–8, 107–8
    neglect of 107–8
    restrictions on 131–2
    specialization of, influences on 12–13
    see also economics major
academic minors, restrictions on 131–2
accountability, of education/faculty
    89–90, 120–21
active learning 97
    in economics major 114–24
    proficiency-based courses 108–13
Adkins, R. 116
Adler, Mortimer 99–100
Advanced Placement examination in
    economics 224
Akron, University of 117
algorithmic knowledge 217–19, 221
American Economic Association
    Committee on Economic
    Education xix, 19, 97, 105, 107,
    173, 222
analytical skills
    acquired in economics major 66–8,
        107, 197–8
    acquired in interdisciplinary
        programs 139–42
    assessment 34, 114–18, 197–8, 334
    see also critical thinking; moral
        reasoning
Association of Advance Collegiate
    Schools of Business (AACSB)
    statement on assurance of learning
    standards 119–20
Association of American Colleges and
    Universities (AAC&U)
    criticism of academic major 19

defining liberal education 3–5, 7, 13,
    83–4, 108, 174
on proficiency-based courses 116, 124
Study-in-Depth Project 116, 119
associationism 68

Bach, G.L. 217
Bartlett, R.L. 64
Batten School of Leadership and
    Public Policy, University of
    Virginia 180
Becker, W.E. 27–8, 97
behavior, human
    economic analysis of 68, 77–8, 111
Beyer, C.H. 107–8
big think questions vs little think
    questions 5–6
    business/employers, relevance to 79,
        152–3, 158, 204–8, 221
    in economics major, whether covered
        43–4, 72–4, 102–3, 164–5, 168–9,
        171–2, 186–8
    and ethical/moral reasoning 53–7
    and interdisciplinary programs
        130–31
    researchers, relevance to 5–7, 14, 18,
        102–3
    teaching methods 6–7
Bok, Derek
    goals of liberal education 202–8
        and academic major, role of 4–5,
            7, 13–14, 108, 124
        and economics major 15, 17, 134,
            216
Borg, J.R. 64
Bowman and Gordon Gray
    Professorships 105
Bransford, J. 33, 84–6
Brasfield, D. 191
breadth vs depth
    balance 19–20, 163–4

242   *Educating economists: the Teagle discussion*

in structured manner 84–5
and students' pre-existing knowledge
     85–7
teacher training 10, 14, 21, 149
   change in, proposals for 21–5, 105,
        150–51, 166, 168, 170–72,
        180, 220
   in graduate education 21–5, 184–5
   lack of 27–8, 185–6
   specialist teachers, need for 220
   teaching qualifications 21–5, 31,
        100–101, 151
   see also interdisciplinary programs
Teaching Innovation Program 105
Teagle Foundation 119
   background to review xix
   economics review proposals
        focus of xx–xxii, xxvii
        main points of consensus/
             disagreement xxii–xxiv
technological change, and the
     economics major 145, 158–60
tenure *see under* faculty
*A Test of Leadership Charting the
     Future of US Higher Education*
     177–8
textbooks, for economics courses 31–3,
     55, 136
   ethical/welfare economics issues,
        coverage of 54–5
   homogenization of 95–7
   in interdisciplinary programs 137–8
   in principles courses 95–6
   role of 217–19
Theory of Justice 70–71
Theory of Moral Sentiments 60–61
'thinking like an economist' 15–20,
     215, 223–4
   and ethical/moral reasoning 53–7
   and expected proficiencies approach
        109–24
   historical development of concept
        16–17
   and intellectual isolationism 72–3
   and interdisciplinary programs
        138–9
   links with other disciplines 57–8
   and promoting expert-like thinking
        84–5

and self-monitoring/self-reflective
     learners 87
student view on economics skills
     learned 197–8
whether appropriate goal for
     economics majors 19, 166–7
see also critical thinking
tragic questions 17
Truth, emergence of 48

UNC-Chapel Hill 101, 105
undergraduate education
   expected proficiencies approach
        118–20, 123–4
   and graduate education
        differing needs of 6–8, 29–30,
             71–4, 100–101, 174
        relevance of courses to 6–8, 29–30,
             71–4, 100–101
   research focus of 6–7, 10, 152, 183–4
universities
   land grant universities 65–6
   *see also individual universities by
        name*
utilitarianism 68

Vassar 148–9, 152
Vickrey, Bill 147
Virginia, University of 180
virtue ethics 56–7
vocational education
   major seen as 8–9, 20, 95, 102
   and pre-professional degree proposal
        26–7
   relevance to future career 99, 220–21

Walstad, W.B. 27–8
Watts, M. 97
The Wealth of Nations 217
welfare analysis 54–6
Wisconsin-Madison, University of
     115
women students', satisfaction with
     courses 202–6
writing skills
   improving, need for 131, 154–6,
        166–7, 185, 188
   neglect in major 5, 101–2, 131
   training methods 5, 10, 15